N

SOLITAIRE

David Parlett

Pantheon Books, New York

SOLITAIRE

Aces Up and 399 Other Card Games

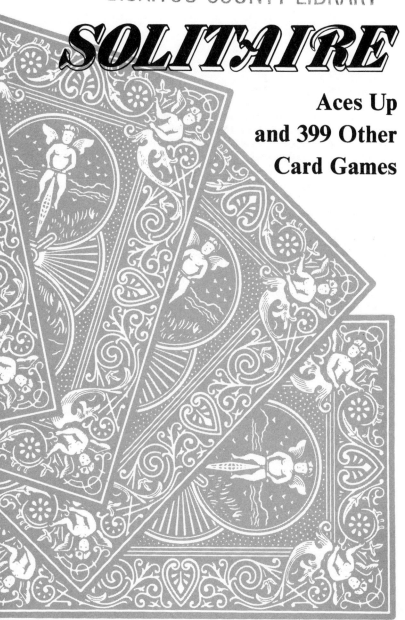

LIBRARY OF CONGRESS CATALOGING IN PUBLICATION DATA
Parlett, David Sidney.
   Solitaire: aces up and 399 other card games.
   British ed. published in 1979 under title: The Penguin book of patience.
   Bibliography: p.
   Includes index.
   1. Solitaire (Game)   I. Title.
GV1261.P27 1980   795.4'3   79-3319
ISBN 0-394-51046-1
ISBN 0-394-73868-3 pbk.

Manufactured in the United States of America
FIRST AMERICAN EDITION

Contents

Only major game headings are listed. For complete alphabetical listing of main games and variants see Index.

Westcliff, Forty-nine, Olga, Triangle, Harp, Suspense,
Wheatsheaf, Ladder, Octave, Marriage, Shah, Diplomat,
British Constitution, Right and Left, Snake, Maria,
Hill of Difficulty, Gargantua, Batsford, Deuces,
Number Ten, Indian, Napoleon at St Helena,
Blind Patience, Double Fives, Highlands, Club,
Simplicity, Limited, Hemispheres, Corona, Colonel,
Big Ben, Napoleon's Square, Bismarck, Lucas,
Empress of India, British Square, Barton

The Patient Pursuit

MINISTER OF WAR   Sir, you try my patience.
RUFUS T. FIREFLY   I don't mind if I do. You must come over
                     and try mine some time.

– Kalmar and Ruby: *Duck Soup* (Paramount, 1933)

Patience is the mental equivalent of jogging: its purpose is to tone the brain up and get rid of unsociable mental flabbiness. As such it belongs to the same class of solitaires as jigsaws, wire puzzles and Chess problems, but with the distinctive feature that its medium is the ordinary pack of playing cards.

Typically, the problem is to transform a shuffled pack into an ordered one, with all its suits occupying separate positions and each one arranged in numerical sequence from Ace (one) to King (thirteen). What distinguishes one game from another is the particular set of rules by which the transformation is to be attempted. In this respect the gamut of Patience ranges from the dispiritingly facile to the compulsively complex. Some are pure gambles that call rather for the exercise of patience than of skill; some call for a high degree of judgement, others for the type of positional analysis more often associated with Chess than cards. Scientists may see in them a struggle against the Second Law of Thermodynamics, which more or less decrees that the whole universe will eventually run down into a mess no matter how much you keep tidying up little bits of it. For the rest of us it is simply a battle of wits between human order and random nature.

Either way, Patience is a subject worthy of greater attention than it has been getting of late, especially in Britain. I cannot judge how it fares in America, but I have always been amused by the sequence in Frankenheimer's film *The Manchurian Candidate* where Raymond, whose hypnotic trance is triggered by the mother-figure of a red Queen, walks into a bar, asks for a pack of cards and starts a game of Solitaire on the counter without anyone looking askance at the event. In England the barman would probably have called the police.

The decline of Patience is something of a mystery, in view of the cheapness of the equipment, the simplicity of the rules, the speed at which things happen, and the incredible variety of situations that can emerge from a single pack of cards. What is certain is that Patience has somehow got itself a bad name. Perhaps this is because patience itself is not the virtue it once was. We live in an age when everything is up for grabs, and anyone who doesn't grab is a 'loser'. Or perhaps it is because the pastime became popular in the much (and wrongly) maligned Victorian period, and gives itself away by its cultured terminology and sometimes simpering titles. It is ironic, but true, that beneath some of the most fey of titles lurk some of the toughest of problems, like wolves in sheep's clothing. Similar mis-associations tell against it. Patience is a commendable activity for invalids or people forced to spend much time alone, but this does not mean (as some appear to assume) that playing it is a symptom of illness or idleness.

Another significant factor working against it is the shortage of good books on the subject. Nearly all the collections published today, and, indeed, over the past hundred years, are short, dull, unreliable, or any combination of the three. As far as I am able to judge, only three good collections have ever been produced, two of which are no longer obtainable and none of which is perfect. As I shall be referring to them quite often by name in the following pages let me introduce them at this point.

Cavendish (pen-name of Henry Jones) published his *Patience Games* in 1890. The collection is short and dull and reads like an army manual, but he was the first writer to distinguish between games of skill ('presenting definite problems') and games of judgement ('presenting indefinite problems'), and the first to show that Patience could and should be regarded as a serious exercise.

Mary Whitmore Jones published several series of games between about 1890 and 1910. Unlike Cavendish, she was quite unanalytical and often haphazard to the point of forgetfulness. On the other hand, she is thoroughly comprehensive and authoritative, and by far the most enjoyable to read. Wherever conflicting accounts occur of the same game, it is usually her judgement I prefer to fall back on.

Albert Morehead and Geoffrey Mott-Smith published their *Complete Book of Patience* in 1950. Although it is nowhere near as 'complete' as the title suggests, the authors do claim to have studied all the literature and to have tidied up conflicting rules, and a commendable effort has been made to classify games and arrange them in some sort of logical progression. Their best contribution was to equip each game with some indication of the chances in favour of or against its being played through to a successful conclusion, given good play where skill is called for. I have borrowed heavily from them in my 'odds in favour/odds against' notes throughout the present book, though my own experience of play leads to the conclusion that many of the actual figures they quote are way off beam.

Although Morehead and Mott-Smith came nearest to it, none of the books available to me when I first discovered an interest in Patience told me the sort of things I most wanted to know. I soon realized that some games struck me as more enjoyable than others and began to notice features of them that were pleasurable or exasperating, but there was no way of telling in advance whether or not a given game was going to be worth pursuing after taking the trouble to read through the rules and set up the layout. So, on the principle that if you want anything done properly you will have to do it yourself, I started doing it myself.

This book does not set out to be more comprehensive than anything published to date (though it does list over 250 main games, or 400 counting major variants, or 500 including minor variants and virtual duplications, which I think is a record). Quantity isn't everything, and it is only a matter of plundering the sources to make up the bulk. Rather, its object is to achieve what has not been properly attempted before: to get all the games sorted out, with duplicates under the same headings and similar games in the same sections, and then to arrange the sections in a logical progression that will act as an easily followed guide through the whole realm of Patience.

The usual way of compiling a Patience book is to wade through the existing literature, pick out the games one likes, divide them into one-pack and two-pack games, and arrange the two halves in alphabetical order. This may be convenient to the compiler, but it leaves the player feeling like a visitor to a zoo where anacondas, ants and aard-varks all jostle together in the first cage on the left. Alphabetical order does not help the American when he looks up Canfield and finds the Englishman's Demon, or the Englishman when he looks up Canfield and finds the American's Klondike. This book's alphabetical listing of games will be found in its proper place – the Index – whereas the games themselves are arranged in related groups.

To this end I have distinguished about a dozen families, proceeding more or less from the simplest and least skill-demanding to the most complex and skill-rewarding. An introduction to each section explains how the games go together and what general principles of play are involved, and the games following it are themselves presented in order from the simplest to the most elaborate.

Although all Patience games should be regarded as belonging to a common stock, I have taken care to credit inventors where their names are known, and hope that others will do the same by me. Games of my own invention included in this book are: Archway, Black Hole, Buffalo Bill, Curds and Whey, Exit, Penguin, and Striptease.

As the nomenclature of Patience games has always been a matter of confusion, I have taken as the main title of each one the name that strikes me as most appropriate and least ambiguous. Alternative titles follow the main name in smaller print, and variant games with names of their own are appended to each main entry.

Each game is prefaced with a note of the cards required to play it (whether one, two or short packs) and a broad indication of whether the odds of bringing the game to a successful conclusion are in favour of or against the player. In this respect it should be understood that where skill is involved the odds assume best possible play, and that some games will only come out if the distribution of cards happens to be favourable.

One thing I have deliberately avoided is the provision of hints or tips on how to win any game. The whole point of trying a new one is to work out how to attack it, and the pleasure is that much greater for doing it yourself. I have never understood why so many compilers seem so anxious to give the game away!

*

Patience is so called not only throughout the English-speaking world other than the United States but also in most European languages except Spanish and Italian. In these it is known as *solitario*, like American *solitaire*, though *paciencia* is encountered in Spanish as the name of a particular game. As the word is either English or French, and the game is certainly not English in origin, it should be regarded as French. Ironically enough, the French themselves now more often refer to the game as *réussite*, as *patience* has also come to mean jigsaw puzzle.

The earliest references to Patience date from the close of the eighteenth century and emanate from the Baltic area of northern Europe – Sweden, Poland, Denmark, Germany. It may have derived from a two-player competitive game in which the winner was the first to get his shuffled pack in order. Bystanders laid bets on the outcome, as card games were inevitably gambling games in those unenlightened days.

It seems not to have reached France until the 1820s, and the reason why it has a French name is simply that French was then the international language of European culture. Associations of Patience with Napoleon are therefore anachronistic. An apparent contemporary reference (1815) to Napoleon at Patience has been shown* in fact to refer to his aide Las Cases, who was espied in a corner forlornly shuffling a sticky pack of cards ('this solitary game of patience' – i.e. the virtue) to make them run smoothly for Napoleon's use at Whist.

Patience became popular in Britain in the 1870s (though Dickens refers to it a decade earlier in *Great Expectations*) following Queen Victoria's revelation in the biography of her late husband that Albert had been a keen Patience player from his German childhood. Similarly, it may be recalled, her son Alfred

* By Professor Alan Ross – see '*The Origins of Patience*' in *Games and Puzzles*, No. 40, September 1975.

had started the Bézique craze and her great-great-granddaughter Princess Margaret was to do much the same P.R. job on Canasta.

The earliest English collection of patiences was compiled by Lady Cadogan in about 1870, closely modelled on such French precursors as *Le Livre Illustré des Patiences* by the Comtesse de Blanccœur – see Bibliography for that and its English translation. It is for this reason that many English patience games are French in nomenclature and Victorian in flavour.

How To Get Started

How poor are they that have not patience

        – Othello (according to Shakespeare)

Given the book of rules, or having taken it, you need a pack of cards and either a large table or a small floor.

CARDS As space is the first requirement of many Patience games, especially some of the more elaborate Victorian concoctions, it is desirable to use special Patience cards rather than ordinary playing cards. Apart from their smaller and more manageable size, proper Patience cards have indices at all four corners instead of just top left and bottom right, which makes for easier identification when they are partly covered during play.

It was Morehead and Mott-Smith's unhappy discovery that some of the older games, even with smaller cards, took up more space than that afforded by the standard folding card-table. Their solution to this problem was to omit the very large games and cut some of the others down in size to the point of meaninglessness. My recommendation is to dispense with the standard card-table and instead use some surface large enough to be seen with the naked eye.

Standard 52-card packs are usually sold in boxed pairs, with back designs of the same pattern but contrasting colours. As some games are played with one pack and some with two this distinction makes it easy to separate the packs and recombine them as required. Better still is to keep a double pack and a separate single pack to save yourself even this small trouble.

RANK, SUIT AND SEQUENCE A 52-card pack is made up of four sets of thirteen cards. Each set is called a suit and distinguished by a particular symbol. Clubs (♣) and spades (♠) are black suits, hearts (♥) and diamonds (♦) red. The thirteen members of each suit are called ranks and run in sequence as follows:

$$A-2-3-4-5-6-7-8-9-10-J-Q-K$$

'A' for Ace is equivalent to 'one'. Beyond the ten numerals run the three 'court' cards: Jack, Queen, King, equivalent respectively to 11, 12 and 13. In some games King and Ace are regarded as consecutive. For example, if you are required to make a sequence starting with a Six, it will run 6–7–8–9–10–J–Q–K–A–2–3–4–5. In others the sequence may keep going round and round or change direction up and down indefinitely.

SHORT PACKS You will find that many games are played with two or even more packs shuffled together, and a few designed for play with one or more short packs. The 32-card pack, for instance, runs A–7–8–9–10–J–Q–K, while the 24-card pack has only A–9–10–J–Q–K in each suit. These should not be regarded as pointless perversions. Although short packs are not used in English card games, they are common on the Continent and in America where such games as Klabberjass, Skat and Pinochle use nothing else. Short-pack patiences are therefore designed for players who only have short packs to hand. I don't think any of them are different enough from full-pack equivalents to make it worth while deliberately stripping a full pack in order to play them.

SHUFFLING The object of most Patience games is to set the cards in order, suit by suit and in numerical sequence. Before you can do this, however, you have to get all the cards back out of order from the previous game. If not, they will come out in part-sequences for the next game, making it either too easy of solution or (less often) utterly impossible.

The usual way of randomizing cards is by overhand shuffling or riffling, but neither method is entirely suitable for Patience cards as they are too small for manipulation. A method often suggested is to spread them all face down on the table and slide them around with a circular motion, group by group, then sweep them all together into a consolidated pack. I prefer to deal them rapidly face up to about ten piles with one pack or twenty with two, trying as far as possible not to get two of the same rank together and often changing direction in the deal. After picking up the piles at random and putting them together I give a final overhand shuffle just to make sure. This system is fast and efficient.

TYPES OF GAME In most Patience games the object is to get all thirteen cards of each suit together in numerical order. This process is called 'building'. For each suit you set out an Ace, and on it build consecutively a Two, a Three, and so on up to the King. To this extent all such games may be referred to as Builders.

In many games this process is assisted by a contrary process carried out in a particular part of the layout called the tableau. While you are building cards in main sequence in one place, you are simultaneously building them in reverse sequence in the other. When the two sequences meet, you can then play off all those on the reverse sequence onto the main sequence. This process of reverse building is known as 'packing'. So many major games make use of it that we may conveniently refer to them under a separate heading as Packers.

Quite a few Builders and Packers make use of other distinctive features. In this book, for instance, I have devoted separate sections to specialized types of Builders under the names Blockades and Planners, and another to a particular class of Packers called Spiders. I could also have made separate groups of Fans (including Belle Lucie and House on the Hill), One-Ups (Golf, Black Hole), Clocks and so on, but as some of these are Builders and some Packers there comes a point at which such cross-classifications become less of a help than a hindrance.

A few games are neither Builders nor Packers. Mostly they involve throwing out cards in matched pairs or other sets, and some are in the nature of mathematical puzzles. For convenience I have brought them together under the heading Non-Builders.

LUCK AND SKILL The fact of classifying a game as a Builder or a Packer, or whatever, serves only to indicate what type of mechanism is involved. It does not say anything about the degree of skill or type of thinking required, or even if any is required at all. Why, then, are some Patience games harder to get out than others? If you do win, how much is success due to skill and how much to chance?

The answers to these questions vary according to the game being played, and it will be useful to identify one or two basic principles of Patience to assist us in our inquiries. The following features are most relevant:

Distribution This means the order in which the cards finish up after you have shuffled them. Obviously, if they come out in the 'right' order the game will be more likely to succeed than if they come out in the 'wrong' order, whatever that may happen to be for the game in question. As the player has no conscious control over the way the cards finish up, we may well feel that the ideal game should always be capable of solution regardless of the distribution, otherwise success is a matter of chance, even if skill is applied.

Discipline I regard the rules of different games as ranging from 'strict' through 'fair' to 'lax'. Let me explain.

A game with strict rules is one that gives you little or no choice of play. At each move there is only one thing you *may* do, and, if you *cannot* do it, the game is lost. Now, where you have no choice of play you clearly have no opportunity of applying skill, so success at a strict game depends entirely upon the chance factor of the distribution – the cards either do or do not come out in the right order. Examples include Accordion and Auld Lang Syne.

At the other extreme is the game with lax rules. This one gives you so many ways of ordering cards and shifting them about that you can hardly go wrong – or, if you do, you can usually put it right again soon after. Such games are likely to come out regardless of distribution, and equally regardless of how well or badly you play. Paradoxically, therefore, they make no more demands on skill than very strict games. Examples include Lucky Thirteen and Empress of India.

Somewhere between the two extremes lies the well-adjusted 'fair' game. This is one that gives just the right amount of play. Theoretically it can always be made to succeed regardless of the distribution, but only if you play perfectly – one foot wrong and you're out! Whether or not any game actually meets this ideal is probably unprovable without extensive computer investigation, as any candidate would need to be tested for (*a*) all possible distributions and (*b*) all possible lines of play. Typical candidates might include Quilt and Terrace.

It is interesting to see how variants of the same game can be produced by tightening or relaxing the rules. Take, for instance, any game played with one pack in which the object is to build four suit-sequences from Ace up to King, and which has a tableau on which packing takes place in reverse sequence.

The laxest rule states that you may pack in descending sequence *regardless of suit*. If you turn a Five, you can put it on any Six, giving you four possibilities. The tightest states that you must pack in descending sequence and *in suit*. If you turn a Five, it will only go on the Six of its own suit – one possibility. A popular rule is that packing must take place in *alternating colour*. In this case a black Five will go on either red Six, or a red Five on either black Six, giving two possibilities for any Five turned. A more rarely encountered rule (see, for example, Thumb and Pouch) is that packing must take place in *different suits*. In this case a Five can go on any Six except the one of its own suit, giving three possibilities. In order of increasing tightness, therefore, the rules are: (1) regardless of suit, (2) in different suit, (3) in alternating colour, (4) in suit.

Other ways of varying the tightness of rules include filling or not filling spaces left by the removal of cards, shifting cards of the tableau in whole sequences, part sequences or one at a time, and reducing or increasing the number of redeals. These are some of the adjustments that can be made to any game in order to secure what the player regards as an ideal balance. A well-adjusted game, clearly, is one that is not too tight and not too lax. It should give you enough choice of play to get the game out regardless of distribution, but not so much as to make success a foregone conclusion. In other words, you need just enough rope to hang yourself with.

Revelation Games vary not only in discipline but also in the degree to which they reveal themselves – i.e. make the distribution known – during the play. This degree also ranges between two extremes, each of which calls for a different type of skill.

At one extreme is the completely 'open' game. In this, all cards are dealt face up before play begins and remain in full view throughout. You therefore have complete knowledge of the distribution at every stage of the game, and the type of skill required to win it is that of *analysis* (positional, as in Chess problems). Cavendish describes such games as presenting 'definite' problems for solution. Examples are Bisley and Baker's Dozen.

At the other extreme is the 'closed' game. In this, you start play by turning cards from the unknown stock and seeing what you can do with them. Whenever you have a choice of play your decision will be influenced by how the remaining cards are most likely to turn out, though you cannot foresee them. By the time they have all appeared it is too late to take advantage of that knowledge. The type of skill involved here is that of *judgement* (of probabilities, as in playing Poker). Cavendish describes such games as presenting 'indefinite' problems. Examples are Sir Tommy and Strategy.

Between these two extremes lie various types of game which can be described as 'half-open'. Typically, you start without full knowledge of the distribution and must therefore work by judgement, but there eventually comes a point at which the position of all cards is known in time for the rest of the game to be worked out by analysis. Such games therefore involve both types of skill (as at Contract Bridge). Cavendish did not distinguish such a hybrid group, but we may follow his principles by saying that they present problems of increasing definition. Examples include Miss Milligan and Interregnum.

To summarize:

Strict games give little or no choice of play: success therefore depends on distribution and takes no account of skill.

Lax games give too much choice of play: success is therefore usually a foregone conclusion and takes no account of distribution or skill.

Fair games give a balanced choice of play: success depends entirely on skill and takes no account of distribution. The type of skill involved is that of analysis if the game is open, judgement if it is closed, both if it is half-open.

TYPE OF SKILL INVOLVED

determined by degree to which game is 'open' or 'closed'

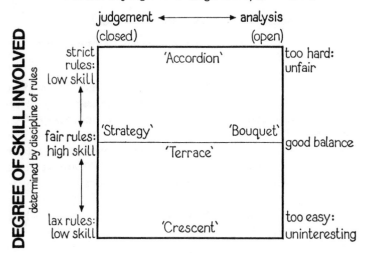

SKILL AT PATIENCE How much skill is involved in a given game depends on the scope it gives for making decisions. With tight rules there is little scope and the game is too hard; with lax rules there is too much and the game is so easy as to be uninteresting. Between these two extremes a well-balanced game gives maximum scope for skill. But then the *type* of skill required varies between two extremes. A completely open game calls for positional analysis (like Chess), a completely closed game for probability judgements (like Poker). This dimension, however, becomes less relevant as less skill is called for. Several particular games are 'plotted' on this diagram according to the type and degree of skill required.

Technical Terms Explained

One technical term is worth a thousand ordinary words.

– Proposed new Chinese proverb

These terms are for reference only – they need not be learnt by heart! But it will be useful to read through them first, as they include some general notes on procedure which are not always spelt out in the text.

This list does not include the family names which I have attached to particular types of Patience, all of which are explained in the separate introductions to the various sections.

ALTERNATING COLOUR Red on black, black on red, where 'red' means hearts or diamonds and 'black' clubs or spades.

AVAILABLE An 'available' card is one which, by the rules of the game, may be taken and put somewhere else. Usually, a card is available if it stands alone or at the top of a pile, but not if it is wholly or partly covered by another card.

BASE Where the object is to build a pile of cards in a given order, the one at the bottom is the 'base' card.

BELOW, BENEATH In this book these words are usefully distinguished as follows. A card *below* another is one nearer the bottom of the board or closer to the player. A card *beneath* another is one that is covered or overlapped by it.

BLOCKED A game is blocked when no more legal moves can be made. In some cases this means the game is lost; in others, a special rule or grace may apply by which the game can be unblocked.

BOARD The area on which you are playing, such as the top of a card table. (In some books it means the same as 'layout'.)

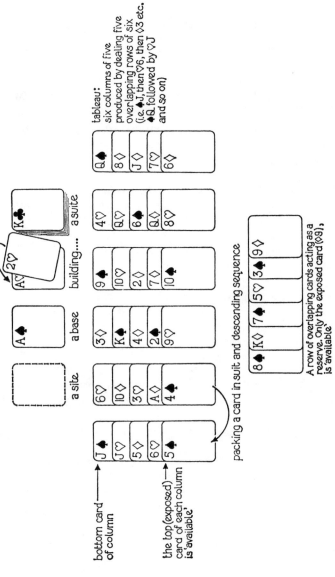

tableau:
six columns of five
produced by dealing five
overlapping rows of six
(i.e. ♠J, then♡6, then ◊3 etc.
♠Q followed by ♡J
and so on)

building....   a suite

A♠   a base

a site

the top (exposed)
card of each column
is 'available'

bottom card
of column

packing a card in suit and descending sequence

A row of overlapping cards acting as a
reserve. Only the exposed card (◊9),
is 'available'

SOME TECHNICAL TERMS ILLUSTRATED   The usual object is to build *suites* on *base* cards, which are either taken out and put in place at the start of play or else must be *founded* on *sites* as and when they become available. An *available* card is usually one that is completely exposed, i.e. not overlapped by another card.

BUILD The object of most patiences is to build piles of cards in sequence, and 'building' is the act of adding a card to such a pile. In some books it is also used with the meaning 'to pack'.

BURIED A card is buried, and therefore not available, if it is wholly or partly covered by another.

CLOSED In this book a game is described as 'closed' if cards that cannot be entered into play are discarded to a wastepile. Such games require the player to make decisions without full knowledge of the position, as there are cards yet to be dealt. See also 'half-open' and 'open'.

COLUMN A line of cards extending towards you. Usually, and therefore unless otherwise stated, they are spread so that all are identifiable but only the one nearest you is 'exposed'.

COME OUT A game is said to come out if you succeed in fulfilling the objective.

COUPLE Two cards in sequence with each other, such as Ten and Jack (as distinct from 'pair', meaning two of the same rank).

COURT Jack, Queen and King are court cards or 'courts' (as distinct from numerals or 'spot' cards).

COVERED A card is covered if there is another one lying wholly or partly on top of it. Usually, a covered card is not 'available'.

CROWN A suite is 'crowned' when the last card is played to it.

DEAL To take cards from the top of the pack and lay them on the table. Cards are always dealt face up unless otherwise stated.

DEUCE The Two of any suit.

DISCARD To lay a card on a wastepile instead of entering it into the business part of the game.

DOWN-CARD One that is lying face down.

EXPOSED A card that is not covered or overlapped by another. Usually, any exposed card is 'available'.

FACE To face a down-card is to turn it face up.

FAN A small number of cards, usually three, laid in an overlapping row so that only one is exposed.

FOUND To lay out a base card ready for a suite to be built on it. In some games the requisite base cards are taken out of the pack and founded before the rest are finally shuffled and play begins; in others they are founded as and when they become available.

FREE To make a card available by removing a card covering it, or by turning it up from the pack in the normal course of events. (Same as 'release'.)

GRACE A special move that may be provided by the rules of the game to get it going again when it blocks – a sort of indulgence or 'official' act of cheating. Usually only one grace may be taken per game.

HALF-OPEN Used here to describe a game which eventually becomes open so that the skill required is one of positional analysis, but which starts off 'closed'.

LAYOUT A formalized arrangement of cards dealt to the table before play begins. In this book it is carefully distinguished from 'tableau'.

NUMERAL A number or 'spot' card, as opposed to a 'court'.

OPEN Used here to describe a game in which play begins with all cards face up on the table, so that there are no unknown factors to take into account when planning the attack.

OVERLAP An overlapping column is one in which each succeeding card half covers the previous card so that the latter can be identified even though it is not available for taking. Where several such columns are to be made at the outset they are usually dealt in overlapping rows – that is, a row of cards separated from one another, then a second row below the first but with each card overlapping the one above it in the previous row, and so on, this being a quicker and easier way to deal. Such an 'overlapping row of cards' must not be confused with a 'row of overlapping cards', in which each succeeding card is so dealt as to overlap the one before.

PACK To place cards on top of one another (overlapping) in a temporary part of the layout called the tableau, in accordance with rules specifying a sequence which is usually the reverse of that required for building the suites.

PACKED SEQUENCE A packing of two or more cards in the sequence required for packing by the rules of the game. In some games such a sequence, if headed by an exposed card, may be shifted as a whole from one part of the tableau to another, provided that the card at the furthest end from the exposed one would be legally packable if it were itself exposed. Of these, in turn, some games require the whole of a packed sequence to be shifted, while others permit the taking of any fraction of it headed by the exposed card. In this book the absence of a reference to shifting a packed sequence means that cards may be shifted only one at a time. Where a rule states that a packed sequence may be shifted as a whole, assume that any fraction of it can be shifted unless otherwise stated.

PACKET A squared-up pile of cards dealt at the start of a game is called a 'packet'. If they are dealt face down except for the top one it makes sense to square them up in order to conserve space. In some older accounts, however, the player is instructed to deal a packet of cards face up. Where the intention is that lower cards should not be known in advance, I have changed this rule to call for them to be dealt face down. Where it is clear that no such restriction applies, I have changed the rule to call for the requisite cards to be dealt in an overlapping column so that all are visible.

PAIR Two cards of the same rank.

PLAY To play a card is to make use of it for building, packing or filling a space, as opposed to discarding it to a wastepile.

RANK The identity of a card irrespective of its suit. There are ten numeral ranks running from Ace to Ten, and three courts.

REDEAL In some games there comes a point at which, when no further play is possible, all the cards that have not yet been built on suites are gathered up and redealt, with or without shuffling as the rules may specify. In others a point is reached at which, when all cards have been either entered into the game or discarded to the wastepile so that none remain in hand, the wastepile is taken, turned upside down and used as a new stock. The term 'redeal' applies to both.

RELEASE To make a card 'available' by removing one that covers it, or by turning it from the stock. (Same as 'Free'.)

RESERVE A group of cards dealt to the layout at the start of play, distinguished from the tableau by the fact that no packing takes place on it. In a replenishing reserve all cards are simultaneously 'available' for packing or building, and when one is taken for this purpose its place may be filled with another card dealt from stock or taken from another part of the layout. In a diminishing reserve the cards are not replaced when taken, and are usually arranged in a pile or column in such a way that only the top card is available.

REVERSAL The transference of a sequence of cards from one place to another one at a time, so that they finish up in reverse order from that in which they started. Many games involve the building of two sequences in the same suit, one from the Ace upwards and one from the King downwards. When a point is reached at which the top cards of two piles in the same suit are consecutive in sequence (such as Ten on one, Jack on the other), the rules may permit you to reverse a number of cards from one to the other, though base cards must always be left untaken. Suite-to-suite reversal is a privilege that must not be assumed where it is not specifically allowed.

ROW A line of cards dealt from side to side. Whether or not they are overlapped depends on the rules of the game.

SEQUENCE The normal sequence of ranks from low to high ('ascending sequence') is Ace–2–3–4–5–6–7–8–9–10–Jack–Queen–

King. Many two-pack games call for suites to be built in descending sequence from King downwards. Some call for 'round the corner' sequences, in which King–Ace are regarded as consecutive. For example, a suite built on a Ten would run 10–J–Q–K–A–2–3– etc. A few vary the interval between consecutive cards, the commonest being the 'alternating sequence' running A–3–5–7–9–J–K–2–4–6–8–10–Q. One or two call for such complicated sequences as alternately up and down, i.e. beginning A–K–2–Q–3–J–4– . . . and ending in reverse . . . 4–J–3–Q–2–K–A.

SHIFT To transfer an exposed card (or a packed sequence headed by an exposed card) from the end of one tableau column to another.

SITE Place in which a base-card is to be founded when one becomes available.

SPACE (or VACANCY) When an isolated card is taken for use, or when all cards have been removed from a tableau column, the rules of the game may declare that the removal leaves a 'space' which may be filled by another card.

SPREAD To overlap cards in a row or column so that all are identifiable but only one is exposed.

STOCK Cards that are not dealt to the layout at the start of play: the remainder of the pack, which is held in the hand and from which cards are turned one by one to continue the game. The stock must be held face downwards, and a card turned from it must be entered into the game or discarded to the wastepile (if any) before the next one is turned. It is, however, permissible to play the first card, then turn the next before deciding whether or not to make any further moves that may be possible before actually playing it.

SUIT Hearts and diamonds are red suits, clubs and spades black.

SUITE Term used in this book to denote the pile of cards whose building in sequence is usually the object of the game. There has never been a satisfactory term for this feature: 'foundation' is inaccurate and 'foundation pile' long-winded. An Ace-suite is one based on an Ace and ascending in sequence, a King-suite one based on a King and descending. See also 'reversal'.

SUIT-SEQUENCE A sequence of cards all of the same suit. Sometimes used instead of 'suite' for clarity.

TABLEAU An arrangement of cards on the table, usually consisting of several columns of overlapping cards, whose distinguishing feature is the fact that packing takes place on the exposed cards of the columns. (If not, then such an arrangement is either a reserve or a number of wastepiles.) Unless otherwise stated, the columns are usually dealt in overlapping rows for convenience: see 'overlap'. In some games a single row of cards is dealt 'to start the tableau', which is gradually built up during the game by the subsequent dealing of other rows across it.

TAKE A card which is 'available' may be 'taken' for building or packing as the case may be.

TURN When King and Ace are regarded as consecutive (see 'sequence'), the sequence is said to 'turn (the corner) between King and Ace'.

UNCOVERED Describes a card which is not covered or overlapped by another; effectively the same as 'exposed'.

UP-CARD A card which is lying face up, usually at the top of a pile.

VACANCY Same as 'space'.

WASTEPILE In some games, cards that are turned from stock but cannot be entered into the layout are discarded face up to form a 'wastepile'. The top card of the wastepile is always 'available' – that is, it may be taken for play if a subsequent move enables it to go somewhere to which it could not go when first turned from stock. Its removal similarly releases the card beneath it, and so on. In many games the wastepile is taken, turned upside down and used as a new stock to continue the game – see 'redeal'. In some games cards are discarded to more than one wastepile, either in an order specified by the rules or, if so stated, in whichever order the player thinks best. In any case, no matter whether there are one or more wastepiles, it is permissible (and desirable) to spread the cards slightly so that those lying beneath the top card are identifiable.

WEAVE, WAVE, WAIVE Term used in the game called Miss Milligan, which see. The original seems to be 'waive', in the sense of waiving a rule to get the game out. (See 'grace'.)

WING A tableau is sometimes dealt in two symmetrical halves with a space between. Each half is a wing.

Terms not used in this book

The following additional terms are often encountered in Patience books and are here explained for completeness.

CHOCKERED Same as 'blocked'.

DEPOT A position in the layout that may consist of a pile of cards, or one card, or a space waiting for a card. It is a very useful word, but as it has gone out of fashion I have replaced it, where necessary, by the non-committal 'position'.

FAMILY Same as 'suite'.

FOUNDATION Strictly, a base card. Loosely, it has come to mean the suite or pile of cards built on it. Though still current, it is awkward and inaccurate. (But see 'found'.)

LANE A space made by clearing out a line or column of cards, or the lower part of one to release the next card up. Like 'depot' it is a useful word but out of fashion.

TALON Same as 'stock'. It has dropped out of use because some writers took it to mean 'wastepile' and the resultant ambiguity rendered it useless. The basic meaning of this French word is 'heel'; a secondary meaning is the part of a loaf of bread which is left when one or more slices have been cut from it. From this developed a third use to denote that part of a pack of cards which is left when one or more cards have been dealt from it. Its application to 'wastepile' was therefore a mistake.

Part One

CLOSED GAMES

presenting indefinite problems
to be solved by care and patience

Simple Builders

In these games the usual object is to put out an Ace of each suit and to build them up in suit and sequence to the King. If played with one pack there will be four such suites, if with two, eight. There are several variations on this theme – for example, building on cards other than Aces (as in Quadrille), or not building in consecutive sequence (as in Musical) – but the underlying principle remains the same.

The usual method of play is simple, offering little or no choice of moves and so demanding no greater skill than that of close attention. You hold the pack or 'stock' face down in one hand, and at each move turn up the top card. If it is the next card required for one of the suites, you build it. If not, discard it face up to a wastepile. If ever the top card of the wastepile can be built on a suite (as the result of further play made since it was discarded) you may take it for that purpose.

Having run out of cards in hand, you may be permitted to take the wastepile, turn it upside down as a new stock, and play through it again. If you were to redeal often enough in this way you would always eventually succeed in building the whole pack into the suites. To overcome this element of inevitability, and to justify the name of 'patience', the rules of each game specify how many redeals may be made, and the game is considered lost if not brought to a successful conclusion within that number.

Robert

One pack
Odds against

This old and rather intractable game has the unusual feature of building a single suite. Compare Golf, King's Way and Black Hole, which share the same feature but require more thinking.

Hold the pack face down and deal the top card up to the table to start a suite. Turn cards from stock one by one. If the turned card is next higher or lower in rank than the top of the suite, regardless of suit, add it to the suite; if not, play it face up to a single wastepile. When you run out of cards, turn the wastepile face down and go through it again. A second redeal is allowed, and if you have not been able to build all cards on the suite by the end of it the game is lost.

Assume (since the original rules do not state) that sequence of rank is not continuous between Ace and King, that the top card of the wastepile is playable to the suite if it fits, and that you are not obliged to play to the suite if you think a card better thrown to the wastepile.

If you play with the stock face up, you should play to the wastepile face down.

Auld Lang Syne

One pack
Odds against

A compulsive but maddening game that might be described as the next best thing to banging your head against a brick wall.

Layout Put the four Aces out in a row.

Object To build them up in suit to the Kings.

Play Deal four cards face up in a row from left to right. Build any that can be built. Deal four more from left to right across the first four, overlapping any that are left or filling spaces as the case may be. Keep dealing rows of four in the same way. After each deal pause and build as many exposed cards as you can. If they cannot all be built off the final layout when no more cards remain in hand the game is lost, as there is no redeal.

TAM O'SHANTER The harder version, for those who are tired of life, is the same as described above except that the Aces are not put out to start with but must be founded as and when they turn up.

Amazons
One 32-card pack
Odds against

Amazons and Puzzler, both old games, are the short-pack equivalents of Auld Lang Syne. Puzzler is simpler; Amazons, described first, more interesting. The first thing to do with Amazons is to discard the Kings, as they have no part to play. (The original Amazons were, of course, the first women's libbers. Indeed, they went one better than their modern counterparts.)

Object To found the Aces as they appear and build them up in suit to the Queens, starting with the Sevens.

Play Deal four cards face up in a row from left to right, and continue this procedure with subsequent cards overlapping those beneath or filling spaces as the case may be. After each deal pause and play any exposed cards that may be possible. As the Aces appear found them in a row above the columns. Any other exposed card may only be built if it belongs to the suit of the Ace lying immediately above the column it falls in.

Redeal Having run out of cards, gather up the columns from left to right, turn them upside down, and continue play with the new stock. Whenever a suite is completed up to the Queen, cease dealing further cards to the column beneath it. Redeal as often as you like, reducing the number of columns by one for each finished suite. Continue until either (*a*) you win by completing the fourth suite, or (*b*) you run through two successive deals without placing a single card, in which case the game is lost.

PUZZLER (32 cards) Deal cards face up four at a time from left to right to form four columns. As they appear, found the Kings and build them down in suit to the Sevens (leaving Aces in the pack). After each deal, pause to build exposed cards where possible. When the stock is exhausted and no more building can be done, gather up the columns from right to left, turn them upside down and continue play. Only one such redeal is allowed. If successful, you finish with a rwo of suites surmounted by Sevens with a row of Aces below them.

Quadrille
Captive Queens, La Française, Partners
One pack
Even chances

A pleasant little pictorial, which may be said to represent the dance of the cardboard court.

Layout and object Arrange the four Queens in the centre. They are for decoration only. Around them arrange the Fives and Sixes as base cards for eight suites. Build the Sixes upwards in suit to the Jacks, and the Fives down in suit to the Kings (which follow on the Aces).

Play Turn cards from stock and build them if possible or discard them face up to a single wastepile if not. Three redeals of the wastepile are allowed.

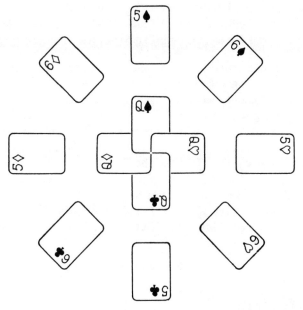

QUADRILLE Arrange the Queens decoratively in the centre, then build the Fives down in suit to the Kings and the Sixes up in suit to the Jacks.

Vanbrugh
One pack
Odds against

Rather more complicated and less pretty than Quadrille, Vanbrugh is presumably named after Sir John of that line, seventeenth-century playwright and architect – though for what reason escapes me. The game is a test of concentration.

Layout and object Place the four Queens in the centre, for decoration only. As base cards, arrange the four Kings radially to each compass point from them, and the four Jacks radiating diagonally in the spaces between, each to the right of his own King. The ultimate objective is to build each King in ascending suit-sequence to the Ten, to be followed by the Jack and finally surmounted by the Queen; but this is to be done in a somewhat roundabout way.

Play Turn cards from stock and build them if possible or put them face up on a single wastepile if not. Upon each King build the Ace, the Two, and then stop. Upon each Jack build downwards in alternating sequence, i.e. J–9–7–5–3. Each Jack suite is then to be reversed onto its King suite as the even numerals become available in ascending sequence. Thus, when the Four is turned, place the Three on the Two and the Four on the Three, exposing the Five. When the Six appears, place it and the Five on the Four. Continue until the appearance of the Ten allows you to add the Nine and Ten to the King suite, and follow with the Jack and finally the Queen. Three redeals of the wastepile are permitted, but will rarely be enough.

Cotillion
Contradance
Two packs
Odds against

The two-pack version of Quadrille is named after another dance. Cotillion comes from a French word for 'petticoat', of which you presumably get a quick flash if you keep your eyes peeled. The cotillion is defined as a country dance. This in turn is said to be a corruption of French *contre-danse*, meaning 'quadrille'. To add to the verbal confusion, the game is not to be confused with Royal Cotillion (described elsewhere).

Layout and object Take all the Fives and Sixes and arrange them in a circle of sixteen base cards, keeping a Five and Six of the same suit next to each other but alternating suits for effect. Each Six is to be built up in suit to the Queen, each Five down in suit to the King. The end product is eight royal marriages.

Play Turn cards from stock and build them if possible or play them face up to a single wastepile if not. Two redeals of the wastepile are allowed.

Precedence
Order of Precedence, Panama
Two packs
Odds against

A legitimist is one who favours royal succession through primogeniture. The other titles are hardly more illuminating.

Object To found, in order and as they turn up, a King, a Queen, a Jack, a Ten, a Nine, an Eight, a Seven and a Six, and to build upon each of these a descending sequence of thirteen cards regardless of suit. The end product is a row of eight piles of thirteen, surmounted respectively by A, K, Q, J, 10, 9, 8 and 7.

Play Turn cards from stock and build them if possible or play them face up to a single wastepile if not. The game cannot start until a King appears, and the other seven bases must be founded strictly in order from Queen to Six. Other cards, however, may be built whenever they fit a suite in progress. Two redeals are allowed.

LEGITIMIST This variant invites you to withdraw a King from the pack first so as to start with a base. It makes little difference.

The Dial
Knaves' Dial
One or two packs
Odds against

Some minor variants on the clockface theme, so called because twelve of the thirteen suites to be built are placed in a circle in such a way that, when complete, their top cards show the numbers

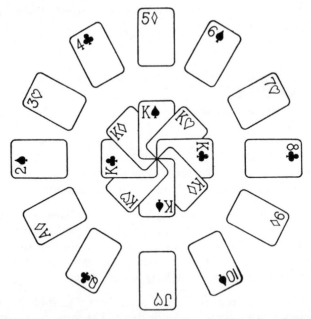

THE DIAL (Two packs)   Build the outer cards up in suit and sequence until the top card corresponds to the right number on the clock face (counting Jack 11 and Queen 12). The Kings play no part but are merely disposed decoratively in the middle.

from one to twelve (counting court cards as numbers where necessary).

DIAL (ONE PACK) The first card turned is a base. Place it in its appropriate clockface position, counting Jack 11, Queen 12. If it is a King, put it in the centre. The other twelve cards of the same suit are to be founded as and when they turn up, and placed in their appropriate positions. Upon each base build the other three cards of the same rank radially outwards as they appear, but in alternate colours. Put unplayable cards on a wastepile, the top of which is always available. Two redeals are allowed.

DIAL (TWO PACK) As above, but build eight cards of each rank in alternating colour on the bases. Three redeals are allowed. In the variant called Knaves' Dial, Queens are 11 and Kings 12, and the Jacks are placed in a row in the middle. Furthermore, cards are arranged in the form of a crescent or semicircle, perhaps rather more like a sundial than a clockdial.

DIAL (TWO-PACK VARIANT) Remove one ♠7, ♥8, ♣9, ♦10, ♠J, ♥Q, ♣K, ♦A, ♠2, ♥3, ♣4, ♦5 and arrange them in a circle with ♠7 in the one o'clock position. Turn cards from stock and build them if possible or play them face up to a single wastepile if not. Upon each base build in suit and ascending sequence until there are eight cards in all, the topmost of which will then represent the appropriate clockface numeral from one to twelve (Queen) – e.g. the Six which originally occupies the one o'clock position will be built up to the Ace, and so on. As the eight Kings have no real part to play, they are merely disposed decoratively in the middle as they appear. Two redeals are allowed.

Musical
Betsy Ross, Fairest, Four Kings, Plus Belle, Quadruple Alliance
One pack
Odds against

This is a form of Calculation (described later), but with less scope for planning. The pretty names for the game were perhaps intended to sweeten the arithmetical pill that it requires you to swallow. It may, in fact, be recommended as a teaching aid when the class gets round to alternative numeration bases or the modulo concept. Of the various titles available, I have preferred Musical because it best combines the mathematic with the aesthetic. The completed suites may also be regarded as cords vibrating at different intervals.

Layout Take any Ace, Two, Three and Four and put them in a row. Below them put any Two, Four, Six and Eight in the same order. The lower row cards are bases, each of which is to be built upwards, regardless of suit, but in four different intervals corresponding to the number shown on the cards above (which

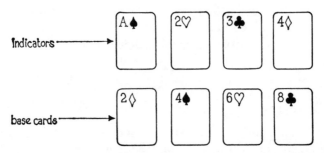

MUSICAL   The upper cards, indicators, are only there to remind you of the intervals by which the suites below are to be built, regardless of suit.

serve only to show the interval). Counting Jack 11, Queen 12, King 13, and anything over 13 as its remainder when divided by 13, the bases will be built as follows:

(A) 2–3–4–5–6–7–8–9–10–J–Q–K
(2) 4–6–8–10–Q–A–3–5–7–9–J–K
(3) 6–9–Q–2–5–8–J–A–4–7–10–K
(4) 8–K–3–7–J–2–6–10–A–5–9–K

The end product explains two of the alternative titles.

Play Turn cards from stock and build them if possible or play them face up to a single wastepile if not. Two redeals are allowed.

Queens and Jacks
Two packs
Odds against

In Queens and Jacks we have what at first sight appears to be a packing game. Closer inspection shows it to be a simple builder with suite-to-suite reversal, but it demonstrates very clearly how Packers may have evolved from Builders.

Layout Take the eight Queens and display them in two rows of four.

Object To found the eight Kings as and when they appear and to build them up in suit to the Jacks (proceeding K, A, 2 etc.).

Play Turn cards from stock and build them if possible or else discard them face up to a single wastepile. Build cards in ascending suit sequence on the Kings and descending suit sequence on the Queens. When the top cards of two suites are in suit and sequence, reverse those from the Queen suite onto the King's, leaving the Queen intact. Lose no opportunity to build the top card of the wastepile, as there is no redeal.

Milton

Two packs
Odds against

For a game that gives virtually no opportunity for skill, Milton is maddeningly difficult to follow at first reading and cannot be recommended to anyone suffering from poor eyesight.

Layout Deal eight cards face up in a row: these are the 'index' cards. If two of them are of the same suit and consecutive in rank, place the higher of them immediately below the other in what will eventually become a second row of cards (and a third in sequence on top of that, if necessary). King and Ace are consecutive, Ace being higher and followed in turn by Two. Fill gaps in the index row from stock, and do the same again if necessary.

Object Ultimately, to finish with an Ace of each suit in the index row above four 25-card suites surmounted by the Kings. Each suite runs from Two to King and then from Ace to King on top of that.

Play Turn cards from stock one by one and play them if possible; if not, discard them face up to a single wastepile, the top card of which is always available.

No building takes place on the index cards: they remain single until taken, and are then replaced from stock or waste.

A turned card of the same suit as and next higher in rank than an index card is to be placed immediately below the card it matches. Upon these cards in the second row build others in suit and ascending sequence, turning the corner from King to Ace as necessary. Go as far as you can, but avoid building the second Ace when it turns up.

When an index card can be built on any other suite than the one immediately below it, build it, together with the suite (if any) immediately below it. This leaves a gap in the index row: fill it with the top card of the wastepile, or, if you think this unsuitable, with the next card turned from stock. Never build an index card on the suite immediately below it, otherwise the game will fail. It will also fail if you are not careful about Aces and Twos, as follows:

The first Ace of each suit that turns up may be founded or built on a King in the second row, but the second Ace of each suit *must* be used as an index-card replacement in the top row, otherwise the game will fail. If there is no vacancy when the second appears, you will have to discard it for the time being. The reverse applies to Twos: the second Two of each suit *should not* be used as an index-card replacement, otherwise the game will very probably fail.

Redeal The wastepile may be turned to form a new stock twice, giving three rounds of play in all.

Weaver's
Two packs
Odds against

Though devoid of skill, Weaver's introduces an appropriate mechanical process that has a pleasing rhythm about it. Something similar will be encountered in Travellers and its variant Spoilt.

Layout Take out the eight Kings and found them at the top of the

board. Deal the remaining cards face up to twelve piles, numbering them from Ace to Queen as you go. If a turned card is of the
same rank as the pile it is about to go to, put it face down to one
side instead and deal the next card to the pile after the one
omitted. These outcasts are the 'shuttles'; the rest of the layout
represents the 'loom'.

Object To build the Kings down in suit to the Aces.

Play The exposed card of each pile is available for building. Build
as far as possible. Then turn up the top shuttle and start 'shuttling'
or 'weaving' as follows: place it at the bottom of the pile whose
number corresponds to its rank, then take the top card of that
pile and put it at the bottom of the pile corresponding to *its*
rank, and keep going. If the top card of a pile corresponds to the
pile it is on, shuttle it to the bottom and take the next one instead.
Keep going until you lift a card that can be built on one of the
suites. Build it, then pause and build as many more exposed cards
as you can.

  With building completed, turn up the next shuttle and start the
process again. Note that a shuttle may not be built directly on a
suite but must pass through the loom first, and that exposed cards
may not be built until a buildable card has actually been lifted
from the top of a pile and built.

Redeal When no shuttles are left and no more building can be
done, gather up the piles in reverse order and deal them out again,
casting out shuttles as before. This time, however, reduce the
number of piles by as many ranks as have all been built on the
suites. For instance, if all Queens and Jacks have been built you
must deal to ten piles instead of twelve. Only one redeal is allowed.

LEONI'S OWN (KINGS) Two packs. Found an Ace and a King
of each suit: the object is to build them respectively upwards and
downwards into thirteen-card suit sequences. Deal the rest of the
cards face up to thirteen piles, numbering them from Ace to King
as you go. When a card you turn is of the same rank as the next
pile, lay it face down to one side as an 'exile' and deal the next
card instead. After dealing, turn the exiles face up: they are all
available for building on suites, as also are the exposed cards on

the thirteen piles and all cards of the King pile, which may be spread so that all are visible. When no more building can be done, take the top exile and start shuttling by placing it at the bottom of the pile corresponding to its rank. Whenever a card on a pile is exposed that can be built on a suite, build it before continuing the shuttle. Shuttling ceases when a King is reached and placed to the bottom of its pile, at which point the next exile is taken and shuttling begins again. Suite-to-suite reversal is permitted. When stuck, gather up the piles from King to Ace, put the unused exiles at the bottom, and redeal. Two such redeals are allowed.

DOG This version, of unexplained title, properly belongs to the Reserved Builders. But it is so obviously Weaver's or Leoni's with the addition of a reserve to make it easier that all three are probably best put together. Found all eight Kings to start with, and play to build them down in suit to the Aces. Deal to twelve piles (as at Weaver's), numbering them from Ace to Queen and discarding correspondence cards to one side (forming the 'dog'). After each deal of twelve, discard three face up to one side to form a reserve called the 'kennel'. Start play by building on the suites any exposed cards on the piles or from the kennel. When stuck, take the first card of the dog and start shuttling. When you lift a buildable card (it is not enough merely to expose one), build it, then pause and build any other exposed cards and cards from the kennel as will go. Turn the next card of the dog and start shuttling again. Having run out of dog cards, gather up the piles from right to left, turn them upside down, add unplayed kennel cards to the top of the new stock (so that they will be dealt first), and redeal. This time, however, deal only eleven piles (Ace to Jack) and discard four to the kennel after each round. A second redeal is permitted, this time to ten piles with five to the kennel after each round. There is no further redeal.

Reserved Builders

These are basically Simple Builders, and the general procedure outlined for that group on page 35 also apply here.

Reserved Builders differ from the previous group in that a certain number of cards are dealt to the table before play begins. These cards form a 'reserve', and can be used for building on suites as and when they are needed. At first sight this makes the games more amenable to success, because whereas before only two cards were available for building (the top of the stock and the top of the wastepile), now the number is increased by as many as are also available in the reserve. The games which follow are, in fact, arranged in increasing order of number of cards initially available.

It may be of interest to note that reserves are of two sorts. In some games cards taken from the reserve are immediately replaced, in others they are not. It is obvious that the advantage created by the reserve is greater in those of the 'replenishing' than in those of the 'diminishing' type. A few games (Captive Commanders, Wheat-ear, Royal Cotillion) have both.

As the cards of the reserve may be arranged in various patterns it is not surprising that many such games are pictorial or thematic in nature. Notably attractive examples include Windmill, Wheat-ear, Pigtail and Diamond.

Attention should be drawn to a general rule of play that can make for an element of choice and therefore of skill. You are never obliged to build a buildable card if you think it may be more advantageously discarded or used to fill a space in the reserve, and you may always look at the next card of the stock before deciding whether or not to fill a space from the wastepile. Where older books give stricter rules they usually spoil the game by reducing the element of choice.

Double or Quits
One pack
Odds against

Double or Quits, a one-suite game like Golf or Black Hole, is basically 'Robert' made slightly more tractable by the addition of a reserve to increase the number of cards available for building. The title refers to the unusual doubling sequence in which the suite has to be built. Apart from increasing the mental complication, this sequence is of no particular significance to the play (which might just as well be carried out in consecutive sequence), but serves the useful purpose of justifying the title.

Layout Deal three cards in a non-overlapping column to the left, three more in a parallel column to the right, and one card in between the top two. These seven form the reserve. Deal the next card between the bottom two. This forms the base of a single suite yet to be built. If any of these cards is a King, put it at the bottom of the stock and deal the next card in its place.

Object To build a single suite on the base running continuously in the following sequence, regardless of suit: A–2–4–8–3–6–Q–J–9–5–10–7–A–2– and so on. This is a doubling sequence, ignoring Kings and subtracting thirteen whenever the previous doubled number exceeds it. Obviously (I hope) the point at which you start this sequence off is determined by the rank of the base you happened to turn. For example, base Three is followed by Six, Queen etc.

Play Turn cards from stock and play them if possible or discard them face up to a single wastepile if not. Available for building are: the turned card, the top of the wastepile, and any card of the reserve except a King. A vacancy in the reserve must be filled at once from waste, or, if none, from stock. Once a King has reached the reserve it stays there as a block, reducing the number of cards available.

Redeal A game consists of three deals, the wastepile being turned twice to form a new stock.

Grand Duchess
Duchess of Luynes, Parisienne
Two packs
Odds against

This old and unusual game nearly defeated my system of classification until I realized that the so-called wastepile amounts in fact to a reserve.

Object To found an Ace and a King of each suit when they become available and to build them respectively upwards and downwards into thirteen-card suit sequences.

Play Deal four cards face up in a row from left to right and two face down to one side to a wastepile or reserve. Found any Aces or Kings that may be visible and do any further building that may be possible. At each subsequent turn deal four more cards from left to right, overlapping any that remain or filling gaps as the case may be, and discard two face down to one side. After each deal pause to build as many exposed cards as possible.

Having run out of cards, turn the discards face up. All of these are simultaneously available for building, together with exposed cards from the four columns.

Redeal When no more building can be done, gather up the four columns from left to right, place the unplayed reserve cards on top, turn the whole pile upside down and continue in the same way. Three such redeals are allowed, but in the last of them no cards are dealt face down to one side.

VARIANT In Parisienne the Aces and Kings are extracted and founded before play begins.

Four Marriages

Two packs
Odds against

An extension of the Quadrille–Cotillion dancing-class theme.

Layout and object Take out one card of each rank. Shuffle these thirteen cards and place them face down in a packet. Turn up the top card. The object is to found one Ace and one Two of each suit as they appear, placing them around the centre pile in the form of a square, and to build in suit and ascending sequence upon them. The Aces are to be built up by odd numbers only, finishing with Jack then King, and the Twos with even numbers only, finishing with Ten then Queen. The end product is eight piles surmounted alternately by Kings and Queens.

Play Turn cards from stock and build them if possible or play them face up to a single wastepile if not. Cards always available for building are: the card turned from stock, the top card of the wastepile, and the top card of the centre packet. When the latter is played, the card beneath it is faced. Two redeals are allowed.

Snail

Two packs
Odds in favour

A creepy little pictorial!

Layout Take out all Fives, Sixes and Jacks and arrange them (in that order) in the form of a spiral representing a snail. Complete the picture with the next four cards dealt face up as a reserve.

Object To build on the Fives downwards in suit to the Kings (which follow the Aces) and on the Sixes upwards in suit to the Queens, omitting Jacks. The Jacks remain where they are and have no part to play.

SNAIL Build the Fives down in suit to the Kings and the Sixes up in suit to the Queens, omitting Jacks as they have no active part to play. The four lower cards are a replenishable reserve, not a tableau for packing.

Play Turn cards from stock and build them if possible or else discard them face up to a single wastepile, of which the top card may be built whenever possible. A reserve card may also be built when possible, its place being filled with the top card of stock or waste.

Redeal The wastepile may be turned and redealt once.

Osmosis

Treasure Trove
One pack
Odds against

Defined as 'the diffusion of two liquids through a porous wall', Osmosis is an apt title for this unusual specimen of the patience-maker's art.

Layout Deal sixteen cards face down in four packets of four each, and place these packets in a column to the left of the board, forming a reserve. Face the top card of each packet. Turn the seventeenth card face up and put it to the immediate right of the top packet as a base card. The other three cards of the same rank as the first base will subsequently be founded as bases in a column below the first as and when they come to hand.

Object The object is to build upon each base card the other twelve cards of its own suit – not necessarily in sequence, but in accordance with peculiar rules as follows. Any card matching the suit of the first (topmost) base may be built as soon as it turns up. As these cards are built, spread them to the right so that all are identifiable. A card matching any of the other bases may only be built if there is a card of the same rank in the row immediately above it. If not, it cannot be used.

Play Cards available for building are: the top cards of the four reserve packets (when one is built, the one beneath it is turned up), the top card of the wastepile, and certain cards from stock as follows. At each turn sweep three cards off the top of the stock and turn them face up in a fan. The exposed card of the fan is available for building. If built, it releases the second card; and the second, if built, releases the third. Any cards of the fan that cannot be built are placed face up on a single wastepile, in the same order. Any number of redeals are allowed until the game either comes out or is blocked. Blockages may occur because certain required cards cannot be got out of the reserve.

PEEK In this variant the cards of the reserve are dealt face up and spread so that all are visible. This increases the skill factor by allowing a certain amount of planning. Count half a Pyrrhic victory for calculating that blockages are inevitable and abandoning play before turning the first batch of cards from stock.

Moojub
One pack
Even chances

This invention of Morehead and Mott-Smith seems to be derived from Osmosis, though it has some peculiar rules that put it outside any framework of classification. The meaning of the name Moojub escapes me, though it happens to be an anagram of Boojum, which is a species of Snark.

Layout Deal four cards face up in a non-overlapping column to the left of the board. These start the reserve, which may be regarded as consisting of four wastepiles. Take the lowest-ranking card among them and position it to the immediate right of the top of the reserve: this is the first base. Below it place the next lowest-ranking card that is different in suit from the first, and below that the third lowest and then the fourth lowest, but only so long as they are of different suits. The reserve must continue to be regarded as four positions, even where there are vacancies due to cards that have been taken as bases.

Object To build all the cards into ascending suit-sequences.

Play Having made as many bases as there were different suits, see if any building can be done. For this purpose, a reserve card of the same suit and next higher in rank than a base is to be built on it to start a pile. Sequence of rank is continuous, passing from King to Ace.

When nothing further can be done, deal four more cards to the reserve from top to bottom, pause and play again. Do the same every time play comes to a halt.

After each deal, resume play by building exposed cards from the reserve on any of the suit piles to which they properly belong. After building, you may found more cards as follows. The first column of bases is to be continued downwards until it contains one of each suit, and, wherever there is a choice, the lowest-ranking of the suit must be chosen. When these four are in place, with or without any cards that may have been built upon them, start another column of bases. You must keep all cards of one suit in the same row, the order of suits from top to bottom being determined by the first four bases. You must also complete each column of bases strictly in order from the top downwards before starting a new column, and, wherever you have a choice of ranks for a base, you must take the lowest-ranking. You must also build whenever you can, and in preference to founding new bases. The game is won if you succeed in getting all cards built from the reserve.

Corners

One pack
Even chances

This looks like a relative of Florentine, or one of the Four Seasons.

Layout and object Deal nine cards face up in three rows of three, but ensure that the four corner cards are of different suits (by dealing each one of them as soon as a new suit turns up in the deal). The object is to build a complete sequence of thirteen cards, following suit, on each of the corners. For this purpose the ranking of cards is continuous, with Ace following King. The five cards other than the corners form a reserve.

Play Play cards from stock face up to a wastepile, building on a corner when possible. A card of the reserve may be built as soon as possible, and must be directly replaced by the next card of the stock (not of the wastepile). Two redeals are allowed.

VARIANT In one old description of the game, the stock is not held in the hand but set face up upon one of the cards of the reserve. This amounts to the same as reducing the reserve to four cards instead of five, which renders the game harder to bring a successful conclusion without adding anything to its interest.

Cock o' the North
Two packs
Even chances

Cock o' the North is a rare avian visitor to the northern shores of Britain, and has given its name to a locomotive and a country dance. The patience is probably named after the dance – compare, for example, Quadrille, Cotillion.

Layout Deal four packets of four cards each face down, and four of four face up. Arrange them in a circle with up and down packets alternating. In the centre deal a packet of eight cards face up. All these cards form a reserve.

Object As they become available, found all eight Aces and all eight Twos. Build on each of the sixteen bases in ascending alternate sequence, following suit. That is, build Ace, Three, Five etc. to the King, and Two, Four, Six, etc. to the Queen.

Play Turn cards from stock and build them if possible or discard them face up to a single wastepile if not. Exposed cards of the reserve are also available for building, as is the top of the wastepile; but if the latter duplicates a card of the reserve, the reserve card must be built in preference. The stock exhausted, examine the cards of the centre packet (originally eight) and build any that will fit. Then face the top cards of the closed packets, build if possible, and face and build any beneath that are released in this way. Finally, take up the closed packets, shuffle them in with the wastepile, and play through it as before. Two such redeals are allowed.

Sultan

Sultan of Turkey, Emperor of Germany
Two packs (or one)
Odds in favour

One of my favourites in the realm of Patience depicts a sultan with eight of his favourites in the realm of domestic bliss. The game is properly intended for two packs, but, as half a harem's better than none, a one-pack version is appended for completeness.

SULTAN The eight cards surrounding the central King (the Sultan) are built up in suit to the Queens. Horizontal cards (the Divan) form a reserve, each being replaced when taken for building. No packing takes place.

Layout Take the eight Kings and one Ace of hearts. Arrange them in a square of three by three, with one ♥K in the centre (the sultan) and the ♥A below him. Deal eight more cards face up, four on each side of the square. These form a reserve called the divan.

Object The sultan remains intact, but the Ace and other Kings are to be built upwards in suit to the Queens. (The Kings are immediately followed by Aces, of course.)

Play Turn cards from stock and play them if possible or discard them face up to a single wastepile if not. A card of the divan may be built when possible, and must be replaced immediately with the top card of stock or waste.

Redeal Two redeals are allowed, and the wastepile must be shuffled before play is resumed.

SULTAN (ONE PACK) This version of the game is not a Builder but a Packer. Place the ♥K in the centre of a cross, with ♥A above and the other three Kings around. Deal a divan of two cards on either side. Play as described above, but with this exception: that cards not playable to a suite may be packed in descending sequence regardless of suit on cards of the divan. Only one redeal is allowed, and in the second round cards must either be built or packed – there is no second wastepile.

Windmill
Propeller
Two packs (or one)
Odds against

Another of my favourites is this well-founded pictorial with an unusual building feature. The two-pack version is the better known, and indeed the better game, though it comes out less often than its one-pack substitute. It is therefore described first.

Layout As illustrated, deal an Ace to the centre of the board, then two cards at random, face up, to north, south, east and west of it. These eight cards form a reserve, representing the sails of the windmill. If there is a King among them, place it diagonally radiating from the centre in a space between two arms, and fill its vacancy from stock. The first four Kings to appear in the course of play are similarly placed. The central Ace and four diagonal Kings are bases.

Object Each of the Kings is to be built in descending sequence, regardless of suit, to an Ace. The central Ace is to be built in ascending sequence, regardless of suit, up to a King, followed by another Ace and its sequence to a King, and so on four times in all, finishing with a pile of fifty-two cards surmounted by a King.

Play Turn cards from stock and build them if possible or discard them face up to a single wastepile if not. A card of the reserve (in a sail) may be built whenever possible, its space being filled

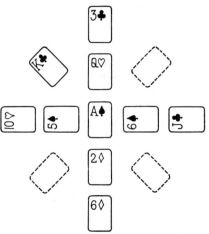

WINDMILL   The central Ace is built up into a single 52-card suite regardless of suit. Found four Kings on the sites indicated and build them down regardless of suit. The eight cards of the sail form a replenishable reserve and are eventually all worked off.

immediately with the top card of waste or stock. If possible and desirable, a card may be transferred from the top of the central Ace suite to any King suite, or vice-versa. But none of the five base cards may be so moved, nor may more than one card be transferred between the same two suites in the same turn. There is no redeal.

WINDMILL (ONE PACK) Place four Aces in a central packet (for decoration only), and two cards north, south, east and west for the sails. As they appear, found the four Twos in the spaces between the original sails, and build them up in sequence to the King, regardless of suit. Rules of play are as above, except that there is no central suite to be built.

Kingdom

Two packs
Odds in favour

This Kingdom resembles a Ruritanian monarchy, in which nothing much ever happens but what does happen usually has a happy ending.

Layout and object Deal eight cards in a row, forming a reserve. Found an Ace under the leftmost of them, and make a row of Aces as the other seven become available during the play. Build these Aces in ascending sequence to the Kings, regardless of suit.

Play Turn cards from stock and build them if possible or discard them face up to a single wastepile if not. A card of the reserve may be built when possible, and is immediately replaced from stock. There is no redeal.

Captive Commanders

Two packs
Even chances

This complicated game evokes that aspect of the Victorian mind which delighted itself in constructing detailed and life-size models of grand pianos out of papier mâché.

Layout Four Kings are rejected from the packs and play no part at all, and the other four (the captured commanders) are placed in a packet at the centre of the layout – where they play no part at all either, except that they have to be 'liberated by the rescuing armies'. Four packets of four cards each are placed face down diagonally to the corners of the central King packet (representing the rebels), and a fifth card (the rebel leader) laid face up outside these packets. In each of the angles formed between consecutive rebel packets two more cards radiate longitudinally from the centre, the innermost of them face down (spies), the outermost

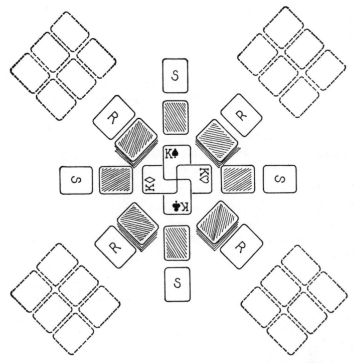

CAPTIVE COMMANDERS Each line marked S (sentries) consists of an outer card face up and an inner card face down. Each line marked R (rebels) consists of an outer card face up and an inner packet of four cards face down. When an outer card (sentry or rebel) is taken, it is replaced by its corresponding inner card, turned face up. The object of play is to release the central Kings, who take no active part in the proceedings. Dotted outlines represent the rescuing armies, each army being of one suit. As the appropriate cards become available, each row of three will consist of a central Ten to be built down in suit to the Ace, and flanked by its Queen on one hand and Jack on the other.

face up (sentries). All these cards form a reserve, any exposed card being available for building.

Object To found all eight Tens as bases, as and when they appear, and to build upon each base a descending suit-sequence of cards to the Ace. (In story-line terms, these suites represent the rescuing armies. As exposed 'rebel' cards are built onto them, the rebel packets eventually disappear and thereby release the captive commanders, who have meanwhile been kicking their heels in the centre of the affray.)

Play Shuffle the remaining cards into a single stock, and turn cards from it one at a time, building them if possible or throwing them face up to a single wastepile if not. As soon as a Ten appears, place it at one corner of the board to form a base, reserving each corner to a particular suit. Jacks and Queens are as useless to the game as Kings, and are simply extracted and piled up in the corner reserved for their suits as and when they appear. Any such Tens and courts exposed in the layout at the start of play may be placed immediately.

When a sentry is built, the spy adjacent to it is turned up and becomes available. When a spy is built, its place is filled immediately with the top card of the wastepile. When a rebel leader is built, its space is filled by the top card of its adjacent packet, turned face up. When the last card of a rebel packet has become a rebel leader and then been built off as such, leaving no rebels in that quarter, its place may be taken by the topmost card of either of the next rebel packets to either side of it, turned face up. This cannot be done, however, if these packets have been already worked off.

Redeals Two redeals are allowed.

Eagle Wing
Thirteen Down, Wings
One pack
Odds against

Though superficially related to Demon and its followers, Eagle Wing offers less scope for skill.

Layout Deal thirteen cards face down in a pile at the centre of the board, forming a reserve known as the 'trunk'. Deal four cards face up in a row on either side of it, forming a reserve of eight cards in two 'wings'. Deal the next card face up above the trunk. This is the first base.

Object To found the three other cards of the same rank as bases as and when they appear, moving them alongside the first base in a row, and to build upon each base an ascending sequence of thirteen cards of the same suit (ranking continuously, with Ace following King).

Play Turn cards from stock and build them if possible or play them face up to a single wastepile if not. Any card of the wing may be built when possible, its place being filled by the top card of the trunk, turned face up. Two redeals are allowed.

Patriarchs
Two packs
Odds against

It is hard to find anything interesting to say about a game with so unprepossessing a title.

Layout and object Take an Ace and a King of each suit, and place the Aces in a column on one side of the board, the Kings in a column on the other. Deal nine cards face up between them in three rows of three, forming a reserve. The object is to build the Aces up in suit to Kings, and the Kings down in suit to Aces.

Play Turn cards from stock and build them if possible or play them face up to a single wastepile if not. A card of the reserve may be built when possible, and must be replaced at once by the top card of waste or stock. It is permissible to reverse one or more cards from an Ace to a King suite, or vice versa, but base cards may not be so transferred. One redeal is allowed.

PICTURE PATIENCE As above, but shuffle the two packs individually without mixing them together. Do not take out the base cards to begin with, but wait until they appear in the course of play. Cards may not be reversed from suite to suite, and there is no redeal. This form of the game succeeds less often.

Odd and Even
Two packs
Odds against

Here is one of several games in which suites are built in alternate sequences, even on Deuces and odd on Aces. See also Four Marriages, Royal Cotillion, etc.

Layout Deal nine cards face up in three rows of three.

Object To found one Ace and one Deuce of each suit, as they become available, and to build upon each of these eight bases an ascending suit-sequence of cards by odds and evens as follows:

A–3–5–7–9–J–K–2–4–6–8–10–Q
2–4–6–8–10–Q–A–3–5–7–9–J–K

Play Turn cards from stock and build them if possible or play them face up to a single wastepile if not. A card of the reserve may be built when possible, and must be replaced at once by the top of the wastepile, or, if none, from stock. One redeal is allowed.

Wheat-ear
Two packs
Odds in favour

A good old pictorial, comparable in design with Pigtail and Herring-bone, the wheat-ear itself is gradually nibbled away.

Layout Deal ten pairs of cards down the centre of the board, each pair in a V-shape and overlapping the pair above, but not overlapping each other. These form a central reserve called the wheat-ear. The next eight cards are dealt four on each side of it, forming two lateral reserves. Deal the next card face up as a base.

Object To found the other seven cards of the same rank as the first as and when they become available, and to build them into thirteen-card ascending suit sequences (passing from King to Ace as necessary).

Play Turn cards from stock and build them if possible or discard them face up to a single wastepile if not. A card of the reserve may be built when possible, and its place filled at any time with the top card of stock or waste. The two exposed cards of the wheat-ear are also available for building, but are not replaced.

Redeal The wastepile may be turned and redealt once only.

Pigtail
Cadenette, Flapper, Plait
Two packs

Odds in favour
Two different patiences called Plait are based on the visually attractive arrangement of overlapping cards in the form of what I have always called a pigtail. As the other belongs to a different family, I have renamed this one to avoid confusion. The same idea evidently occurred to some previous writer who renamed it Flapper – which, for those too young to remember, was the term denoting a modish young woman of the 1920s.

Layout Deal twenty cards overlapping one another in V-shaped pairs down the centre of the board. This forms a reserve called the pigtail, of which only the uncovered card is available. Deal the next four cards to the corners of the pigtail, two at the top and two at the bottom: these constitute the corner reserves. Deal the next eight horizontally, four down each side of the pigtail: these

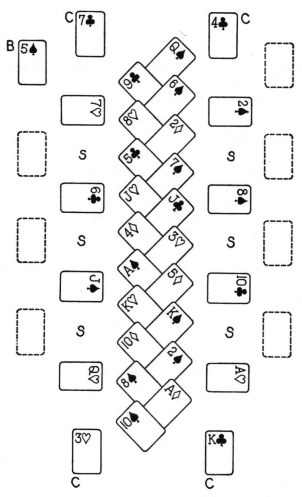

PIGTAIL Twenty cards form a diminishing reserve called the pigtail, of which only the exposed card is available. (In this diagram the removal of ♠10 exposes ♦A, and so on.) C denotes four corner reserves, S eight side reserves, and B the first base. Dotted lines indicate sites on which the other seven bases (in this case Fives) are to be founded when available. The fact that two bases lie in the pigtail will cause some difficulty.

are the side reserves. Finally, deal another card face up wherever you can find room for it: this is the first base.

Object To found the other seven cards of the same rank as the first base as soon as they become available, and to build them all into thirteen-card ascending suit-sequences, turning the corner from King to Ace as necessary.

Play The exposed card of the pigtail, all four of the corner reserves and eight of the side reserves are available for founding or building. A vacancy in the side reserves may be filled only from stock. A vacancy in the corner reserves is filled with the exposed card of the pigtail. Cards of the pigtail are not replaced, but the play of each releases the one below it until all are gone.

When stuck, turn cards from stock one by one, building them or filling side reserves if possible, or discarding them face up to a single wastepile if not.

Redeal Having run out of cards, turn the wastepile and use it as a new stock. Three such turns are allowed, giving four rounds of play in all.

VARIANT A variant of 'Plait' has fifteen cards in the pigtail, four corner reserves (as above) and six side reserves. With bases founded before play, four Aces and four Deuces are built up in suit to Kings, the other Aces being eliminated as they turn up.

Pyramid
One pack
Even chances

As good a way as any of passing eternity in an Egyptian burial chamber. See also Khedive.

Layout and object Deal fifteen cards face up in the form of a pyramid, with one at the apex and five in the bottom row. This forms the reserve. Take the four Aces and place them two on either side, for symmetry. Build the Aces up in suit to the Kings.

Play Turn cards from stock and build them if possible or play them face up to a single wastepile if not. A card of the reserve may be built when possible, its place being filled by the top card of stock. One redeal is allowed.

Matrimony

Two packs
Odds against

There are several patiences called Matrimony, as it is a theme conducive to illustration on the cards. Perhaps the alternative title 'Teenagers' was intended to abolish any confusion. But times change, and teenagers now sound more dated than matrimony. At time of writing, genuine teenagers are mostly in their thirties.

Layout and object Place one ♦J to the left of one ♦Q as two base cards. As they become available, found two Jacks of hearts to the left of ♦J and the four black Tens to the right of ♦Q as six additional bases in an eventual row of eight. The object of play is to build a suite of cards of the same suit on each base. The Queen is to be built upwards to the Jack, but the Jacks downwards to the Queen and the Tens downwards to the Jacks.

Play Deal sixteen cards face up as a reserve. Found or build any of them that may be appropriate, but do not close up the gaps they leave. This done, deal sixteen more cards face up on the reserve from left to right, filling gaps or covering previous cards as the case may be. Cards may be overlapped so that all are visible. Again, build any exposed cards that will fit. A card beneath an exposed card is not available until it is uncovered. Keep building and dealing in this way. (The last deal will comprise only six cards.)

Redeal When the stock is exhausted and all possible builds have been made, take the sixteenth pile of unbuilt cards, turn it upside down to form a new stock, and deal it around as far as it will go, the top card to the vacancy left by that pile, and subsequent cards on piles one, two, three etc. Build again. When stuck, do the same with the fifteenth pile, and subsequently with all piles down to the first. If this fails, the game is lost.

TEENAGERS The effect of this minor variant is to change the picture slightly. Start with a Jack and Queen of hearts, and found, as they become available, four black Tens and the two Tens of diamonds. Build the Queen up to the Jack, the Tens down to the Jacks and the Jack down to the Queen. From a representational point of view, the end product is perhaps more meaningful.

Queen's Audience
King's Audience
One pack
Odds in favour

This pictorial changes title to suit the reigning monarch.

Layout Deal sixteen cards face up in such a way as to enclose a square, with four cards to each side. These form a reserve called the antechamber, and the space enclosed is the audience chamber.

Object To found a Jack of each suit, as and when they become available, and upon these four bases to build descending sequences, in suit, to the Deuces. Aces, Kings and Queens are disposed of as described below.

Play Turn cards from stock and build them if possible or play them face up to a single wastepile if not. The top card of stock, the top of the wastepile, and all cards of the reserve are available for building. When a card is played from the reserve, fill its vacancy at once from the wastepile, or, if none, from stock. As soon as a Jack and an Ace of the same suit are simultaneously available, lay them together at the bottom of the audience chamber with the Jack on top. The Jack is then to be built down to the Deuce. Whenever a King and Queen of the same suit are simultaneously available, place them together above the Jack suite of the same suit, with the Queen on top (or, in the variant called King's Audience, with the King on top). There is no redeal.

Royal Rendezvous
Two packs
Odds in favour

An interesting variation on the odds and evens theme.

Layout Remove one Deuce of each suit and all eight Aces. Put the Aces in two rows of four, and two Deuces on both sides of the lower row, extending it to eight cards. Below them, deal the next sixteen cards, face up, in two non-overlapping rows of eight. These sixteen form the reserve.

Object Build the top four Aces up in suit to the Queens. Build the lower Aces up in suit and alternate sequence (A–3–5 etc.) to the Kings, and the Deuces up in suit and alternate sequence (2–4–6 etc.) to the Queens. The other four Kings are placed separately above the Deuce suites as they become available, but none may be placed until its duplicate has appeared on the appropriate Ace suite.

Play Turn cards from stock and build them if possible or play them face up to a single wastepile if not. A card built from the reserve must be at once replaced by the top waste card, or, if none, the top card of stock. There is no redeal.

Twenty
Two packs
Odds in favour

The chief, if not the only, merit of this patience is that it should succeed more often than not.

Layout and object Put out an Ace and a King of each suit, and build them respectively upwards and downwards into thirteen-card suit sequences.

Play Deal twenty cards face up in four rows of five, none overlapping. Build any that can be built, and then fill gaps from stock. Build and fill again until none of the twenty will fit. At that point deal another twenty over the layout, card upon card, and in the same order of dealing as for the first twenty. Then build from the exposed cards, filling gaps made by the removal of both cards from a position with one card from stock. Continue in the same way, dealing twenty each time the game blocks. The last deal will usually consist of fewer than twenty cards, and if all cannot then be built off when the stock is exhausted, the game has failed.

Carpet
One pack
Odds in favour

An unspectacular game to play on the floor.

Layout and object Deal twenty cards face up in four rows of five, forming a reserve. Found the four Aces as and when they become available, and build them up in suit to the Kings.

Play Turn cards from stock and build them if possible or play them face up to a single wastepile if not. All cards in the reserve are available. When built, each must be replaced at once from stock or waste. (This is called 'repairing the holes in the carpet'.

For slightly greater pictorial effect, the Ace foundations are placed two on either side of the 'carpet'.) There is no redeal.

Royal Cotillion

Two packs
Odds against

Dancing again (compare Quadrille, Cotillion, Cock o' the North), but this time with the building of suites in alternate sequences, odd and even – as in the patience of that name.

Layout Found an Ace and a Deuce of each suit, and lay them in parallel columns down the centre of the board: these are the bases. To their left, deal twelve cards face up in three rows of four, forming the left wing of the reserve; to their right, deal sixteen in four rows of four, forming the right wing.

Object To build suit sequences on the eight bases by odds and evens thus:

A–3–5–7–9–J–K–2–4–6–8–10–Q
2–4–6–8–10–Q–A–3–5–7–9–J–K

resulting in eight piles surmounted by Kings and Queens – four royal couples.

Play Turn cards from stock, building them if possible or playing them face up to a single wastepile if not. Every card of the right wing is available: when one is built, fill the space with the top waste card, or, if none, from stock. In the left wing, only the four cards of the bottom row are available. They are not replaced when built, but the play of each releases the one above it for building, so that the whole of the left wing eventually disappears. There is no redeal.

GAVOTTE (ODDS AND EVENS) In this variant, both wings consist of sixteen cards in four rows of four. The bases are not necessarily Aces and Deuces; instead, after examining the wings, you may select any two consecutive ranks (including King–Ace), and subsequently found these bases as and when they appear. Before playing, you have also to decide which of the two wings is to be the replenishable reserve (fill gaps as cards are played out) and which the diminishing (only the lowest cards in columns are available, and these are not replaced). As before, build the suites up in alternating sequence.

Khedive
Two packs
Odds in favour

As a patience, this is merely a bigger pyramid than the one of that name, and therefore easier to demolish. Deriving from the Persian word for prince, 'khedive' was also the title of the viceroy of Egypt for almost fifty Victorian–Edwardian years of the Empire.

Layout and object Deal twenty-five cards face up in the form of a pyramid, with one at the apex and nine in the bottom row. This is a reserve. Choose any card of it to act as the first base – preferably one which is accompanied by consecutive higher cards of its own suit in the pyramid, or as which you can see several other cards of the same rank. As the other seven of that rank become available, establish them as bases, with a column of four such bases ascending on either side of the pyramid. The object is to build these bases up in ascending suit sequence (ranking continuously, with Ace following King) until each contains thirteen cards.

Play Turn cards from stock and build them if possible or play them face up to a single wastepile if not. All cards of the reserve are available for building. Fill gaps from the wastepile, or, if none, from stock. There is no redeal.

Fort
Two packs
Odds against

Though the layout of Fort is strongly reminiscent of Wheat-ear, Herringbone and Pigtail, its theme is military rather than rustic or domestic.

Layout and object Take an Ace and a King of each suit, laying the Aces in a column down one side of the board and the Kings likewise down the other. These are bases, and the object is to build the Aces in ascending suit sequence to the King and the Kings in descending suit sequence to the Ace. From the shuffled packs, deal another column of four side by side with the Aces, and four side by side with the Kings. These form a reserve known as the walls of the fort. Two more laid face up at the top of the board and two at the bottom continue the reserve, representing the gates of the fort. Finally, deal twenty-one cards face up and overlapping one another, in pairs, down the centre of the pattern. These form a diminishing reserve known as the garrison.

Play Turn cards from stock and build them if possible or play them face up to a single wastepile if not. Cards in the wall and gate reserves are available for building. When a card is built from the wall, its place is taken by the top card of the wastepile, or, if none, from stock. When a card is built from a gate, its place is taken by the exposed card of the garrison. As this is the only way in which the garrison can be worked off the board, it is desirable to play from a gate rather than from a wall whenever you have the choice. Two redeals are allowed – or three, if you insist. (Accounts vary.)

Golf

Fan Tan, One Foundation

One pack
Odds against

To judge from the variety of its titles, Golf is a long-popular game despite its estimated one-in-twenty chance of coming out. It is aptly named. The single suite represents a hole, into which the cards of the reserve must be putted one by one. The number left unputted at the end of play is your handicap for the round. In respect of the title Fan Tan, Mary Whitmore Jones, writing at the turn of the century, says: 'This game . . . is of Chinese origin, and is said to be the oldest patience known. It is also much played in California, and forms a gambling game, with the high forfeit of a dollar for every card not worked away.' I think she may have been confusing several other games of the same name with Canfield–Klondike, but stand to be corrected on this point.

Layout Deal five overlapping rows of seven cards each and regard the result as a reserve of seven columns. Deal the next card to one side as a base.

Object To clear all the cards off the reserve by building them into a continuous suite on the base.

Play Take exposed cards of the reserve one by one for building on the base in ascending or descending sequence regardless of suit, changing directions as often as necessary. Ace and King are not consecutive: only a Two can be built on an Ace, and only a Queen on a King. When stuck, deal the next card from stock onto the suite and continue play from this new base. If you run out of stock before the reserve has been emptied, you have lost.

VARIANT One account states that a Queen may not be built on a King. The building of a King ends the sequence, and another card must be turned from stock.

King's Way

Two packs
Even chances

The original account of this interesting variant on Golf requires all cards of the tableau except the lowest row to be dealt face down. By dealing all except the top row face up, as described here, an element of choice and therefore skill is injected into what would otherwise be a purely mechanical exercise. It should come out as often as not.

Layout Put the eight Kings face up in a row at the top of the board. Half cover them with a row of eight cards dealt face down, and on these deal four more overlapping rows of cards face up. Regard the tableau as eight columns of five (not counting the Kings).

Object To clear all the columns off the board by playing exposed cards to a single wastepile, thus leaving each King's Way free.

Play Turn cards from stock and play them face up to a single wastepile, but hold out Aces if they appear to hinder the game. After each turn, pause and pack onto the wastepile any exposed cards which continue the sequence upwards or downwards in alternating colour. (Example: having turned a red Four, you could pack exposed cards such as black Five, red Six, black Five, red Six, black Seven, and so on.) Aces are not consecutive with Queens. A Queen can only follow or be followed by a Jack, and an exposed Ace on the tableau can only be played on a Two.

Grace During the deal, however, if you turn an Ace from the stock you are not obliged to play it to the wastepile, where it can only be followed by a Two. Instead, you may hold it out. If, then, you run out of stock before you have cleared every King's Way (turning face down cards face up when exposed), you have the following grace. Turn the wastepile upside down and count off as many cards from the top of it as there are Aces held out. These few cards may then be played as a new stock, and may just be enough to get out the last remaining royal obstructions.

Note Since Queens are just as awkward as Aces, why not permit them also to be held out for the same purpose?

Gateway
Three packs
Odds against

For this patience, you need an extra pack of cards and an extra pair of eyes.

Layout and object Deal forty-eight cards in eight columns of six each – rejecting, as you do so, all Aces and Kings as bases. The Aces are arranged in two rows of four at the top of the board, with two Kings extending the lower row on each side of it. The object is to build the Aces in ascending suit sequence to the King, and the Kings in descending suit sequence to the Ace.

Play Turn cards from stock and build them if possible or play them face up to a single wastepile if not. The exposed card of each column is available for building, thus releasing the one above it. If a column is cleared away, any available card may be transferred to its space. One redeal is allowed.

Note Miss Whitmore Jones, my only source for this patience, does not make explicit how many Aces are built up to Kings and vice versa, nor whether cards may be reversed between up and down suites. You could start with all twelve Aces and Kings out, and consolidate opposite suit-sequences when they meet in the middle.

Diamond

Two packs
Even chances

Diamond has several unusual features. Cards are laid out in rows and columns, not overlapping one another, so that those in the middle are surrounded by cards on each of their four sides. Such a card is blocked, and does not become available until one of the four surrounding it is removed. Edge and corner cards, being surrounded by fewer than four, are available at the start of play, and gradually unblock others as they are played off. The array of exposed cards is thereby gradually eaten away from the outside inwards.

Layout and object Deal forty-one cards face up in the form of a diamond, with a row of nine in the middle, seven above and below, five above and below those, then similarly three and then one. This forms a reserve. The object is to found all eight Aces, as and when they become available, and to build each of them up in suit to the King.

Play Turn cards from stock, building them if possible or discarding them face up to three wastepiles in rotation if not. That is to say, the first three unusable cards are laid in a row from left to right, the next three upon them in the same order, and so on. The top card of each wastepile is available for building. Also available is any card of the reserve which is not surrounded by four others – initially, those eighteen forming the edges and apexes.

Redeals Two redeals are allowed. When the stock is first exhausted, take the wastepile on the left, turn it upside down, and deal cards off the top to fill gaps in the diamond. If there are not enough, do the same with the second pile. Then shuffle the wastepiles together and start playing again as before. (If, however, you were unable to play any cards from the diamond, stack the wastepiles together without shuffling them.) When you have played through the stock a second time, the redeal is carried out differently. Gather together all cards of the wastepiles and those of the diamond, shuffle thoroughly and lay out a new but smaller diamond, with only seven cards in its middle row. Play as before, and if the game does not come out this time, it has failed.

Simple Packers

Packers are games in which if (for example) you are building cards in ascending sequence in one part of the board, then cards that turn up in the wrong order may be built in descending sequence in another, so that they can subsequently be picked off in reverse order and built right way up on the main suites as required. The 'other place' in which cards are temporarily built for this purpose is called the *tableau*, and the process of storing them in reverse order is called *packing*. Hence the name.

Although a few of the following games exhibit unusual and specialized features, nearly all are based upon a common pattern of play. To start with, a number of cards are dealt face up to the board to form a tableau. These are the cards on which auxiliary sequences are packed in the opposite direction to that of the main suites. Games vary according to the number of cards dealt, and therefore the number of auxiliary sequences that may be in progress, and in the following pages I have arranged them in order from those with fewest (four in Single Rail) to those with most (seventeen in Barton).

Cards are turned from the stock one by one, and each is built on a suite if possible, or else packed on an auxiliary sequence if possible. If neither can be done, it is played face up to a single wastepile. The top card of this is always available for building or packing if a suitable card becomes exposed to take it, and in games where there is no redeal of the wastepile it is always essential to play off the top card whenever the opportunity arises.

As cards are packed on the tableau they form columns of overlapping cards extending towards the player. Only the exposed card of a column is available for building on a suite or packing on another exposed card in the tableau, but its removal automatically exposes the one below it for treatment in the same way. Thus it is that runs of cards in descending sequence of suit may be built off one by one onto the appropriate ascending suite. In some games, however, the rules of packing are deliberately designed to prevent the playing off of long runs onto a single suite by stipulating that packing be carried out in descending sequence but not of the same suit. Most often the requirement is to pack in alternate colours. Thus a red Seven goes on a black Eight, to be followed by a black Six, red Five, and so on.

There are two respects in which rules are most likely to differ. First, in some games only one exposed card may be moved at a time. In others, a sequence packed on a column may be lifted as a whole and placed on an exposed card, provided that the join follows the rule. For example, a sequence of ♥7–♣6–♦5–♣4 etc. may be taken as a unit and packed upon an exposed black Eight. Existing rules are somewhat hazy about whether or not a part sequence may be moved in this way – for example, whether from the above four-card packing you would be permitted to take just the ♦5–♣4 and place this couple upon an exposed (say) ♠6 in order to release the ♣6 for building. A very few state that you may take either the single exposed card or the entire sequence, but not just a part of it. This has logic on its side, as it regards the sequence as a single card, and I am inclined to favour it. But it is a point on which you should make up your mind, and remain consistent in all the games you play.

The second most variable rule concerns the refilling of a vacancy made when all the cards of a column have been built or packed off. The kindlier games allow you to refill it with any available card from stock, waste or tableau, or with a sequence from another column, and may even invite you to leave it vacant until you can fill it with a more advantageous card. The stern ones state that it must be refilled immediately with the top card of the wastepile, and if you don't like it you can lump it. There are varying degrees of laxity and strictness in this respect, and you must take note of the exact rule before starting play as it will often affect your strategy.

Few of the games in the following section permit 'worrying back' – i.e. reversing cards from a suite to a packed column in order to unblock something else – and you should not assume this privilege to apply where it is not stated.

The games also vary as to whether or not you are permitted

to turn the wastepile and use it as a new stock when the old one is exhausted, and, if so, how many such redeals are allowed. Some games are bound to come out if enough redeals are taken, and it is always tempting to take them in order to justify the effort of embarking upon the game in the first place. I suggest you count half a victory for succeeding in one more redeal than the official allowance, and a double defeat for taking a second unauthorized redeal and still failing. There is, after all, an element of skill in determining that a given position cannot possibly result in a win.

Talking of skill, note that many of the following games give you wide choices of alternative lines of play, and that these are the ones that give most scope for skill. It is also true to say that the more exposed cards there are at any given time, the more opportunity you have for either working out a winning line or determining that the position is lost.

Single Rail

Auxiliary Sequences

One or two packs

Odds in favour

This game is so simple in format that it must be one of the earliest of its type, if not of all patiences – a suspicion reinforced by its gawky titles. The one-pack form is described first.

Layout and object Lay the four Aces out in a row (the 'rail', so called because they are traditionally laid out in horizontal orientation). The object is to build them up in suit and sequence to the Kings.

Play Turn cards from stock one by one, building them on the suites whenever possible, or else discarding them face up to a single wastepile. The first four cards turned from stock, if not buildable, may be placed face up in a row below the Aces. These form the base cards of 'auxiliary sequences', which may be packed in descending sequence regardless of suit. It is not obligatory to use the first available cards as bases if you consider them better discarded or packed on top of other auxiliaries. Cards of the four auxiliary sequences should be spread towards you in columns, so that all remain visible. Considerable latitude is allowed in the play. The top of the wastepile is always available for transfer to a main or auxiliary sequence if it fits. The top (exposed) card of an auxiliary may be transferred to the top of another if it continues the downward sequence, or a sequence of two or more may similarly be shifted *en bloc*. It is even permissible to transfer the top card of a main sequence to an auxiliary, provided it fits, if it seems advantageous to do so. Whenever a space is formed by the removal of the last or bottom card of an auxiliary, it may be filled as and when desired with any available card, or with a sequence taken from the top of another auxiliary.

Grace As if all this latitude were not enough, you are permitted one grace if you get through the whole stock without concluding the game. This entitles you to draw any one card from the wastepile and use it as you see fit. If the game still does not come out, you should be ashamed of yourself.

DOUBLE RAIL The two-pack version of Single Rail is played in exactly the same way, except that the object is to found and build on eight Aces instead of four, and unbuildable cards may be packed on five auxiliary sequences instead of four.

Octagon
Two packs
Even chances

The title refers to the pattern made by the initial layout of cards, but the pattern is of no particular significance to the play and can be simplified if found too space-consuming.

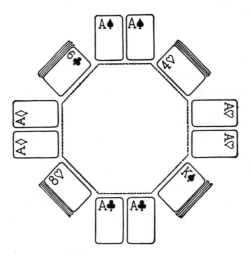

OCTAGON The corner packets of five cards each may be spread to reveal the lower cards.

Layout Set out the eight Aces in matching pairs, one pair at each compass point of the table. Deal the next twenty cards face up to make a tableau consisting of four packets of five, each packet to be laid anglewise at the corners of the table to complete the outline of an octagon (see diagram). To facilitate play, it is permissible to spread the cards of each packet so that all are visible.

Object To build each Ace upwards in suit and sequence to the King.

Play Turn cards one by one from stock and play each one to a suite or a packet if possible. If not, discard it face up to form a wastepile in the centre of the tableau. The packets are to be packed in suit and descending sequence. When such a sequence is played off to a suite, the next card of the packet becomes available for play or for packing on, and so on. When the last card of a packet has gone, the space is to be filled with the top card of the wastepile.

Redeals When the stock is exhausted, turn the wastepile and go through it as a second stock. Three such redeals are allowed.

Vanishing Cross
Corner Card, Corners, Czarina
One pack
Odds against

Vanishing Cross strikes me as the best of several titles, being a compromise between the exotic but irrelevant Czarina, and the relevant but prosaic Corners. Little Windmill, the title used by Cavendish for almost the same thing, implies a relationship with the splendid two-pack Windmill which in fact it does not bear. Almost identical is Florentine, the difference being that its centre card is not used for packing but acts as a reserve, so transferring the game to a different category.

Layout and object Deal five cards face up in the form of a cross, and a sixth in one of the corner spaces. The sixth forms the base of a suite, which is to be built in suit and ascending sequence until it contains thirteen cards (turning the corner from King to Ace where necessary). The other three cards of the same rank are to be founded as bases in the other corners as and when they appear, and similarly built upwards in suit.

Play Turn cards from stock and play them if possible or discard them face up to a single wastepile if not. The top card of stock or wastepile may be built on a suite if it fits, or packed on one of the five cards of the cross. Each of these is to be built in descending sequence regardless of suit, turning the corner from Ace to King where necessary. A space in the cross may be filled from stock, waste or an auxiliary. There is no redeal.

LITTLE WINDMILL The same, except that the suites are to be based on Aces and built up to the Kings. One Ace is extracted and founded before play. The others are founded as and when they appear.

Wholesale and Retail
One pack
Odds against

An extension of games of the Sir Tommy type (see 'Planners'), Wholesale and Retail has as its chief point of interest an unusual method of building the suites. In my view it is spoilt by the fact that the second deal may produce a completely blocked position; but at least it is possible to see this at a glance and so avoid wasting your time on it.

Layout Take out the four Aces. Deal three overlapping rows of five cards each and regard this tableau as five columns of three.

Object Found the four Aces in pairs of opposite colour, and build each pair up to the Kings in alternating suits. For example, if clubs and hearts are paired, build as follows:

♣A ♥2 ♣3 ♥4 ♣5 etc.
♥A ♣2 ♥3 ♣4 ♥5 etc.

. . . and do likewise with spades and diamonds.

Play Exposed cards of the tableau are available for building on suites and for packing on each other. Pack in suit and descending sequence, moving only one card at a time, and fill a vacancy with any available card.

Deal the rest of the cards from stock one by one. Build them if possible or pack them if you can and will; otherwise discard them face up to any of up to four wastepiles. These may be spread towards you so that all cards are visible, and the exposed card of each pile is available for building on a suite or packing on the tableau (but not on another wastepile).

Redeal Having run out of stock, gather up all cards of the tableau and wastepiles and shuffle them together thoroughly. Deal another tableau of five three-card columns and play again to four wastepiles. There is no second redeal.

Note This is more of a building than a packing game, as most packing is likely to hinder rather than help the progress of play. The title is flimsily explained by stating that the exotically packed suites represent the retail establishments, and the slightly miscellaneous and humdrumly packed tableau represents the wholesale.

Pas Seul

One pack
Odds in favour

The title of this otherwise unremarkable patience brings us back to the dancing class, being a ballet term for what might be called a solitaire performance – literally a 'solo step'.

Layout Deal six cards face up in a row to start the tableau.

Object To found the four Aces in a row above the tableau, as and when they turn up, and to build them up in suit to the Kings.

Play Turn cards from stock and play them if possible or else discard them face up to a single wastepile. The top cards of stock and

waste and exposed cards of the tableau are available for building
or for packing on the tableau. Pack in descending sequence and
alternating colour. Any length of properly packed sequence may
be shifted as a whole, provided that the join follows the rule. Fill
a space made by clearing out a column with any available card or
packed sequence. There is no redeal.

Herring-bone
Two packs
Odds in favour

There are two Herring-bones, both of which are nicely pictoriai.
This is the simpler of the two.

Layout Deal six cards face up in two rows of three. If a Jack
appears, put it to one side and replace it.

Object To found the eight Jacks, as and when they appear, in a
non-overlapping vertical column, and to build each one down in
suit to the Ace.

Play Turn cards from stock and play them if possible or discard
them face up to a single wastepile if not. The six initial cards are
to be packed upon in suit and ascending sequence (not higher
than Ten), and may be played off onto Jack suites as and when
they fit. A part suit-sequence of cards in the tableau may be
shifted to the top of another pile provided that it continues the
sequence. When a space is made in the tableau, it must be filled
from hand or waste.

   As they become available, Kings and Queens are placed on
either side of their Jacks of the same suit to form the herring-bone
pattern as illustrated. But they may not be put into position before
the accompanying Jack is there. Therefore, unplayable Kings and
Queens turned from stock must go to the wastepile, and any dealt
in the initial tableau are frozen until playable to a Jack.

Redeals One redeal is allowed.

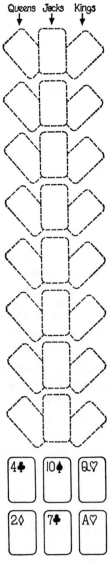

Queens Jacks Kings

HERRING-BONE In this diagram the ♥Q cannot be put in place in the herring-bone until one ♥J has been founded. The central Jacks are built down in suit to the Aces and flanked by their Queens and Kings.

Following

One pack
Odds against

The structure of this game is much the same as that of Pas Seul, but it imposes an unusual order in the following of suits.

Layout Deal six cards face up in a row to start a tableau.

Object To found the Aces in a row above, as and when they appear, and to build each Ace in ascending order to the King of the same suit – but not following suit. Instead, always play a club on a heart, diamond on club, spade on diamond and heart on spade. So, for example, the ♥A base will proceed ♣2, ♦3, ♠4, ♥5 and so on, finishing with ♠Q, ♥K.

Play Turn cards from stock and play them if possible or else discard them face up to a single wastepile. The six cards of the tableau may be packed upon in columns, in descending sequence and in the same rotation of suits as for the suites – i.e. heart on spade etc. Note that this makes it impossible to play more than one card at a time from a column to a suite, as the suits will come off in reverse order from that required for building. As usual, a card may be packed or built from hand or from the top of the wastepile, and a single card or properly constituted sequence of cards may be transferred from one column to another, provided that the join follows the rule. Fill vacancies from hand, waste or tableau as preferred.

Redeals One turn of the wastepile is allowed.

Blind Alleys
One pack
Odds against

Blind Alleys is but a slightly elaborated form of Single Rail.

Layout and object Set out the four Aces as base cards, and play to build them up in suit up to the Kings. Below them deal three overlapping rows of six cards each, the first two rows face down, the third face up. Regard these as six columns of three.

Play Turn cards from stock and play them if possible or else discard them face up to a single wastepile. Exposed cards are to be packed upon in descending sequence and alternating colour, from hand, waste, or the top of other columns. When a down-card is uncovered, turn it face up. An empty column may be filled with any available card either immediately or when it suits you.

Redeals One redeal is allowed.

Q.C. (K.C.)
Two packs
Odds against

Said to have been the preferred recreation of an eminent Victorian barrister when not able to make up his rubber of Whist, this patience is called Q.C. at time of writing, but is due to become K.C. upon the accession of Charles III.

Layout Deal four rows of six cards each, face up, and regard the result as six columns of four.

Object To release the eight Aces as they appear, and to build them up in suit to the Kings.

Play Turn cards from stock and play them if possible or else discard them face up to a single wastepile. Exposed cards may be packed in suit and descending sequence from hand, waste or other columns, but only one card may be shifted at a time. A space made by clearing out a column must at once be filled with the top waste card. Whenever the top card of the wastepile can be built on a suite, it must be, even if its duplicate is available from a column. (This sometimes prevents long runs from being cleared off columns and is a particularly aggrieving feature of the game.)

Redeal Strictly speaking, the game permits of no redeal. But it is so difficult without one that a redeal may be necessary to restore one's faith in pasteboard nature.

Thirty-six
One pack
Odds against

Of these numerically similar games Thirty-Six is the simpler and its variant Six by Six the more intriguing.

Layout Deal cards face up in six overlapping rows of six and regard this tableau as six columns of six. Any Ace that turns up in the deal is to be extracted as a base card and replaced by the next one turned, but no cards other than Aces may be transferred to suites during the deal.

Object To found the four Aces as and when they become available and to build them up in suit to the King.

Play Turn cards from stock and play them if possible or else discard them face up to a single wastepile. Exposed cards in the columns are to be packed upon in descending sequence but regardless of suit. They may be shifted singly or in any length of packed sequence. A space made by clearing out a column may be filled by any available card or column sequence. There is no redeal.

SIX BY SIX This variant is altogether harder on the player. Layout and object are as before. Unplayable cards turned from stock are played not to a separate wastepile but to the leftmost column, whether in sequence to the exposed card or not, though that column may also be packed upon in the usual way. A sequence of two or more cards may be shifted as a whole to another only if they happen to be of the same suit. As there is no redeal, this version requires even greater care than the other.

Klondike

Canfield, Chinaman, Demon, Fascination, Small Triangle
One pack
Odds against

As the number of alternative titles might imply, Klondike is perhaps the most popular of all the perennial favourites in the realm of patience. For many players no other game exists: it is simply called 'Patience'. In England the same game is traditionally known as Canfield, but as the name Canfield is used by American players to denote the game known to their English counterparts as Demon, it seems advisable to drop this title altogether from English-language anthologies in order to avoid any confusion. The original English title 'Triangle' is more accurately descriptive, but 'Klondike' has more flavour and is satisfyingly distinctive. Why the game itself should have achieved such popularity defies explanation, considering that it offers one of the lowest success rates of any patience. Morehead and Mott-Smith put it at one in thirty games. If 'patience' means 'suffering', Klondike is akin to masochism.

Layout Deal seven packets of cards in a row, all face down. The first consists of one card, the second of two, the third of three, and so on to the seventh of seven. Then turn the top card of each packet face up.

Object To found the four Aces as and when they appear, and to build each one up in suit and sequence to the King.

Play Turn cards from stock and play them if possible or else discard them face up to a single wastepile. Exposed cards on the packets are to be packed in descending sequence and alternating colour, with their constituent cards spread towards you in columns. A card or properly packed sequence of cards may be transferred from one column to another provided that the join follows the descending–alternating rule. Whenever a down-card is exposed, turn it face up. Whenever a space is made by clearing out a column, fill it only with a King (and any other cards that may be packed upon it in proper sequence). There is no redeal.

VARIANTS Some players turn cards from stock in fans of three, of which only the uppermost (after turning) is available. If played, it releases the one below, and so on; if it is unplayable, all three must be discarded to the wastepile in the same order. If this method is used, the wastepile may be turned twice, giving three rounds of play in all. Some permit shifts between columns only of sequences: they may not be broken up for the transfer of individual cards of part-sequences.

THUMB AND POUCH As Klondike, except that a card may be packed on the next higher rank only if it is of a different suit, not necessarily of a different colour. Any card or sequence may be used to refill a space. These changes considerably increase the chance of success – to perhaps one in four.

Whitehead
One pack
Odds against

Whitehead, probably not named after a co-author of *Principia Mathematica* (but in that case I know not after whom), is a more open version of the triangular patience well known as Canfield on one side of the Atlantic and Klondike on the other. It exhibits the unusual feature of packing in colour.

Layout Deal seven overlapping rows of cards, face up, with seven in the first row, six in the second, and so on down to one in the seventh. Regard this tableau as seven columns. Deal the twenty-ninth card face up above the first column as a base.

Object To move the other cards of the same rank as the first base into line with it as and when they become available, and to build them all into thirteen-card ascending suit sequences, turning from King to Ace as necessary.

Play Turn cards from stock and play them if possible or else discard them face up to a single wastepile. Pack the tableau in descending sequence of the same colour (red on red, black on black). A packed sequence of cards in the same suit may be shifted as a whole if there is a suitable card to receive it. A space made by clearing out a column may be filled with any available card or packed suit-sequence headed by an available card. There is no redeal.

Westcliff
Aces up
One pack
Odds in favour

Westcliff is much the same as Blind Alleys described earlier, differing only in the number of cards dealt.

Layout Deal three overlapping rows of seven cards each, the first two face down and the third face up. Regard the tableau as seven columns of three.

Object To found the four Aces as and when they appear, and to build them up in suit to the Kings.

Play Turn cards from stock and play them if possible or else discard them face up to a single wastepile. Exposed cards in the tableau are to be packed upon in descending sequence and alternating colour, and may be shifted either singly or in any length of properly packed sequence provided that the join follows the rule. Whenever a down-card is exposed, turn it face up. A space made by clearing out a column may be filled with any available card or descending-alternating sequence. There is no redeal.

EASTHAVEN This is the name given by Morehead and Mott-Smith to the game described above. According to them, Westcliff is played with a tableau of ten columns of three instead of seven. It may be noted that if the cards are dealt as fans of three instead of columns, the game is substantially similar to Fan or Belle Lucie.

Forty-nine
Two packs
Odds against

These are straightforward members of the family, representing an increase in number of cards. 'Alternation' is somewhat more difficult, as a number of cards are dealt face down to start with.

LAYOUT Deal forty-nine cards face up in seven overlapping rows of seven cards each, and regard the tableau as seven columns of seven. All must be dealt before any play begins.

Object To found the eight Aces as and when they appear, and to build them up in suit to the Kings.

Play Turn cards from stock and play them if possible or else discard them face up to a single wastepile. Exposed cards are to be packed in descending sequence and alternating colour. Only individual exposed cards may be shifted from column to column, not part-sequences. A space made by clearing out a column may be filled with any available card or part-sequence at whatever stage seems most advantageous.

Grace There is no redeal, but an unusual grace is permitted. A suite in course of building may be taken as a whole and placed on the exposed card of any column, provided that the top card of the suite is next lower in rank (regardless of suit) than the exposed card concerned. It is then permissible to pack on the top card of that suite. At a later stage the suite can be put back in position. In other words, a suite can be treated exactly as if it were a single available card.

ALTERNATION This is also laid out as a seven column by seven row game, but the second, fourth and sixth rows are dealt face down, so that each column consists of alternately faced and unfaced cards. Play as before, and whenever a down-card is exposed turn it face up. There is no redeal and no grace.

Olga
Four 32-card packs
Odds in favour

Most patience packs are sold in pairs. If you have two such pairs you need only discard cards lower than Seven (but retaining Aces) to be in a position to try this unusually sumptuous game, which may take a good half hour of your time. Structurally, it is much like Forty-Nine, but the play is quite different and more challenging.

Layout Deal cards in seven rows of seven, not overlapping one another. The second, fourth and sixth rows are dealt face down, the others face up. Whenever an Ace is turned for a face-up row, put it to one side as a base and fill its place with the next card from stock. Similarly, if the Seven turns up of a suit of which an Ace is already out, build it on the Ace and deal a substitute. In the same way, an Eight may be built on a Seven, Nine on Eight, and so on.

Object To found all sixteen Aces as and when they appear, and to build upon each one a suite ascending in suit from Seven to King.

Play Before turning any cards from stock, examine the layout to see what plays may profitably be made in accordance with the following rules. Only the bottom card of a column (that is, in the row of cards nearest you) is available for building on a suite. The removal of such a card releases the card above it for building, and so on up the column. Whenever a face-down card is released, turn it face up. All face-up cards in the layout are, however, available for packing on one another at any time, for which purpose they are to be packed in descending sequence and alternating suit. Note that a space made by packing a card off does not in itself release the card above it for building purposes: such a card is released only when it becomes the lowest in its column. When you cannot or will not carry the game further, deal cards from the stock and build or pack them if possible, or discard them face up to a single wastepile if not. The top card of the wastepile is always available for building or packing. A space in the tableau may be filled only with a King, which may come from the hand, the top of the waste-pile, or elsewhere in the tableau (in order, for example, to release a card in the column above it). Note that the filling of a space with a King may block the card immediately above it in the same column, which previously was available for building.

JUNCTION is another good game if you happen to have four 32-card packs to hand and no one to play with. Found sixteen Aces as they become available and build them up in suit to the Kings. (Sevens go on Aces.) Deal cards from the stock face up to a single wastepile unless you can build them or pack them as follows. Up to seven unbuildable cards may be held out and put in a row. These may be packed in descending sequence and alternating colour, using other exposed cards or the top card of the stock or wastepile. There is no redeal. (The game is an adaptation of Single or Double Rail, which see if more details are needed.)

Triangle

Two packs
Odds against

This species of the triangular genus has some unusual positional rules. Another game called Triangle is a variant of Batsford.

Layout Deal cards face up in eight non-overlapping rows, the topmost of eight cards, the next of seven, and so on down to one. Regard the result as eight columns, of which the left-hand has eight, the second-left seven, and so down to one card at the top right.

Object To found the eight Aces as and when they appear, and to build them up in suit to the Kings.

Play Turn cards from stock and play them if possible or else discard them face up to a single wastepile. The lowest card of each column is available for building or for packing upon the lowest card of another column, packing to be done in suit and descending sequence. However, such a card may never be packed upon the lowest card of a longer column: it may go only to a column of the same or shorter length. For this purpose any packed sequence counts as a single card, and may be packed as a whole. A space made by clearing out a column may be filled with any available card or packed sequence whenever it seems most advantageous to do so.

Redeal The wastepile may be turned once, giving two rounds of play.

Harp
Two packs
Odds against

Both Harp and Triangle may be regarded as two-pack versions of Klondike. A cross between Harp and Miss Milligan, unimaginatively called Milligan Harp, more closely resembles the latter and will be found among the Half-open Packers.

Layout Deal overlapping rows of cards face down, with nine in the first, eight in the second and so on down to one in the ninth. Regard this triangular tableau as consisting of nine columns of diminishing length, and turn up the exposed card of each column.

Object To found the eight Aces as they become available and to build them up in suit to the Kings.

Play Turn cards from stock and play them if possible or else discard them face up to a single wastepile. All exposed cards are available and may be built on suites or packed on the tableau. Pack the tableau in descending sequence and alternating colour, moving only one card at a time and facing the down-cards when they are exposed. A space in the tableau made by clearing out a column may be filled only with an available King. For this purpose, however, a properly packed sequence of cards based on a King may be moved as a whole into the space. (In no other circumstance may more than one card be shifted at a time.)

Redeal The wastepile may be turned and redealt – some say twice, some three times, some as often as necessary. Take your choice.

STEPS In this variant the triangle consists of seven rows and columns. Play as above, except that any length of properly packed sequence may be shifted as a whole and a space may be filled with any available card or sequence. There is one redeal.

Suspense

One pack
Odds against

Its best friend (if any) could hardly describe Suspense as more than an assortment of bits and pieces from other games, and I would not be the first to rush out and recommend it to the attention of Alfred Hitchcock.

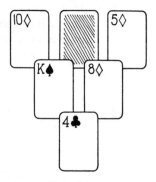

SUSPENSE The layout consists of four groups of six randomly dealt cards, each group arranged with one face down and others face up, overlapping as illustrated.

Layout Deal four groups of six cards as illustrated. Each group consists of a face-down card (the 'centre') flanked by two face-up cards (the 'wings'); these three overlapped by two face-up cards, and those in turn by one face-up, which for the time being is the exposed card of the group.

Object To build four suit sequences of thirteen cards each as described below. Those built on bases will ascend in sequence, those built only in the tableau will descend in sequence.

Play Phase One requires the removal of those cards temporarily covering the four centre and eight wing cards. This is done as follows. Turn cards from stock face up to a single wastepile. Whenever an exposed card of the groups is consecutive in rank with the top of the wastepile, regardless of suit, play it to the top of the pile. King and Ace are consecutive. When a wing card is uncovered, put it to one side as the first card of a tableau pile. When a centre card is uncovered, put it face up to the other side as the base of a suite.

Phase Two begins as soon as tableau and base cards enter play, though Phase One continues simultaneously until the other covering cards have been worked off.

On each base card build upwards in suit, turning the corner from King to Ace as necessary. If two or more are being built in the same suit, place one pile on the other as soon as they become consecutive. Any suit not represented among these suites can only be built within the tableau.

On each tableau card pack, downwards in suit, passing from Ace to King as necessary. When two or more of the same suit become consecutive, join them up. Tableau cards may be reversed onto suites of the same suit when they become consecutive, but not vice versa.

Available for building or packing are: the exposed card of a group not yet worked off, the top of the wastepile, the card turned from stock, and the exposed card or sequence of a tableau column. When the stock is exhausted, turn the wastepile and deal through it again. Two such redeals are allowed.

Note A wing card may be packed on the wastepile, provided that it is not the only card of its suit available for building a sequence; but this is not recommended. If a suit is not represented on any of the centre or wing cards (an unlikely event), discard all of that suit as they turn up and build only three suites. Note that a tableau column, when moved elsewhere, is not replaced.

104

Wheatsheaf

Two packs
Odds against

These closely related games are only slightly elaborated forms of Single or Double Rail with which this section began. Some of them are semi-pictorial as the titles vaguely suggest, but not enough interest attaches to the pattern to merit illustration. Wheatsheaf comes first.

Layout and object Take out an Ace and a King of each suit and found them as bases, the object being to build them respectively upwards and downwards into thirteen-card suit sequences. Deal the next eight cards face up in a row to start the tableau.

Play Turn cards from stock and play them if possible or else discard them face up to a single wastepile. Pack the tableau in suit and sequence, up or down ad lib but shifting only one card at a time. A space made by clearing out a column must be filled at once with the top card of the wastepile, if any, or else from the stock (but never from the tableau).

CONGRESS (PRESIDENT'S CABINET) The same, except that all the Aces are founded and built up in suit to the Kings, and packing is done in descending sequence only and regardless of suit. (Now you know what goes on in Washington behind closed doors.)

DIEPPE As Congress, but with some easement. After dealing the first row of eight, building any that can be built and filling gaps from stock, deal another row of eight across the first and pause to build again. Having filled any gaps, deal yet a third row of eight. After that, play to the wastepile in the usual way and start packing where possible. Any length of packed sequence may be shifted to another column provided that the join follows the rule (descending, regardless of suit), and a space made by clearing out a column may be filled with any available card.

RED AND BLACK In this version, the eight Aces are set up as

bases and are to be built up in sequence to the Kings, not following suit but in alternating colours (red Ace, black Two, red Three
etc. and vice versa). Eight cards are dealt to start the tableau, and
these too are to be packed in alternating colour, but in descending
sequence. There is no redeal. This game is also known as Blonde
and Brunette, Light and Shade, Noir et Rouge, and even Rouge
et Noir. The wording of the account in Whitmore Jones's First
Series of Patience Games seems to suggest that the concept of
alternating colours was something of a novelty in the 1890s, and
not a particularly popular one with many players. It is a supposition reinforced by the various titles of the game, which draw
attention to that feature.

Ladder

Two packs
Even chances

An unusual and exasperating game, which at first sight appears
to offer so many escape routes that you either suppose it to be
ridiculously easy or conclude that you have misunderstood the
rules. It takes some time to play, most of which must be spent
looking before you leap. The layout is vaguely descriptive of the
title, or vice versa.

Layout Deal the first four cards face up in a column down the left
of the board, with no overlapping, and the next four similarly on
the right. Leave enough space between them to take two columns
of horizontally disposed cards, which presumably represent the
rungs of the ladder. If any of the first eight cards are Aces or
Kings, set them up as bases and deal substitutes.

Object To found eight bases, consisting of an Ace and a King of
each suit, and to build the Aces up in suit to the Kings and the
Kings down in suit to the Aces.

Play Deal six separate spreads of four cards each, face up, and pause to consider the play. The exposed card of a spread or of the tableau may be built on a suite if it fits. Exposed cards in the tableau may also be packed in ascending or descending order ad lib, changes of direction being permitted provided that all sequences follow suit. Individual cards (not sequences) may come either from other columns in the tableau or from the exposed ends

LADDER Dotted lines indicates sites on which an Ace and a King of each suit are to be founded. Given this deal and first six spreads it is possible to found one Ace (spades) and build it as far as the Five.

of the six spreads, but not from hand. A space made in the tableau by playing off the last card of a pile or column need not be filled immediately, unless all four depots on one side or the other are missing, in which case they must be refilled with exposed cards taken from the spreads. Other than in this circumstance, it is not necessary to fill a vacancy with the top card of a spread. If there is one vacancy, either of the top two cards of any spread may be used to fill it; if there are two vacancies, any one of the top three cards of a spread may be taken; and so on pro rata. When you are quite certain that you cannot or will not proceed further, deal six more spreads of four across any of those that may be still left, then pause and play again.

Redeal When you have run out of cards and can get no further, gather up the spreads in rotation, consolidate them into a new stock, and play through them once again. If it still fails, you will see why the game is much more difficult than it looks.

Octave
Two packs
Odds against

This is an unusual patience, with some features reminiscent of the 'spiders' described in another place. I hope I have got it right: my only source (Whitmore Jones) sails into a fog patch at a critical point in the description.

Layout Set the eight Aces up as bases in a row, alternating the colours. Deal the next twenty-four cards in three overlapping rows of eight each, the first two face down and the third face up, and regard the tableau as eight columns of three.

Object The Aces are to be built up in suit and sequence as far as their respective Tens. Below each suit in the final tableau is to remain a column consisting of King, Queen and Jack in alternating colours, with the King at the bottom and the Jack exposed.

Play Cards in the tableau are to be packed in descending sequence and alternating colour. Whenever a down-card is exposed, turn it face up. Turn cards from stock and play them if possible or else discard them face up to a single wastepile. Only one card may be shifted at a time. When a space is made by clearing out a column it may be filled with any available card at any time. (Clearly, it is desirable to reserve such spaces for Kings.) When the stock is exhausted, gather up the cards of the wastepile, turn them face down, and deal a row of eight cards face up. These are all available for building or packing in the tableau (but not on one another). When one is taken, its place may be filled with the next card from stock. When no more moves are possible a final chance remains: you may turn the next card from stock and use it if you can; if not, the game is lost.

Marriage

Two packs
Odds against

The theme is not so much about marriage as marriage settlements – an old custom by which a father could provide his married daughter with money that would (in theory at least) be her own. No doubt this will be smugly regarded as a thing of the past in these enlightened days characterized more by wage settlements and marital breakdowns. 'The eight concealed cards,' says Whitmore Jones, 'are the settlements, which in this game of patience, as in real life, wreck many a hope, for how often do we hear of a promising match "gone off upon settlements"; and here, if they remain undisclosed, it is impossible for the Kings to marry the Queens.' Those who like happy endings are not advised to try this one.

Layout (simplified). Leave room for eight suites at the top of the board, and below that deal eight cards in a row, face down. These are the settlements. Deal three more rows of cards across them, face up, and regard the result as eight columns of four.

Object To found the eight Aces, as and when they become available, and to build them upwards into thirteen-card suit-sequences with the Queen and King displayed on top.

Play Do any founding and building that can be done, and start packing on the tableau. Pack in descending sequence regardless of suit, shifting only one exposed card at a time. When a settlement card is exposed, turn it face up. If you succeed in clearing out a column, refill it with the next three cards dealt face up from stock. (They must be dealt as a group: only the third of them is immediately available for building.)

Then turn cards from stock one at a time and play them if possible or else discard them face up to a single wastepile. The top card of the wastepile is also available for building or packing. When the stock runs out and no further play is possible, make a new stock by gathering in all the face-up cards on the tableau and shuffling them in with the wastepile. Deal another eight columns of three cards each, face up, covering again any settlement cards that may not have been disclosed. Only one re-deal is allowed.

Grace The game often founders on the obstruction of a King at the exposed end of a column. When you create a vacancy by clearing out a column, you may, instead of dealing three stock cards to it, fill it with an exposed King from a column obstructed by it. In this case, however, the King may not be packed upon, and should be placed horizontally to give warning of this restriction. Until this King is used to crown a suite it reduces the number of columns available for packing.

Shah
Star
Two packs
Odds against

The alternative titles for this patience are not only quite similar but also equally appropriate – Shah for the similarity of its final effect to that of Sultan, Star for the pattern it makes on the table. Shah is preferable, if only because Star has already been used.

Layout Remove Aces and Kings. Place the Kings in a packet in the centre with a ♥K face up on top. Around him arrange the eight Aces in a pattern radiating from the corners and edges of the packet.

Object To build the Aces up in suit and sequence to the Queens, so as to finish with the representation of a Shah surrounded by his seraglio (or whatever it is called in that part of the world).

Play Deal another circle of eight cards radiating outwards from the Aces, but not overlapping them. If any of these are Twos, build them on their Aces and replace. Deal another circle of eight cards, this time overlapping the previous eight, and build or pack if possible; then deal a third circle and do likewise. After that, turn cards from stock and play them if possible or else discard them face up to a single wastepile. The radial lines are to be packed in suit and descending sequence, but only one card may be moved at a time. When a space is made by clearing out a ray, it may be refilled with any three cards taken from the exposed ends of other rays. (As at the start of the game, these three need not be in suit or sequence.) There is no redeal.

Diplomat
Two packs
Odds against

This game and its variants below all have in common that the initial tableau consists of eight columns of four. In some cases they are actually designated eight rows of four (with cards overlapping by their long edges), and dealt in two 'wings' of four rows each in order to conserve space, or apply symmetry, or both. This accounts for such a title as Spread Eagle, which is more or less pictorial. The games also differ from one another in minor details, probably owing to copyists' errors.

Layout and object Deal eight rows of four overlapping cards each, four rows on each side of the board. Leave enough space between the two wings to accommodate eight base cards in two non-overlapping columns of four. Any Aces so dealt may be taken, used as bases and replaced with fresh cards, but no further building may yet be carried out. The object is to found all eight Aces as and when they appear, and build them up in suit to the Kings.   *Cop. 1*

Play Turn cards from stock and play them if possible or else discard them face up to a single wastepile. The rows of the tableau may be packed in descending sequence regardless of suit, but only one card may be shifted at a time. A space made by clearing out a row may be filled only with a King.

Redeal One turn and redeal of the wastepile is permitted. (This is a compromise between conflicting accounts, one of which allows two redeals and the other none.)

VARIANTS In Diplomat and Lady Palk it is permissible to worry back from suites to tableau. In Spread Eagle and Princess, a vacated row may be restarted with the top card of stock or wastepile, or with an exposed King from another row (but not with any other exposed rank). In Lady Palk, a sequence may be shifted from one row to another provided that the join continues it. In Princess, there is an unusual rule whereby only the fourth or later card of a row may be packed upon, not any of the first three. To compensate, however, any exposed card may be transferred to any column consisting of three or fewer cards. Aces may not be taken during the deal.

British Constitution

Two packs
Odds in favour

The Victorian era is here encapsulated in a single game of patience. Patriotic in theme, it is at once symbolic, representational, and sumptuously space-consuming. The Queen packet at the centre represents Victoria R.I. on her throne, and of the Kings surrounding her in alternating colour the black represent bishops and the red judges. The lowest of the four rows forming the Constitution (tableau) represent 'the people', who are to ascend, in order, through the next three rows symbolizing respectively the House of Commons, the House of Lords, and the Privy Council. Not until they reach these dizzy heights may they presume to enter the circle immediately surrounding THE SOVEREIGN. (Capital letters by courtesy of Lady Cadogan, our only source for this game.)

Layout Extract all the Queens, Kings and Aces. Make a packet of the Queens near the top of the board. Surround this packet by the eight Aces radiating outwards from the corners and edges of the packet, alternating in colour. Surround the Aces with the Kings, laying their long edges parallel to the short edges of the Aces, and also alternating colour for effect. Beneath this circular pattern deal the next thirty-two cards face up in four rows of eight, not overlapping one another. These rows form the 'Constitution'.

Object The Aces are bases (representing 'the Government'), and are to be built up in suit and sequence to the Knaves (appropriately, some might think). The Kings and Queens are for decoration only.

Play The rules of play are somewhat unusual, so pay attention. The only cards available for building on the Ace-suites are those exposed in the top row of the Constitution. All other cards must gradually work their way upwards into the top row from the row they are already in, and those not yet dealt can only be entered in the bottom row when vacancies occur there. Within the Constitution, any card in the bottom three rows may be packed on any of the eight cards in the row immediately above it, provided that it is placed upon a card next higher in rank and of opposite colour. In other words, cards in the Constitution may be packed in descending sequence and alternating colour, but

BRITISH CONSTITUTION (*opposite*)   The Aces are to be built up in suit to the Jacks with cards taken only from the 'privy council' (top row of the tableau or 'constitution'). Unlike some elaborate patiences this one is as interesting to play as it looks.

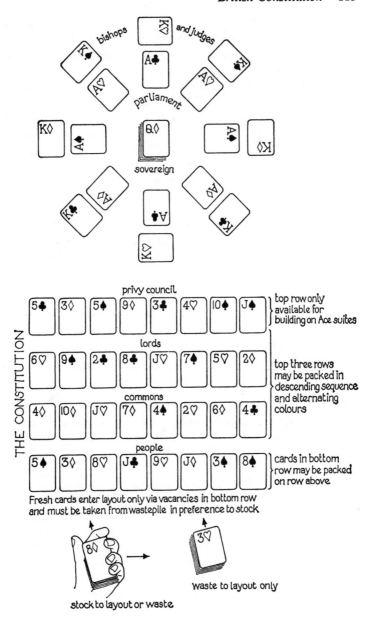

privy council

top row only available for building on Ace suites

lords

top three rows may be packed in descending sequence and alternating colours

commons

people

cards in bottom row may be packed on row above

THE CONSTITUTION

Fresh cards enter layout only via vacancies in bottom row and must be taken from wastepile in preference to stock

stock to layout or waste

waste to layout only

forming piles rather than overlapping. Only the top card of a pile may be moved in any one turn. Whenever a vacancy occurs in one of the top three rows, it must be filled immediately with one of the eight exposed cards in the row below. Whenever a vacancy occurs in the bottom row, it must be filled immediately with the top card of the wastepile if any, or of the stock if not. Having made all opening moves that may be possible, turn cards from stock and enter them in the bottom row if this will progress the game, or discard them face up to a single wastepile if it seems more useful to delay their entry. If there is no vacancy in the bottom row, and none can be made by judicious play elsewhere in the Constitution, the game is lost. There is no redeal.

Note The game described by Morehead and Mott-Smith under the title 'Constitution' seems to be based on a misreading of Lady Cadogan's text, even allowing for their republican dismissal of the pretty bits at the top.

Right and Left

Two packs
Odds against

This is another straightforward packing game, which in effect amounts to eight columns of four but in fact is dealt in rows in partial justification of the title.

Layout Deal eight rows of four non-overlapping cards each, in two wings of four rows. Leave enough space between the two wings to accommodate eight suites. The deal is to be carried out in a particular manner, the purpose of which is to slightly increase the chances of success. When dealing each row of four cards, consider the rank of the first one turned from the pack. If it is an Ace, set it up as a base at the centre of the board and turn the next card. If it is a Seven or lower rank, deal the row from the outside (nearer the edge of the board) inwards (towards the centre). If it is an Eight or higher rank, deal the row from the centre outwards.

Object To found the eight Aces, as and when they become available, and to build them up in suit to the Kings.

Play For convenience, the cards of each row may now be overlapped, for which purpose the exposed card must be the one nearer the edge of the board. Turn cards from stock and play them if possible or else discard them face up to a single wastepile. Exposed cards in the tableau, and cards from hand and waste, are available for building on suites or packing on other exposed cards. Packing is to be carried out in descending sequence and regardless of suit. Only one card may be moved at a time. A vacancy made by clearing out a row may be filled only with an available King. There is no redeal.

Note Comparison with original accounts of the game will show that I have made some slight modifications, which I regard as desirable rather than vital improvements.

Snake
Les Huit
Two packs
Odds against

We have already encountered the idea of attaching the wastepile to the tableau in Six by Six, where it grows longer and longer, like a snake, and may have to be coiled around to make best use of the space available.

Layout and object Deal sixty-four cards in eight overlapping rows of eight, and regard the tableau as eight columns of eight. The object is to release the Aces and build them up in suit to the Kings.

Play The exposed card of a column may be built on a suite or packed on another column, packing to proceed in descending sequence and regardless of suit. A part sequence may be moved from one column to another, provided that the join follows the rule. Turn cards from stock and build or pack them if possible. An unplayable card from stock is placed on the end of the left-hand column, where, until covered, it remains available for building, packing, or being packed on in the normal way. It is permissible to worry back from a suite to the tableau, but there is no redeal.

Maria
Two packs
Odds against

The close relationship between Maria and its variant Midshipman seems to confirm, as an old war-time song has it, that all the nice girls love a sailor.

Layout and object Deal four overlapping columns of nine cards each. Play to release the Aces and build them up in suit to the Kings.

Play Turn cards from stock and pack, build or discard them to a single wastepile. In the tableau, pack in descending sequence and alternating colour. Only one card may be moved at a time. A space may be filled with any available card. There is no redeal.

MIDSHIPMAN The same, except that the first two rows are dealt face down and the second two face up. When a down-card is exposed, turn it face up.

Hill of Difficulty

Two packs
Odds against

The title supposedly refers to the infrequency with which the game comes out, but my chief difficulty has lain in determining how best to make up deficiencies in the original account of the rules, which I find unintelligible. Hill of Difficulty introduces the unusual feature of building in alternate sequence as well as alternate colour. The effect of this is to double the number of suites and halve their size, which should make for an easy game. It is complicated, however, by the difficulty of packing in the tableau.

Layout Take all the Aces and Twos and arrange them in a V-formation pointing away from you, none of them overlapping. These constitute the 'hill'. At the base of the hill, in the space between its sides, deal the next nine cards face up in a pyramidal shape with one at the top, three in a row below it, and five in a row below that. These constitute the tableau or 'mound'.

Object The Aces and Twos are bases, and the object is to build them up in alternating sequence and colour to the Kings and Queens respectively. (Thus: red Ace, black Three etc. to red King; red Two, black Four etc. to black Queen; and vice versa.)

Play Of the cards in the mound, only those in the bottom row are available for building on the hill. When a vacancy is made in the bottom row, the card immediately above it (if any, because the end cards are single) is freed for use anywhere in that row, either to fill the vacancy or to be packed upon a card elsewhere in it. Any space made in the mound must be filled at once with the top card of stock or waste. Turn cards from stock and use them to build, pack or fill vacancies if possible, or else discard them face up to a single wastepile. Cards in the mound may also be packed upon in descending alternating sequence, regardless of suit. (Example: any Four on any Six, any Nine on any Jack etc.) Presumably the creation of a vacancy in the bottom row frees only the top card of the packed pile immediately above it, and does not permit the descent of the whole pile into that space. There is no redeal.

Gargantua
Double Klondike
Two packs
Even chances

This two-pack version of Klondike, described earlier, was re-named Gargantua by Morehead and Mott-Smith. It has no novel features.

Layout Deal nine packets of cards face down, the first consisting of one card, the second of two, and so on up to the ninth of nine. Turn the top card of each packet face up.

Object To found all the Aces, as and when they appear, and build them up in suit to the Kings.

Play Turn cards from stock and play them if possible or else discard them face up to a single wastepile. Exposed cards in the tableau are to be packed in descending sequence and alternating colour, and part-sequences may be shifted from column to column provided that the join follows the rule. When a down-card is exposed, turn it face up. A space made by clearing out a column may be filled only with a King – either an available King or a part-sequence packed on a King. One redeal is allowed.

Batsford
Two packs
Odds against

Batsford is Gargantua with slight modifications. Triangle is Batsford with slight modifications. Both have slightly novel features.

Layout Deal ten packets of cards face down, the packets containing one to ten cards each in order from right to left. Turn the top cards face up.

Object To found the Aces as and when they appear, and build them up in suit and sequence to the Kings.

Play As for Gargantua, but with no redeal and with this difference: that if a King turns up when there is no space for it, it may be put face up to one side and held in reserve until it can be used. Up to three Kings may be held in reserve at a time, but no more.

TRIANGLE As Batsford, but with these differences. The Aces are to be built up to the Queens, leaving their corresponding Kings in a row below them. When a space is made by clearing out a column, it must be filled at once with all the face-up cards of the column nearest the right-hand side of the board which still contains one or more face-down cards. As before, there is no redeal; but if the game blocks when the stock is exhausted you may worry back one card from a suite if it will match the end of a column and progress the game. This privilege may be taken more than once, but only one card may be taken at a time. Further play must ensue before another is taken.

Deuces
Les Deux, Twos
Two packs
Even chances

The only distinctive features of Deuces are its layout and the fact that the suites are founded on Twos and are built up to their corresponding Aces. Neither of these superficial differences is of any significance to the play of the game, which otherwise remains an orthodox member of the family under discussion.

Layout and object Extract the eight Twos, set them up as foundations in two rows of four, and build them up in suit and sequence to the Aces. Deal the next ten cards face up in a partly encircling pattern – four in a row above the foundations, and three in a column down each side of them. (The pattern is not important.)

Play Turn cards from stock and play them if possible or else discard them face up to a single wastepile. The ten cards of the tableau are to be packed (in piles if the pattern is followed, otherwise overlapping one another in columns) in descending sequence and following suit. Any length of properly packed sequence may be shifted to another column, provided that the join follows the rule. A space made by clearing out a pile or column must be filled at once with the top card of stock or waste – not with an exposed card from the tableau.

Redeal Two redeals are permitted.

SQUARE (COURTYARD, PLUTO) The same, except that the Deuces are not removed to start with but are founded as and when they turn up. To compensate for the extra difficulty, the tableau consists of twelve cards – four along the top and four down each side if the pattern is followed. Pluto is an alternative title. Courtyard denotes the same game but with suites based on Aces and built up to the Kings.

Number Ten
Two packs
Odds against

Another unremarkable member of the family, of which Indian (below) may be regarded as a more interesting extension.

Layout and object Deal three overlapping rows of ten cards each, the first two face down and the third face up, and regard the tableau as ten columns of three. Play to release the Aces and build them up in suit to the Kings.

Play Turn cards from stock and play them if possible or else discard them face up to a single wastepile. On the tableau, pack in descending sequence and alternating colour. Only one card may be moved at a time. When a down-card is exposed, turn it face up. When a column is emptied, refill it with any available card whenever you like. There is no redeal.

Indian
Two packs
Odds against

Some unusual features of a game structurally similar to Number Ten may provide you with an intriguing challenge.

Layout and object Deal three overlapping rows of ten cards each, the first face down and the other two face up, and regard the tableau as ten columns of three. Play to release the Aces and build them up in suit to the Kings.

Play Turn cards from stock and play them if possible or else discard them face up to a single wastepile. On the tableau, pack in descending sequence and differing suit. (E.g. a spade may be packed on any suit other than a spade.) Only one card may be moved at a time. When a down-card is exposed, turn it face up. It then becomes a 'protected card', and may neither be packed upon nor used for packing: instead, it must remain in position until either it can be built on a suite, or the stock is exhausted. When it has been built, the vacancy must be filled from stock (if it is not yet exhausted) in the same way as in the original deal – one card face down and two overlapping it face up. When the stock runs out, protected cards become free for packing in the usual way, and a vacancy may be filled with any available card. There is no redeal.

Napoleon at St Helena

Big Forty, Cadran, Forty Thieves, Roosevelt at San Juan
Two packs
Odds against

The Napoleonic flavour and number of alternative titles show us
to be at the centre of a circle of old and popular games. Closely
related, differing only in the number of cards dealt initially, are
some of the preceding and some of the following patiences, such
as Maria, Number Ten, Emperor and Napoleon's Square.
References to the number forty allude to the 10 × 4 tableau, and
that to Roosevelt (showing American popularity) presumably to
the domestic period between F.D.'s terms of office. Napoleon at
St Helena is not wildly exciting or unusual, but we may conclude
from its popularity that it represents the best balance of forces
amongst the seemingly myriad games of its type. Fans of the
game who are looking for something similar but more challenging
should try Blind Patience, which follows.

Layout and object Deal four rows of ten cards each, face up, and
regard the tableau as ten columns of four. Play to release the Aces
and build them up in suit to the Kings.

Play Turn cards from stock and play them if possible or else discard them face up to a single wastepile. Pack on cards of the
tableau in suit and descending sequence. Only one card may be
moved at a time. When a column is emptied the space may be
filled with any available card at any time. There is no redeal.

STREETS The same, except that cards in the tableau are packed
in alternating colour. (A variant called Alley has more restrictive
rules.)

EMPEROR (DEAUVILLE, DRESS PARADE, RANK AND FILE)
As Napoleon at St Helena, except that the first three rows are
dealt face down and the fourth face up, and cards are packed in
alternating colour.

Blind Patience

Two packs
Odds against

This cruel game might be represented as Napoleon at St Helena with the additional disadvantage of having his eyes put out.

Layout and object Deal four overlapping rows of ten cards each, all face down. Play to release the Aces and build them up in suit and sequence to the Kings.

Play Turn cards from stock and consider how best to deal with each one. If it is an Ace, start a suite; if it can be built, build it. Otherwise, you are at liberty to discard it face up to a single wastepile, or to lay it face up overlapping the exposed (but face-down) card of a column, or to pack it on the tableau if it is headed by an appropriate faced card. Packing is to be done in descending sequence and alternating colour. The exposed card of a blind column may be turned face up at any time, and built or packed if possible. If it cannot be used, it remains face up on its column, blocking the cards beneath it. A sequence may not be shifted as a whole, but individual exposed cards may be taken and either packed elsewhere or placed upon the top card of a blind column. A space made by emptying a column may be filled with any available card at any time. There is no redeal, but you are permitted to examine the exposed cards of blind columns to see if any are worth turning.

Note Although sequences may not be shifted, it is sometimes possible to get them onto another column by playing exposed cards off one at a time to the head of blind columns, and then gathering them onto another column in reverse order. For this purpose you need to keep some columns blind, rather than indiscriminately face the exposed card as a matter of principle. At the start of play, it is generally advisable to discard high ranks to the wastepile and use low ones for opening up the tableau. Blind Patience calls for a considerable degree of judgement.

DEAUVILLE (BLIND HOOKEY, DRESS PARADE, RANK AND

FILE) The same, but deal the fourth row face up. This makes it harder to place the first cards turned, as they may only enter the tableau if packable in accordance with the rules.

EMPEROR As above, but with the privilege that cards may be worried back from suites into the tableau, provided that they will properly pack.

Double Fives

Two separate packs
Odds against

Double Fives is one of several patiences in which you have a choice of bases, and if you choose the wrong one you may live to regret it. The skill factor is high.

Layout From one of the two packs deal five overlapping rows of ten cards each, face up. (Strictly, but not essentially, in two square 'wings' of five rows and columns each, with enough space between them to accommodate eight bases. This adds nothing to the play, but accords neatly with the quinary theme of the game.) Choose one of the two remaining cards to act as a base, and lay the other to one side for the moment.

Object To found the other seven cards of the same rank as the first base, and to build them up into thirteen-card suit sequences, turning the corner from King to Ace where necessary.

Play Columns in the tableau are to be packed in suit and descending sequence, a King following an Ace where necessary. A space made by emptying a column may be filled with any available card at any time. Only one card may be moved at a time. Having made all opening moves that may be possible, turn cards from the second pack in groups of five, and lay each group face up on the table. All five cards (and the one left over from the other pack on the first turn) are available for packing or building. When no further moves are possible or desirable, put any unplayable cards face down to one side and turn the next five from stock. Continue until the stock is exhausted.

Redeal Continue the game by making a new stock of the unplayable cards. Now turn cards from stock one by one, playing each one if possible or discarding it face up to a single wastepile if not. This time there is no redeal, so it is essential to play from the top of the wastepile whenever possible.

QUINARY This is like a quandary, only more so. My variant of the game starts with two packs shuffled together. The layout is the same, but this time you have the additional choice of building either upwards or downwards on your chosen base. If you decide to build in descending sequence, then you must pack on the tableau in ascending sequence, and vice versa.

Highlands

Two separate packs
Odds against

In the old days, when patience-players had tables like barn doors, they used to lay their full-size cards out individually in rows and columns without overlapping. This explains how a game could come to be called Highlands; for packing took place on the top card of a column, and columns were worked off downwards towards the player instead of upwards away from him as is now the case when overlapping is necessary to conserve space. In defiance of the title, I shall describe it in the usual columnar way, from which it will be seen that the game is no more than an extension of the Napoleón at St Helena type.

Layout Deal the first pack face up in five overlapping rows of ten cards each. Start a sixth row with the two left over, and complete it with the first eight cards from the second pack. Regard the tableau as ten columns of six.

Object To found all eight Aces as and when they become available, and build them up in suit to the Kings.

Play Turn cards from stock and play them if possible or else discard them face up to a single wastepile. Pack the tableau in suit and descending sequence. Part sequences may be shifted from column to column provided that the join follows the rule. When a column is emptied it may be filled with any available card or part sequence at any time. There is no redeal.

Club

Two packs
Odds against

The slightly pictorial layout of this patience suggests that the title denotes an implement for beating people over the head with, rather than an organization from which one would be expelled for cheating at Patience. The pattern has some significance to the play, as will be seen.

Layout Deal three concentric and overlapping arcs of eight cards each, the first face down and the others face up. We will refer to this part of the layout as the arc. Beneath it, deal three overlapping rows of three cards each, also with the first face down and the others up. This forms the square.

Object To found the Aces, as and when they appear, and build them up in suit to the Kings.

Play Turn cards from stock and build or pack them in either half of the layout if possible, or else discard them face up to a single wastepile. Packing within the tableau is to be done in descending sequence and alternating colour. Only the eleven exposed cards of the tableau are available, and they must be moved singly, not in sequences. No card in the square may be moved at any time into the arc, or used to fill a space in the arc made by emptying

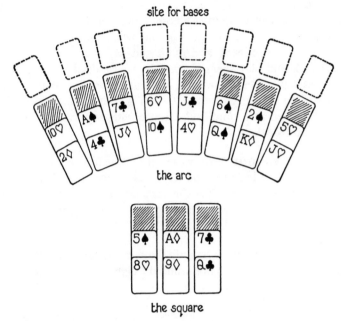

site for bases

the arc

the square

CLUB The eleven exposed cards are available. Exposed cards may be packed from the arc on the square, but not vice versa.

a column. This restriction does not apply in reverse: any exposed card in the arc may be packed on a suitable card in the square, or used to fill a vacancy in it. There is no redeal.

Simplicity

One or two packs
Odds in favour

The following four games start with a tableau of twelve single cards ready for packing, and follow the usual rules of play. Some of them specify particular patterns for the initial layout, but none of them is pictorially strong enough to be worth detailing.

SIMPLICITY (One pack) Deal twelve cards in two rows of six and turn up the thirteenth card as a base. The other three cards of the same rank are to be founded as and when they turn up, and built into thirteen-card ascending suit-sequences. Turn cards from stock and play them if possible or else discard them to a single wastepile. On the tableau, pack in descending sequence (a King can go on an Ace) and alternating colour. Only one card may be moved at a time. Fill a space with any available card. There is no redeal.

FORTUNE'S FAVOUR (One pack) Set out the four Aces and play to build them up in suit to the Kings. Deal twelve cards face up. Play to a single wastepile. Pack in descending sequence, following suit. Move only one card at a time. Fill a space from waste or hand. There is no redeal.

BUSY ACES (Two packs) Exactly the same as Fortune's Favour, but use two packs and do not found the eight Aces until they turn up in the deal.

THE SPARK (Two packs) Upside-down version of the above. Take out the eight Kings as bases and build them down in suit to the Aces. Turn cards from stock in sweeps of three at a time, and play the sweeps alternately to two wastepiles. Playing the top card of a sweep releases the one below it. Fill any gaps made in the tableau from either of the wastepiles. There is no redeal.

Limited

Two packs
Odds against

The limitation referred to is the unusual one of allowing only two cards at a time to be packed together. (A similar but 'open' game with one pack is Reversible Sequences.) Although the odds are against success if the strict rules are followed, Limited will nearly always come out if the redealt stock is played to a second waste-pile.

Layout Deal three rows of twelve cards each, face up and not overlapping. Regard this tableau as consisting of twelve columns of three.

Object To found the Aces as and when they become available and build them up in suit to the Kings.

Play Only cards in the bottom row are available for founding and building, but when one is taken it releases the one immediately above it, and the play of the second releases the one above that in the top row. A vacancy made by clearing out a column may be filled with any single exposed card, but not with a packed couple as described below. Start by doing any packing and building that may be possible.

   Limited packing is carried out to this extent: that any available card from stock, waste or tableau may be placed upon any single tableau card which is of the same suit and next higher in rank to form a consecutive couple. A packed couple may not be further packed upon, and may only be moved as a unit when it can be built on an appropriate suite.

   Play as far as you can, then turn cards from stock and build or pack them if possible. If not, discard them face up to a single wastepile, of which the top card is always available.

   Having run out of stock, turn the wastepile face down and deal out the top four cards face up to a reserve. If any of these can be built, paired or used for filling vacancies, use them and fill their place from the new stock. If the game blocks again and none of the four reserves can be used, your last chance is to turn the next card from stock and see if it can be used. Should this last resort fail, so does the game.

Hemispheres

Two packs
Odds in favour

For all its apparent complexity, Hemispheres is basically quite simple. If you spread out the cards of the wastepile, you will soon see whether the distribution contains a particular kink that will render it impossible to get out, so no time is wasted. And in that event you may legitimately allow yourself a redeal, in which case the game hardly ever fails.

Layout Take the four black Kings and radiate them from the centre of the board in the form of a cross. Take the four red Aces and use them to extend the arms of the cross. Extend them further with an Ace of clubs and of spades, and a King of hearts and of diamonds, but align their long edges with the short edges of the four red Aces. Then deal the next twelve cards in a circle, three to a quadrant, starting above the westernmost card and proceeding in a clockwise direction.

Terminology The black Aces and red Kings are barriers dividing the races. The six cards of the northern hemisphere are associated with Europeans (north west) and Asiatics (north east), both being represented by red suits. Those of the southern hemisphere are associated with Australians (south east) and Africans (south west), these being represented by black suits.

Object The four black Kings are bases, and are to be built down in suit to the Aces. The four red Aces are also bases, and are to be built up in suit to the Kings. The four barrier cards are not used in any way during the game, but at the end of play (if successful) go to crown the suites on which they belong.

Play The twelve cards of the circular tableau are available for building on suites and packing on one another, but only if they are in their proper hemisphere – red suits in the north, black in the south. A card in its wrong hemisphere (caused by the randomness of the deal) may not be built or packed until it has been put in its proper hemisphere. This may only be done by exchange –

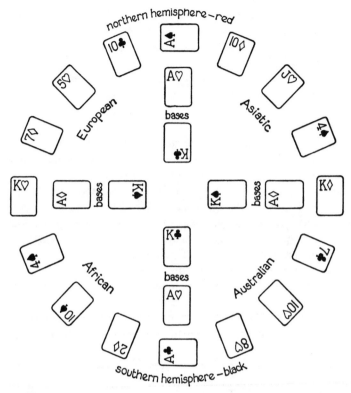

HEMISPHERES Only cards of the proper colour may be built or packed – red in the north, black in the south. But cards of the 'wrong' colour may be exchanged on a one-to-one basis, e.g. in this diagram ♣10 for (say) ♦2 and ♠4 for ♥10, leaving ♥8 temporarily unusable. Build central Aces and Kings respectively up and down in suit. Peripheral Aces and Kings are 'barriers' dividing the ethnic quadrants, and are used to crown the suites when completed. An unusual and challenging game.

any red card in the south may be exchanged for any black card in the north. If you were lucky enough to have dealt six of each colour, all can be properly arranged; if not, some will have to wait until the game has progressed before they can be moved.

Before turning any cards from stock, make such north–south exchanges as may present themselves. (Given a choice, prefer high ranks in the north and low in the south.) Carry out any packing that may be possible, packing northern red cards in suit and descending sequence, and southern black cards in suit and ascending sequence. Also carry out any building that may be done on the suites.

When you can get no further, turn cards from stock and use them to fill up vacancies in the circle. For this purpose you must start in the west and proceed clockwise, as in the original deal, allowing the cards to arrange themselves as they happen to come. Then exchange, pack, build and refill in the same way.

Eventually you will reach a point at which there are no vacancies in the hemispheres, and no more exchanging, packing or building can be done. Thereupon you start turning cards from stock one by one. Each one turned may, if possible, be built on a suite or packed on an appropriate exposed card in either hemisphere. If not, discard it face up to a single wastepile. The top card of the wastepile is always available for building or packing.

Whenever vacancies are made in the hemispheres, fill them from stock in the same way as in the initial deal, or else fill each one as soon as it occurs.

When, towards the end of a successful game, there are no cards left in the stock or the wastepile, a card in its wrong hemisphere may be transferred to a vacancy in its proper one, without necessarily exchanging with a card of opposite colour.

Note My only source for this game (Lady Cadogan) leaves many questions unanswered. For example, I have assumed from my own experience of the game that it is permissible to build a card directly from the stock or wastepile, though the original account does not refer to this possibility one way or the other.

Corona

Round Dozen
Two packs
Odds against

The following three games are based on a tableau of 12 × 3 cards and follow the rules of play common to most games in this section. They differ only in detail.

CORONA (Round Dozen) Deal three rows of twelve cards and regard the result as twelve columns of three. (Strictly speaking, the columns radiate from a common centre to make a twelve-rayed star, whence the circular titles; but this space-consuming feature is not essential.) Found the eight Aces as they appear and build them up in suit and sequence to the Kings. On the tableau pack in descending sequence and following suit. Only one card may be moved at a time, and a vacancy must be filled with the top card of the stock or waste. Play from stock, putting unplayable cards on a wasteheap. There is no redeal.

QUADRANGLE Deal three rows of twelve again. Turn up the thirteenth card and use it as the first base: the other seven of the same rank are to be founded as and when they appear, and all are to be built up in suit and ascending sequence until each suite contains thirteen cards. Play as for Corona, turning the corner between King and Ace where necessary. (The title refers to an unimportant opening pattern similar to that of the game called Deuces.)

TRIPLE LINE A suitable game for parliamentary whips. Deal three rows of twelve. Found the Aces as they appear and build them up to the Kings. Pack in suit and descending sequence, moving only one card at a time. One redeal is allowed. (This game is considerably against the player. Later accounts allow packing in alternating colour and shifting packed sequences, but this makes the game altogether far too easy. Corona may be regarded as having the best combination of rules.)

Colonel

Uncle Walter's
Two packs
Odds against

Two different titles introduce the one game, though Whitmore Jones describes them separately in the same book and says that Colonel is similar to Limited while Uncle Walter's is similar to Barton! In fact it is only a slight extention of Triple Line, but with a sufficiently crippling rule to put it in a class of its own.

Layout and object Deal three rows of twelve cards, but do not overlap them. Play to release the Aces and build them up in suit and sequence to the Kings.

Play Turn cards from stock and play them if possible or else discard them face up to a single wastepile. Exposed cards in the bottom row of the three may be built on suites or packed on other exposed cards in descending sequence of the same suit. A card in a higher row does not become exposed until there is a gap immediately beneath it in the next row down. An exposed card may be packed on another exposed card in the same or a higher row, but not on a card in a lower row than itself. To avoid confusion, packing should be done in piles rather than columns, though of course you may look through a pile to see what it contains at any time. Only one card may be moved at a time, and there is no redeal.

VARIANT An even more horrible version of the game prohibits you from packing a card from one row onto another in the same row, such transfers being allowed only to higher rows.

Big Ben
Clock, Grandfather's Clock, Father Time
Two packs
Even chances

The representation of a clock face is a natural, not to say obvious, theme and pattern for a form of patience, and one that is expressed in several other games. Here we have a two-pack version going under various titles, of which on the whole I prefer Big Ben. (That I am a Londoner by birth and inclination is pure coincidence.) Although this patience has a slightly unusual layout, little analysis is required to show it to be at root an orthodox member of the family of games under discussion.

Layout Extract the following twelve cards and arrange them clockwise in a circle starting at the one o'clock position: ♠6 ♥7 ♣8 ♦9 ♠10 ♥J ♣Q ♦K ♠2 ♥3 ♣4 ♦5. Deal the next thirty-six cards face up in twelve columns of three overlapping cards each, in such a way that each column radiates away from one of the first twelve cards without touching it. These columns form the tableau, and the original twelve cards are bases.

Object To build each base card up in suit and sequence, turning the corner from King to Ace where necessary, until the top card of the suite exhibits the number corresponding to its position on a clock face. For this purpose eleven and twelve are represented by Queen and King respectively.

Play On the tableau, pack cards in suit and descending sequence, turning the corner from Ace to King where necessary but always moving only one card – the exposed one of a column – at a time. Turn cards from stock and play them if possible or discard them face up to a single wastepile if not. Special rules apply to the replenishing of columns when they become short or entirely consumed. A column containing fewer than three cards must be refilled up to three again using only cards taken from stock, not from the wastepile or from elsewhere on the tableau. When you decide to make the refill, you must refill *all* the deficient columns at once, starting at the one o'clock position, proceeding in a clockwise direction, and restoring a column to three cards before dealing with the next. There is no redeal.

Napoleon's Square
Quadruple Line
Two packs
Odds in favour

When the uninteresting pattern of the initial layout is ignored, Napoleon's Square proves to be Napoleon at St Helena with twelve columns instead of ten. Although the game is perpetuated in many books, no two accounts detail exactly the same combination of rules. The following version is that of Cavendish, who claims that 'with reasonable skill' the chances of success are just in favour of the player.

Object To build the eight Aces up in suit to the Kings.

Layout Take the Aces and put them in position to start with. Then deal cards face up in four overlapping rows of twelve and regard the tableau as twelve columns of four. Pause after dealing each row and do any building and packing that may be possible, but do not fill spaces except by the next deal of twelve. (Strictly, cards are dealt in twelve packets of four, the twelve forming three sides of a square enclosing an area big enough to accommodate the eight suites. This can be ignored.)

Play Turn cards from stock and play them if possible or else discard them face up to a single wastepile. Pack the tableau in suit and descending sequence, moving only one card at a time. A space made by clearing out a column may be filled with the top card of stock or waste, or with an exposed King (nothing else) from the tableau. There is no redeal.

METTERNICH is much the same, except that the two packs are kept separate to start with – perhaps out of deference to Metternich himself, the reactionary Austrian prime minister renowned for his opposition to German unification. Extract the Aces from one shuffled pack, set them up as bases, and deal the remaining forty-eight face up in four overlapping rows of twelve cards each. Regard the result as twelve columns of four. Found the other Aces as bases when they turn up, and build all eight up in suit and sequence to the Kings. Turn cards from the second pack and play them if possible or discard them face up to a single wastepile if not. On the tableau, pack in suit and descending sequence, moving only one card at a time. A vacancy made by clearing out a column must be filled at once with the top card of the wastepile. There is no redeal.

Bismarck

Two packs
Odds in favour

We continue this historical who's who by abandoning Metternich in favour of the father of German unification. I'm not sure how we got onto this subject in the first place, but suspect that Napoleon had a lot to do with it. As for the workings of the game, they include a novel feature which gives it some distinctiveness from the one discussed above.

Layout and object Deal four overlapping rows of twelve cards each and regard the result as twelve columns of four. All must be dealt before any move is made towards founding or building a suite, but if two Kings of the same suit turn up in the deal you may bury one in the pack and deal the next card in its place. The object is to found all eight Aces and build them up in suit and sequence to the Kings.

Play Turn cards from stock and play them if possible or discard them face up to a single wastepile if not. On the tableau, pack in suit and descending sequence. A whole sequence may be moved to another column provided that the join follows the rule.

The distinctive feature is that a space made by clearing out a column puts an end to further packing in that line. The space may be filled only with a two-card descending suit-sequence, which may be taken as a couple from the exposed end of a packed column or else made up if two appropriate cards happen to be available from hand, wastepile and/or tableau. Such a couple may not then be packed upon or moved, except to take their proper place on a suite. The space they leave in turn becomes open to another couple, to which the same rules apply.

Redeal The wastepile may be turned once for use as a new stock.

Lucas

Two packs
Odds in favour

Hardly worth dignifying with a separate entry, Lucas (named after I know not whom, but probably not Maigret's right-hand man) may be represented as Napoleon at St Helena played with thirteen columns of three instead of ten of four. And if the thirteen sets of three are dealt as fans instead of columns, then it becomes a minor variant of Belle Lucie and other members of the Fan club (see Open Packers).

Found the eight Aces and build them up in suit to the Kings. Deal thirteen rows of three. Play from stock to tableau or wastepile. Pack in suit and descending sequence, moving either single exposed cards or packed sequences as a whole. Fill a vacancy with any available card. One redeal is allowed.

WANING MOON Essentially the same, but cards are dealt in faced packets of three in the form of a crescent. Aces are taken out as they occur and ranged in a parallel crescent as bases for building up to the Kings. Cards on the tableau may only be moved one at a time and there is no redeal of the wastepile. With

WANING MOON (variant of Lucas)   In this aptly-named pictorial the Aces are founded on the sites (dotted) as they become available and are built up in suit to the Kings. When all are complete, the thirteen outer packets of three will have disappeared – the moon will then be seen to have waned.

these restrictions, Waning Moon – a remarkably apt pictorial, by the way – succeeds less often than Lucas. (A similar but preferable game is Crescent.)

Empress of India

Four packs
Odds in favour

A fitting climax to the historical who's who provided by our last few titles is this apotheosis of Victorian endeavour, centred upon the person of the matriarch herself (who, incidentally, seems to have upset other European dignitaries by adopting the style 'R.I.' – *regina et imperatrix*). It probably sprang from the same mind as the British Constitution described several pages ago. The patience has some unusual and complicating features, but, like most of the more elaborate members of the tribe, is designed to come to a successful conclusion more often than not. It would hardly be fitting for so patriotic a concept to come to a sticky end.

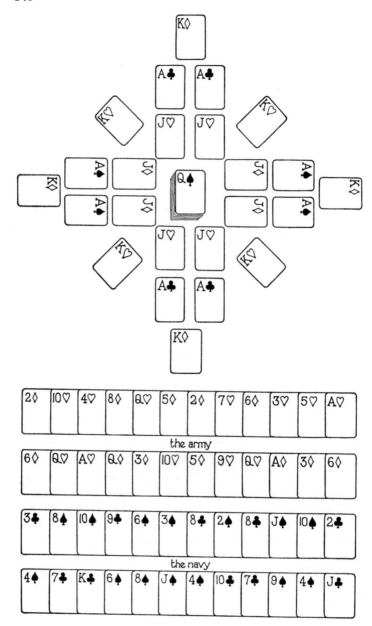

the army

the navy

Layout Extract all the black Queens and Aces and red Jacks and Kings before shuffling the four packs thoroughly together. Found the eight Aces and eight Kings as base cards of sixteen eventual suites. If you have enough room, make a packet of the eight Queens, representing Victoria on her throne, and surround it with the red Jacks to represent her guards or courtiers. If not, discard them, as they serve only a decorative function.

Then deal more cards face up from the stock to make four *non-overlapping* rows of twelve cards each, the first two rows consisting entirely of red cards (representing the army) and the bottom two of black (representing the navy). Any surplus cards of one colour are to be discarded face up to start a wastepile until the four rows are complete.

Object To build the Aces up in suit to the Kings (jumping from Jack to King because the black Queens are out), and the Kings down in suit to the Aces (jumping from Queen to Ten because the red Jacks are out).

Play Cards may be built on the suites only in couples from the tableau, each couple consisting of a red and a black card whose face values total thirteen, counting King 12 and Jack or Queen 11. (The purpose of this is to keep pairs of opposite-coloured suites building apace with one another, since, for example, an Ace suite requires a Two when a King suite requires a Queen, and so on.)

On the tableau, a red card may be packed upon a single black card with which it couples to make thirteen, and vice versa. No other packing is done, but the process of coupling and building creates spaces which are then to be filled with the top card of the red or black wastepile, depending on whether the space concerned lies in the upper (red) or lower (black) two rows.

Turn cards from stock and use them to fill vacancies so long as they are of the right colour. Turned cards may not be used for

EMPRESS OF INDIA (*opposite*)   The eight black Queens and red Jacks play no active part in this four-pack game. All Aces and Kings in the upper part are bases, to be built respectively up and down in suit with cards taken from the army and navy stores (below).

building or coupling. If there are no vacancies, discard them face up to two wastepiles, one reserved for red and the other for black cards. When a vacancy is created by coupling or building, fill it with the top card of the appropriate wastepile, if any, or with the first card turned of the appropriate colour if not. There is no redeal.

Note The only elements of skill in this game lie in deciding whether or not to couple a valid pair of cards, having regard to their suits and the relative progress of the suites; and, if so, whether to place the red upon the black or vice versa, having regard to the relative numbers of cards in the two wastepiles.

British Square

Two packs
Odds in favour

This patience, whose title distinguishes it from Napoleon's Square, is based on an unusual mode of suite-building.

Layout Deal sixteen cards face up in the form of a square of four by four, and regard the result as sixteen 'columns' of one card each.

Object To found the Aces as and when they appear, and to use each one as a base of an eventual 26-card suite running from Ace to King and then from the second King down to the second Ace, all following suit.

Play Build as far as possible from the initial layout and refill vacancies from stock, then turn cards from stock and play them if possible or else discard them face up to a single wastepile. On the tableau, pack in columns or piles of cards following suit and in either ascending or descending sequence, but not in both directions in the same column. Only one card may be moved at a time, but of course it will be found possible to reverse sequences from column to column in this way. A vacancy must be filled at once with the top card of the stock or wastepile, but not from the tableau. There is no redeal.

Barton

Four packs
Odds against

Barton is the four-pack version of Colonel (Uncle Walter's) described elsewhere – that exasperating game in which cards may only be packed on higher rows.

Deal 102 cards in six rows of seventeen, preferably not over-lapping, and regard the result as seventeen columns of six. Only Aces dealt in the bottom row may be taken; these and the others (sixteen altogether!) are to be founded as they become available and built up in suit to the Kings. Play to a wastepile in the usual way. On the tableau, pack in suit and descending sequence, shifting only one card at a time. Packing should be done in piles so that you do not lose count of the rows. An exposed card in the tableau may be packed upon a suitable exposed card in another column only if the latter is in a higher row: it may not be packed off either laterally or to a lower row. As there is no redeal, you may count yourself lucky if you succeed in building half the required number of suites.

Reserved Packers

The games in this section are all Packers and therefore follow the same general rules as those outlined in the introduction to the preceding section.

In addition, however, they include besides the tableau an extra card or group of cards known as a 'reserve', usually dealt face up but sometimes face down. Unlike the tableau, the reserve is not used for packing on. There are two types of reserve. In a diminishing reserve, of which the classic example is Demon (Canfield), the cards of the reserve are played off into the game one by one, either by packing or by building, until they have all been absorbed. Frequently one's strategy is governed by the need to play in such a way as to facilitate the removal of the reserve cards, the classic example of this type being Terrace. In a replenishing reserve, all cards of the reserve are simultaneously available, and when one is played into the game its place is taken by another dealt from hand or waste. Thus, in games of this type, the reserve acts as a sort of escape hatch. (The principles are well illustrated in Casket, which includes two reserves, one diminishing and one replenishing.) In several replenishing reserve games, of which perhaps the neatest example is Step-up, the reserve is less an escape hatch than an air-lock, in that cards may only be built on the suites from the reserve, into which they must be entered as the opportunity arises.

If the replenishing reserves give more scope for the application of skill and foresight by increasing the number of cards visible (if not available) at any time, the diminishing reserve games produce some of the best pictorials by the representational pattern into which the cards of the reserve are arranged. The classic games of this series are Backbone and Plait.

Alhambra

Two packs
Odds against

These variations on a simple theme may be regarded as forerunners of Quilt, in that packing takes place on the wastepile or
one-card tableau and cards have to be unblocked from the reserve
to enter the game. It is not clear why the game should be named
after the palace of the Moorish kings of Granada.

Layout and object Found an Ace and a King of each suit to start
with, and play to build them respectively upwards and downwards into thirteen-card suit sequences. Below them deal eight
piles of four cards each, forming the reserves.

Play Turn cards from stock and build them if possible or else
discard them face up to a single wastepile. The top card of each
reserve is available for building a suite or for packing on the
wastepile, to which it may be played if consecutive in rank (regardless of suit) with the top card. For this purpose an Ace may
be played on a King and vice versa. The wastepile may be turned
and redealt twice.

Note Decide beforehand whether to spread the reserves in columns
towards you so that all are visible or to deal them face down so
that only the top card (turned up when exposed) can be seen. The
former seems preferable in view of the odds against success,
estimated at nine to one.

THE RESERVES The same as Alhambra, but with four reserve
piles of twelve cards each. Chances of success are more like one
in twenty.

FIFTY Deal the first forty-nine cards face down in seven piles of
seven each and the fiftieth above the first of them to start a row
of bases. Found other cards of the same rank as the first base
when they become available, and build them into thirteen-card
ascending suit sequences (turning from King to Ace as necessary).
Turn cards from stock three at a time to a single wastepile,

pausing to play the top card of the wastepile as long as possible. The top of each reserve, turned face up as it becomes exposed, may be built on a suite or packed on the wastepile, provided, in the latter case, that it is consecutive in rank and opposite in colour to the top card of the waste. Ace and King are consecutive. When the last card of a reserve is played, the space may be re-filled with any available card other than the top of the stock. If the stock ends with two cards discard them as if they were three; if with one, put it to one side and make it the bottom card of the first three to be dealt from the new stock, which is made by turning the wastepile. Only one redeal is allowed.

Quilt

Crazy Quilt, Indian Carpet, Japanese Rug
Two packs
Odds in favour

Quilt is so called from its patchwork appearance, and has one of the most attractive layouts ever devised.

Layout and object Take an Ace and a King of each suit and found them as bases. The object is to build them respectively upwards and downwards into thirteen-card suit sequences. Shuffle the other cards and deal the next sixty-four into a square array of eight rows and eight columns, not overlapping. In doing so, alternate the orientation of all adjacent cards, placing the first vertically, the second horizontally, and so on. This forms the 'quilt'.

Play Turn cards from stock one at a time and build them if possible (and desirable) or else discard them face up to a single wastepile. The top of the wastepile is always available for build-ing, and may also be packed upon from the quilt. Pack in upward or downward sequence regardless of suit, noting that Aces and Kings are not consecutive.

Any card in the quilt is available for building on a suite or packing on the wastepile if at least one of its shorter edges is free.

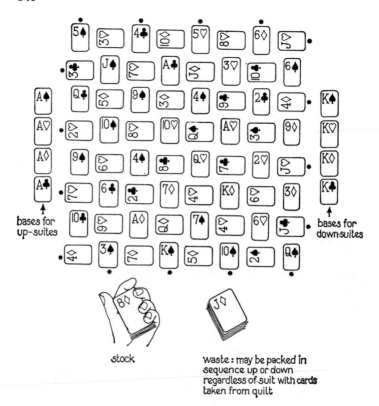

stock

waste : may be packed in
sequence up or down
regardless of suit with cards
taken from quilt

QUILT Cards with at least one short edge free (marked with a
spot in this initial layout) are available for building on suites or
packing on the wastepile. The ♥2 may be built immediately, releasing
♣Q for ♣K.

In the initial layout, for example, sixteen cards are available – to
wit, all those projecting from the edges of the quilt. The play of an
available card will free for use any card whose short edge was
adjacent to its long one, and in this way the patchwork quilt
will gradually be picked to pieces.

Suite-to-suite reversal is permitted whenever top cards of the
same suit are consecutive in rank, except that Ace and King bases
may not be moved.

Redeal Having run out of stock cards, you may turn the wastepile once and deal through it again.

Note Technically, Quilt is an advanced reserved packer with a one-card tableau. The quilt is the reserve, and the so-called wastepile is by definition a tableau because packing takes place on it.

Demon

Canfield, Fascination, Thirteen
One pack (versions for two)
Odds against

Demon has long been one of the most popular patiences on both sides of the Atlantic, as its multiplicity of titles and variants may suggest. If we assume that 'packing' patiences are a later development from 'building' forerunners, then we may see the Fly as a possible ancestor of the Demon. The alternative name Canfield is or was American, but has since come to be applied to the game entered in this collection under the name Klondike. It would appear that the game of Demon had become so popular under the name Canfield that when it was ousted from that position by the more recently developed Klondike, the name itself (which for many players had become synonymous with 'Patience') automatically got transferred to the newcomer.

The original Canfield, whose name has become perpetuated to the point of confusion and ought really to be dropped, is reported to have been the owner of a gambling saloon in Saratoga during the 1890s. His gimmick for making money out of patience – no mean feat – was to sell punters packs of cards at $50 apiece and to pay them $5 for every card they managed to build upon their suites at a game of Demon before it blocked. A frequently quoted average expectation of playing off five or six cards would give Canfield an average of $20–25 per game. Out of curiosity I have just played ten games to test this figure. With the most thorough shuffling between deals I managed to play off an average of 11.9

cards, the actual range being from none from twenty-four. I conclude that the estate of Mr Canfield owes me $95, and look forward to hearing from his descendants.

As you may gather from this paltry (though profitable) result, the game does not come out very often. Morehead and Mott-Smith estimate success at an average of one in thirty games. Truly, Demon is enough to try the patience of a saint.

Layout and object Deal a packet of thirteen cards face down and turn the top one face up. These form a reserve called the demon. Deal the next card face up to the top of the board to form the first of four base cards, then deal four more cards in a row beneath it to start the tableau. As the three other cards of the same rank as the first base become available, move them up into a row next to it. Build these up in suit and sequence until each suite contains thirteen cards, turning the corner from King to Ace as may be necessary.

Play On the tableau, pack in descending sequence and alternating colour, turning the corner from Ace to King as necessary. You may move either one card at a time or complete sequences from column to column, provided that the join follows the rule. Turn cards from stock in sweeps of three at a time and play them to a single wastepile, pausing then to play from the top of the waste-pile on the suites or the tableau so far as may be possible. The top card of the reserve must be built or packed whenever possible, and the card beneath it is then turned face up. A space made in the tableau must be filled at once from the top of the reserve, but when the reserve has been played out it may be filled at any time from the top of the wastepile (never from the stock or tableau).

Redeal Keep turning the wastepile and redealing until the game either blocks or comes out.

RAINBOW The same as Demon, but turn cards from stock one at a time. Only two redeals are allowed.

SELECTIVE DEMON The same as Demon, but after forming the reserve deal the next five cards face up and choose any one of them to act as the first base, putting the other four in a row beneath it and playing as usual.

SUPERIOR DEMON The same as Demon, but with modifications intended to make things easier for the player – or to give him more scope for skill, depending on your point of view. The reserve is dealt face up and the cards are spread so that all are visible, though they must be taken strictly in order. A space made in the tableau may be left open as long as may be desired. It is permissible to shift just part of a sequence from one column to another if desirable. Other rules unchanged.

CHAMELEON The same as Demon, but deal only three cards to start the tableau, and pack downwards regardless of suit. There is no redeal.

STOREHOUSE (PROVISIONS, RESERVE, THIRTEEN UP) The same as Demon, but start by founding the four Deuces and build them up in suit to the Aces, which rank above King. Pack downwards in suit, without turning the corner. Redeal twice.

VARIEGATED DEMON The straight two-pack version of Demon is as follows. Found the eight Aces to start with and build them up in suit to the Kings. The demon is a reserve of thirteen cards dealt face up so that the lower ones may be examined. The tableau is started with a row of five cards to be packed into columns. Follow the rules of Demon, except that only two redeals are allowed.

AMERICAN TOAD This two-pack variant of Demon is presumably so called to distinguish it from the common or garden Toad, or Frog, which is described in another place and is a horse of quite a different colour. The toad is a reserve of twenty cards dealt face up. The next card turned determines the first base. Others of that rank are founded as and when they appear, and all are to be built into thirteen-card ascending suit sequences. Deal eight cards to start a tableau and pack them in descending suit sequence, shifting cards either singly or in full sequences. Turn cards from stock one at a time and play or discard them. Fill vacancies only from the toad until it is exhausted, and then from the wastepile. Cards of the toad must be played whenever possible. One redeal is allowed.

Seven Devils

Two packs
Odds against

Yet more variation on a demonic theme: this one is the triangular member of the family.

Layout Deal cards face down in overlapping rows, with seven in the first, then six, and so on down to one in the seventh. Regard the triangular tableau as consisting of seven columns of varying length, and turn up the exposed card of each column. Deal the next seven cards face down in a packet, and turn up the top one.

Object To found the eight Aces as they become available, and build them up in suit to the Kings.

Play Turn cards from stock and play them if possible or else discard them face up to a single wastepile. Pack the tableau in descending sequence and alternating colour, moving only one card at a time and facing down-cards as they become exposed. A space made by clearing out a column may be filled with any exposed card of the tableau or the top card of the stock. The top card of the reserve is only available for building, and the one beneath is turned up when exposed. Cards of the reserve are never to be entered into the tableau. There is no redeal.

Note My source, the pseudonymous Tarbart, states that the reserve contains eight cards – which is nonsensical in view of the title, as they must represent the devils most likely to prevent the game from coming out. He also states that they are dealt face up. If so, you should be allowed to spread them so that all are visible, thereby improving the skill of the game (but at the same time spoiling the significance of the title).

The Plot

Two packs
Even chances

With its unusual restriction on the building of suites, whereby the first must be completed before any others commence, this game's title at first suggests a plot to drive you mad. When it proves to be not as difficult as it sounds, one begins to suppose that the layout might be intended to represent a squarish plot of land, or small-holding, or something of the sort. It has, in either case, a clearly Demonic background or inspiration.

Layout Deal a reserve of thirteen cards face down in a pile, and turn the top one face up. Below it deal twelve cards face up in three rows of four (not overlapping) to form the tableau. Deal the next card face up in a position immediately north-west of the top left card of the tableau and in line with the reserve. This is the first base. When the other seven cards of the same rank become available by the special rules of this game, the first three will form a column below the first base, and the other four a corresponding column down the right-hand side of the tableau.

Object To build the first base up in suit and sequence until it forms a suite of thirteen cards, turning the corner from King to Ace as necessary. Thereafter, to found the other seven bases as and when they become available and build them up in the same way. The first suite must be completed before any others are started, but the others may then be built simultaneously.

Play Any cards in the tableau of the same rank as the first base are temporarily frozen, and can be neither moved nor packed until the first suite is built. They must then be taken as bases and re-placed from stock, waste or tableau. The cards of the tableau may be packed on (forming piles rather than columns) in descending sequence of the same suit; but a base card may not be packed, and if one turns up before the first suite is built it must be discarded to the wastepile. The top card of the reserve is only available for building on a suite, never for packing on the tableau. Its play releases the one beneath it, which is accordingly turned face up and follows the same rules. Throughout play only one card may be moved at a time.

Turn cards from stock and build or pack them if possible, otherwise discard them face up to a single wastepile. A vacancy made in the tableau must be filled with the top card of the stock or wastepile only, but may be left open until a suitable filler turns up. There is no redeal.

Gate

One pack
Odds against

An ordinary member of the family, exhibiting a somewhat prosaic pictorialism.

Layout Deal two columns of five non-overlapping cards some way apart to represent the posts of the gate. Between them deal two rows of four cards each to represent the rails, leaving room for a third rail above them to consist of the base cards as they appear.

Object To found the Aces as and when they turn up, and to build them up in suit to the Kings.

Play The rails are the tableau, which may be packed in descending sequence and alternating colour to form eight piles or columns. You may move either the exposed card of a column or an entire sequence (not just part) headed by an exposed card. The two gate-posts are the reserve, and only the bottom card of each one is available. It may be built or packed when the opportunity arises, thereby releasing the one above it. Turn cards from stock and play them if possible or else discard them face up to a single wastepile. A vacancy in the tableau must be filled at once from the bottom of a gatepost or, when both are exhausted, from the top of the wastepile. Vacancies in the posts are not refilled. There is no redeal.

Backbone

Two separate packs
Odds against

My favourite Dickens is inhabited by a young lady who neither regards herself nor would wish to be regarded 'in a boney light'. No doubt she would find Plait, which follows, a more pleasant patience, and leave the following ingenious pictorial to be articulated by her osseous inamorato.

Layout Any Aces that turn up in the deal are to be taken and put to one side. Down the centre of the board deal eleven pairs of cards, each pair in the form of a 'V'. The two cards of a pair should not overlap each other, but the eleven of a column may do so for convenience. At the lower end of this spinal array deal the next card horizontally – unless it is a King, in which case bury it in the pack and deal the next card in its place. This array represents the vertebrae. On each side of the backbone deal four more cards to represent the ribs.

Object To found the Aces as and when they appear, and build them up in suit and sequence to the Kings.

Play The twenty-three cards of the backbone form a reserve that is gradually depleted and not replaced. Only the bottom card is available to start with, but when it has been taken the two immediately above it are released for play, and throughout the game the bottom card on each side of the backbone is available for packing, building, or filling a vacancy.

The eight cards of the ribs form the tableau, and are to be packed in suit and descending sequence. Only one card may be moved at a time. A vacancy must be refilled at once, but from hand, waste or backbone as preferred.

Having made any opening moves that may be possible, turn cards from stock and put unplayable ones on a single wastepile, or bone-bed. This may be turned and played through once more.

Note No source states that a vacancy in the ribs may be filled from the backbone, but I am convinced that this is an unintentional omission and have therefore repaired it.

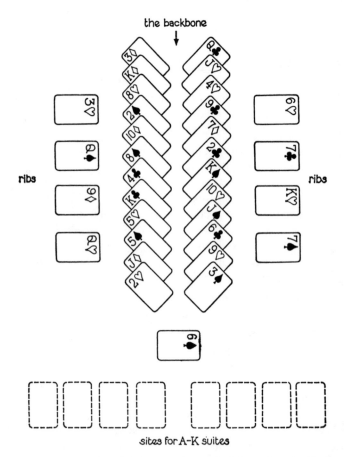

the backbone

ribs

ribs

sites for A-K suites

BACKBONE The eight 'ribs' are to be packed down in suit. Cards of the central 'backbone' become available from the bottom up. A start may be made by playing ♥Q to ♥K, then ♠6 to ♠7 releases ♥2 for play to ♥3, while ♦J may be played to the vacancy left by ♥Q. Then ♠5 to ♠6 and ♥5 to ♥6 leaves ♣K and ♠3 available but with nowhere to go. Play then continues with cards turned from stock.

HERRING-BONE is essentially the same as Backbone. (There is also a 'Builder' of the same name, which does not help matters.) The reserve depicting the herring-bone consists of twenty-four cards arranged as follows: a fan of three at the top with a single card below it, followed by five more such groups of four dealt down the board. The single cards together with the centre cards of adjacent fans form a centre spine, from which lateral fan-cards project like vertebrae. As each single card is taken it exposes the fan above it, and the three cards of each fan are available one by one as they become exposed. The cards of this reserve are available for packing and building, and are not replaced when taken.

On either side of the top and bottom of the bone deal another card face up. These four corner reserves are available for building but not for packing, and, when taken, are replaced from the bone. Deal four more cards to start a tableau, two on either side of the bone, and deal the thirty-third card face up to one side as a base. Found the other cards of the same rank as they become available, and build all eight bases into thirteen-card ascending suit sequences, turning from King to Ace as necessary. Play to a single wastepile, and pack the tableau in descending suit sequence, turning from Ace to King as necessary. A vacancy in the tableau may only be filled from the wastepile, but need not be filled at once. One redeal is allowed.

Plait

Two packs
Even chances

The passage from bones to hair brings us to a game similar to Backbone but as much cleverer as prettier, the theme of unwinding the plait being particularly apt for the act of playing cards from the reserve, and providing a pictorial which is lively rather than static. The version described here is the thirteen-card plait with packing. The other game usually given under the same title, in-

158

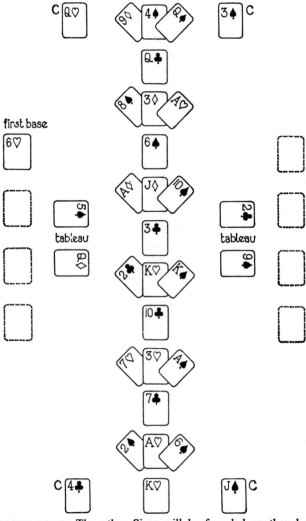

HERRING-BONE The other Sixes will be founded as they become available and built into thirteen-card suit sequences. Cards marked C are corner reserves: they may only be built, not packed, and are replaced when taken. The four tableau cards may be packed or built. In this layout only ♥K is immediately available from the herring-bone. When taken, it will free ♠6, which in turn frees ♥A, and so on.

volving a twenty-card plait without packing, I have renamed Pigtail and dealt with in its proper place.

Layout Deal four overlapping rows of eight cards each and regard the resultant tableau as eight columns of four. Deal the next thirteen cards down one side of the board in the representaton of a plait, with each succeeding pair of cards laid V-wise with one overlapping the other and both overlapping the previous pair. These form the 'plait' or reserve. Deal the next card face up to the top of the board, where it acts as the first base.

Object To release the other cards of the same rank as the first base, and to build all eight up in suit and sequence until each suite contains thirteen cards.

Play Turn cards from stock and play them if possible or discard them face up to a single wastepile if not. Pack the tableau in descending sequence and alternating colour, turning the corner from Ace to King where necessary. Single exposed cards or complete sequences headed by them may be moved to other columns provided that the join follows the rule. A vacancy in the tableau may be filled at any time with any available card or tableau sequence. Only the exposed card of the plait is available, and it may be used for building, packing or refilling a vacancy. There is no redeal.

Great Wheel
Two packs
Odds against

This rather silly pictorial patience, as befits the fairground theme, demands more skill in understanding the rules than in bringing it to a successful conclusion. It contains some unusual features, of which perhaps more could have been made.

Layout A verbal description of the circular layout would defy comprehension, so either copy the illustration or simplify it as follows: take out the eight Kings and lay them face up in a row, alternating the colours. They take no part in the play and are neither moved nor covered. Above each King deal a fan of four cards face up.

Object To found the eight Twos in a row beneath their corresponding Kings as and when they become available, and to build them up in suit by even numbers as far as the Queens; simultaneously, to found the eight Threes in a row below the Twos and build them up by suit and odd numbers to the Jacks. The eight Aces, as they become available, are simply piled up, but they must be piled in alternating colours.

Play The fans constitute a reserve, the exposed card of each one being available for building to the even, odd or Ace suites. The play of an exposed card releases the one below it for similar usage. Play as far as you can from the initial layout. Then turn cards from stock and either build them on suites or discard them face up to a single wastepile. There is no tableau, and no packing takes place (yet) on the reserve. When a fan is cleared out, fill the vacancy with the top four cards of the wastepile, retaining their order and keeping the same exposed card on top.

Packing When the stock is exhausted there is no redeal, but now the reserve becomes a tableau and packing may take place upon the exposed cards. This is to take place in suit and descending sequence. (For example, a Six on a Seven of its own suit.) Cards may be packed from the wastepile or from other fans, but only one may be moved at a time.

Note The final result in circular form depicts a Great Wheel centred on the Aces, which are stacked crosswise with those of one colour horizontally and those of the other vertically. From the centre radiate eight arms, each of which displays a Jack, Queen and King of the same suit in a line. In the original account the 'fans' are described as face up packets; but as 'face up' usually implies that you may see what cards lie beneath, you might as well deal them as fans and save yourself the trouble of continually looking through them.

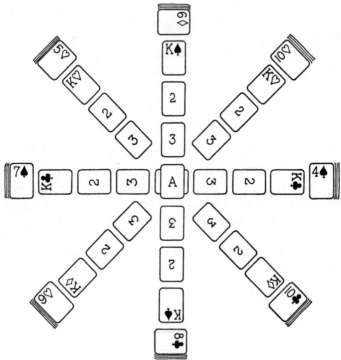

GREAT WHEEL Place the Kings as illustrated and deal a packet of four cards face up outside each one. As the Twos, Threes and Aces turn up place them in the positions marked. Build Twos up in suit and even numbers, Threes in suit and odd numbers, and Aces on one another in alternating colour.

Duchess

Glenwood
One pack
Odds against

The invention of Morehead and/or Mott-Smith, Duchess is perhaps best regarded as a one-pack version of the delightful Queen of Italy (Terrace).

Layout Deal a reserve of twelve cards in four face-up fans of three cards each. Deal four more cards in a row, face up, beneath the fans but far enough apart to leave space for four base cards in a row between them. Examine the fans and choose any one of the four exposed cards to act as the first foundation, moving it down into position.

Object To release the other cards of the same rank as the first base and to build each one up in suit and sequence until it contains thirteen cards, turning the corner from King to Ace as necessary.

Play Turn cards from stock and play them if possible or else discard them face up to a single wastepile. Pack the tableau in descending sequence and alternating colour, moving either single exposed cards or complete sequences. Exposed cards in the reserve may be built or packed whenever possible. A vacancy in the tableau must be filled with an exposed card from the reserve until it is exhausted, and then from the top of the wastepile.

Redeal One redeal is allowed.

Terrace

Queen of Italy, Signora
Two packs
Odds in favour

These variations on a theme give you some choice in the selection of a suitable base card, forcing you to make a strategic decision at the outset. This additional element of skill makes Terrace one of my favourites.

Layout At the top of the board deal eleven cards face up and overlapping one another in a row. This forms a reserve (the 'terrace'). Below it, deal the next four cards face up. Having regard to the availability of cards in the terrace, choose one of these four to act as the first base, and lay the other three in a row below that to start a tableau. Deal six more cards in line with these three to complete a tableau of nine cards, which will extend towards you in columns when packing begins. If any of these cards is of the same rank as the first base, move it up into the base row next to the first and replace it. If the exposed card of the terrace is of the base rank do likewise, but do not replace it.

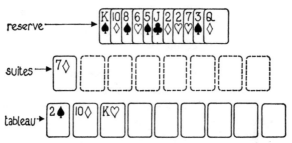

TERRACE Of the first four turned cards the King must be rejected because of the awkward placing of a Queen and King in the reserve. The Ten is rejected because another base would then lie too far down, and the Two because the top Queen would continue to block the reserve for too long. With the Seven chosen and the other three placed below, it is time to deal six more cards to complete the first row of the tableau, after which play begins.

Object To found the other cards of the same rank as the first base in line with it, and build them up in sequence and alternating colour until each contains thirteen cards, turning the corner from King to Ace as necessary.

Play Turn cards from stock and play them if possible or else discard them face up to a single wastepile. Pack the tableau in descending sequence and alternating colour, turning the corner from Ace to King where necessary. Only one card may be moved at a time. A space made by clearing out a column in the tableau must be filled at once with the top card of the stock or wastepile (not from the terrace or the tableau). The exposed card of the terrace is available only for building on a suite – it may not be packed on the tableau. This exposes the card beneath it, and the whole strategy of the game is determined by the need to free all the cards of the terrace in the required order.

Redeal There is no redeal, but it seems reasonable to follow the relaxation of this rule permitted in the game called General's Patience. This allows you to turn the wastepile once and go through it so long as you can pack or build the top card. But you may not form a second wastepile, and as soon as you come to an unplayable card the game is lost.

THE GENERAL'S PATIENCE (THIRTEEN) As Terrace, but: Deal a reserve of thirteen instead of eleven, and build in suit rather than alternating colour.

FALLING STAR As Terrace, but: The twelfth card turned from stock determines the first and subsequent bases – there is no choice. (The reserve represents 'stars' which must 'fall' if the game is to succeed.)

BLONDES AND BRUNETTES (WOOD) As Terrace, but: Deal a reserve of ten instead of eleven, turn the next card to determine the bases (no choice), and deal a row of eight to start the tableau. Wood is the same, but has a tableau of nine.

Cable

Three separate packs
Odds against

In this game, unusual for its employment of three packs (representing the three strands of a cable to be twined together), there is a simple reserve of four face-down cards. These are not revealed until the game blocks, when they may or may not set it going again. Whitmore Jones estimates the chances of success at one in twenty, and adds: 'the pleasant feeling of complacency when success is attained quite makes up for the nineteen previous disappointments'.

Layout Deal the first pack face up in five overlapping rows of ten cards each, and place the two undealt cards face down to one side

as a reserve. Extend this tableau by dealing five more rows from
the second pack, and add the last two face down to the reserve.
Regard the result as ten columns of ten.

Object To found all twelve Aces as and when they become available, and to build each one up in suit to the King.

Play Turn cards from the third pack and play them if possible or
else discard them face up to a single wastepile. Pack the tableau
in suit and descending sequence. For this purpose exposed cards
may be taken singly, as may descending sequences in whole or
part provided that there is a suitable card to pack them on. A
vacancy in the tableau may be filled at any time with a single
available card or a packed sequence.

Redeal and reserve When the third pack is exhausted, you may
turn the wastepile once only for a second and final deal. The cards
of the reserve are not touched until the game is blocked. Only
then may they be faced, and all are then available for packing or
building in the hope of unblocking the game and bringing it to a
successful conclusion.

Florentine

One pack
Odds against

This, the first of the reserves that is refilled when emptied, is almost identical to Vanishing Cross or Four Seasons. It is a pleasant
little game, but has been rather ill-served by a succession of
compilers who all fail to notice that the account from which they
crib gives no detailed rule as to the management of the reserve. I
have therefore devised an arbitrary rule to repair the omission,
which is better than no rule at all.

Layout Deal five cards in the form of a cross and a sixth at an
angle in one of the corner spaces, forming the first base.

Object To found the other three cards of the same rank as the first base as and when they appear, and to build them up into thirteen-card suit sequences turning the corner from King to Ace as necessary.

Play The centre card is a reserve. It may only be played to a suite or to a vacancy in the tableau, and must not otherwise be moved or packed upon. When it it has been played, its place must be filled at once from the top of the wastepile if any, or from stock if not.

The four arms of the cross form a tableau to be packed in descending sequence regardless of suit, turning the corner from Ace to King as necessary. They may be packed on one another, but only one card may be moved at a time. A vacancy in the tableau must be filled at once, either with the reserve card or from the top of the wastepile.

Turn cards from stock and play them if possible or else discard them face up to a single wastepile.

Redeal The wastepile may be turned and redealt once.

Note Existing rules state only that the reserve card must not be packed upon but may be moved into a space. I have added the reasonable supposition that it may be played to a suite when possible, and the probable restriction that it may not be packed on the tableau. If this restriction is removed, I think the chances of success are about even.

The Pyramids
Pyramid
Two packs
Odds in favour

Although this is described by Whitmore Jones under the heading Pyramid, I have pluralized the title partly to avoid confusion with a better-known Pyramid and partly because three of them are depicted in the full pictorial version. This one has features reminiscent of the Hill of Difficulty, and, like that problematical game, is most inadequately explained at source. Once again I have had to patch up the gaps with guesswork.

Layout Deal a 'pyramid' of nine cards face up, one at the apex, three in a row below it, and five in a row below them. This forms the Great Pyramid, of which the top four cards are a reserve and the bottom five a tableau for packing on.

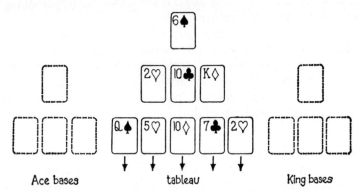

THE PYRAMIDS The initial layout shows the Great Pyramid consisting of a four-card reserve and five-card tableau. Completion shows two lesser pyramids, each consisting of four thirteen-card suites.

Object To release one Ace and one King of each suit as and when they become available, then build the Aces up in suit to the Kings and the Kings down in suit to the Aces. The Ace suites are based and built on one side of the Great Pyramid and the King suites on the other, and in each case are composed into a lesser pyramid with one base as the apex and three in a row beneath it.

Play Exposed cards in the bottom row are available for building, or may be packed on one another in either ascending or descending sequence of the same suit (but changes of direction are not allowed in the same column, and Aces and Kings are not consecutive). Only one card may be moved at a time.

The four cards in the upper part of the Great Pyramid are not available for packing but only for building on an appropriate suite, and then only when freed by the play of a card below. As soon as a vacancy is made in the bottom row, the reserve card immediately above it is available for building if possible, and the play of the middle card in the second row releases the single card above that. We must assume from Miss Jones's diagram that the play of the first *or* second card in the bottom row releases the first in the middle row, and the play of the fourth *or* fifth releases the third. All vacancies made in the Great Pyramid must, at the end of the series of moves that created them, be filled from the wastepiles if any, or from hand if not.

Having made any opening moves that may be possible and re-filled vacancies thereby created, turn cards from stock three at a time and deal them face up to three wastepiles from left to right. Then pause and play: the top card of every wastepile is available for packing or building, and its play releases the one below it for the same purpose. Keep dealing in threes until the stock is exhausted.

Redeals After running through the first stock, gather up the wastepiles from left to right and consolidate them into a new stock without shuffling. Play through this stock again, this time dealing them to only two wastepiles. When this is also exhausted, turn the two piles into a new stock and deal for the last time to only one wastepile. No further redeals are allowed.

Casket

Two packs
Odds against

This ingenious pictorial has the unusual feature of two reserves, one diminishing (as at Demon) and one to be kept replenished. It does not come out as often as you might expect.

Layout Deal a packet of thirteen cards face down at the centre of the board and turn the top card face up. These form a diminishing

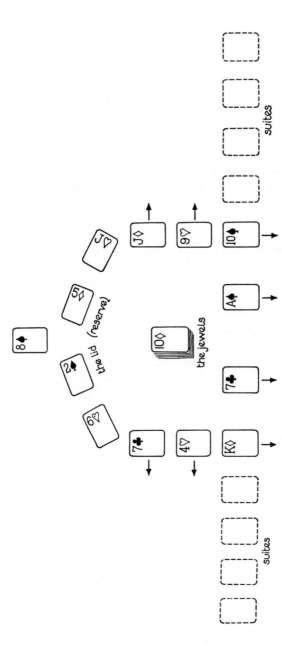

CASKET The topmost jewel may only be played to a suite in the five-card reserve (the lid), and a card of the reserve only to a suite when it fits. The other eight cards of the casket form a tableau to be packed down in suit as indicated by the arrows. Eight Aces are to be founded and built up in suit to Kings. In this diagram ♠A may be founded at once and ♠2 built. The ♦10 then occupies the space left by the Two (it may not be packed on the Jack, by the rules of the game). The space left in the bottom row is then filled from stock and play continues.

reserve representing 'the jewels'. Deal the next thirteen cards face up to form the outline of a casket enclosing the jewels. Eight of these form a tableau representing the base and sides of the casket; the other five form a reserve representing its curved lid and handle.

Object To found the eight Aces as and when they appear and to build them up in suit to the Kings.

Play Play as far as possible before turning cards from the stock. Any Aces and succeeding cards forming the casket may be taken and built, and their spaces refilled from stock. Both now and throughout play the top card of the jewels may only be taken to fill a vacancy in the five-card reserve formed by the lid, the card beneath it then being faced in its turn. (This process is supposed to depict the opening of the lid and removal of a jewel.) The five-card reserve may only be filled in this way until the jewels have all gone, after which it may be filled only from the wastepiles.

The eight cards of the tableau may be packed on one another in suit and descending sequence. Only one card may be moved at a time. A vacancy in the tableau must be filled at once from hand or waste (presumably – the rules are not explicit on this point).

Turn cards from stock three at a time and deal them face up on three wastepiles from left to right. Then pause to play what you can from the tops of the wastepiles before turning from stock again. There is no redeal.

Step-up
Two packs
Odds in favour

Dimly related to the Queen of Italy, this patience uses its reserve in an unusual way that calls for a goodly amount of skill and judgement. I should point out that the chances of bringing it out successfully only favour the player if there is no obvious difficulty in the thirteen cards of the reserve. Sometimes it is clear from the start that the game is likely to fail, and the correct recognition of such arrangements may be regarded as a victory rather than a defeat.

Layout Deal thirteen cards face up in a row, forming a reserve known as the middle step. Deal the next card face up at the top of the board as the first of eight bases, which will form a row immediately above the middle step. Immediately below the middle step deal a row of nine cards to start a tableau known as the bottom step.

Object To found the other cards of the same rank as the first base as and when they appear, and to build them all up into thirteen-card suit sequences, turning the corner from King to Ace as necessary. And to do this with the restriction that cards may only be built from the middle step, through which all those in the tableau must pass in their turn.

Play Any base cards in the middle or lower step may be put into position immediately, as may any that turn up during the play, and any cards in the middle step that can be built on a suite may follow without delay. A vacancy in the middle step may (but need not yet) be filled with any card from the bottom step, and a vacancy in the bottom step must be filled at once from the stock (or, during subsequent play, from the wastepile if preferred). Exposed cards in the bottom step are available for filling vacancies in the middle step, or for packing on one another in descending sequence and alternating colour, turning the corner from Ace to King as necessary. Such packing may only take place with one card at a time.

When all opening moves have been made and vacancies filled, turn cards from stock and pack them on the tableau if possible or else discard them face up to a single wastepile. They may not be played to the middle step or built directly, except for base cards.

The following important rule gives the game its whole point. A vacancy in the middle step may only be filled with an exposed card from the tableau. But it need not be filled immediately: it may be left open for up to three more turns of cards from the stock, after which it must be filled with a tableau card if still unoccupied.

There is no redeal.

Squadron
Two packs
Odds in favour

Squadron is an ordinary packer with the addition of a three-card reserve.

Found the eight Aces as and when they become available and build them up in suit and sequence to the Kings. Deal a tableau consisting of ten columns of four, and a face up reserve of three separate cards. Pack on the tableau in suit and descending sequence, moving only one card at a time. The exposed cards of the tableau and all three of the reserve are available for building, packing or filling vacancies. A space in the reserve is filled at once with any available card. Play to a single wastepile. There is no redeal.

Besieged City
The Frame
Two packs
Odds against

Not to be confused with Beleaguered Castle, Besieged City is a typically elaborate specimen of the Victorian patience-maker's art, and hard to bring to a successful conclusion. But it is well worked out and gives many opportunities for the exercise of skill – or for the making of mistakes, if you are not careful.

Layout Deal twelve cards face up in a 3 × 4 array, without overlapping. These form the reserve and represent the inhabitants of the city. Deal the next fourteen cards face up around them to form an enclosing square, laying each card in the opposite orientation to that of the row or column aligned with it. These form a tableau known as the ramparts.

Object As and when the first Ace of each new suit becomes available, found it at one corner of the layout. Build each of them up in suit to form a twenty-six card suite running in the following order: A–K–2–Q–3–J–4 . . . and so on up to J–3–Q–2–K–A, i.e. ascending and descending simultaneously.

Play One or more suites may be started immediately if there are any Aces and consecutive building cards in the ramparts. Each card taken for this purpose must be replaced at once with any one of the reserve cards in line with it, and a space in the reserves must at once be filled from hand.

Next, if possible, cards in the ramparts may be packed on one another. Any exposed card may be packed on another if it is of the same suit and consecutive in rank, whether in ascending, descending, or building order. (For example, a Jack may be packed on a Ten, Queen, Three or Four of its suit.) Sequences may change direction in the same line of packing. A vacancy in the ramparts must be filled with a reserve card in line with it, and a vacancy in the reserve must be filled from hand.

Then turn cards from stock one at a time and build or pack them if possible or else discard them face up to a single wastepile. The same rules apply, except that a space in the reserve must be filled from the wastepile (if any, or from hand if not). The top of the wastepile may not be directly built or packed, but may enter the game only by means of a vacancy in the reserve. Similarly, a card in the reserve may not be built or packed, but may enter the game only by occupying a vacancy made in one of the ramparts in line with it.

There is no redeal, but when the stock and wastepile are exhausted you may, if no reserve card can be moved into the ramparts, transpose two reserve cards to unblock the game. This privilege may be exercised any number of times.

Non-Builders

The following games differ from the usual run of patiences in that the object is not to build cards up in suit and sequence. Most of them may be described as Eliminators, the object being to discard the whole pack in pairs of cards of the same rank or making up the same numerical total. Others are unclassifiable. Despite their nondescript status, many are popular, all have their points of interest (especially to mathematicians), and quite a few offer scope for more than a little skill.

Pairs

One pack

These games are based on the principle of eliminating pairs of cards of the same rank. Win by eliminating all cards from the layout.

PAIRS Deal nine cards face up. Eliminate any two of the same rank and fill spaces from stock. If impossible, turn the next card from stock and eliminate it together with any exposed card with which it pairs. If this also fails the game is lost.

DOUBLETS Deal cards face down in twelve piles of four and one fan of four. Turn up the top twelve cards. Eliminate any two of the same rank and turn up those beneath. Continue. When a pile is emptied, fill it with the top card of the fan.

MONTE CARLO (DOUBLE OR QUITS, WEDDINGS) Deal twenty-five cards face up in five rows of five. (*Variant*: twenty in four rows of five.) Eliminate any pair of the same rank lying next to each other, whether edge-to-edge or diagonally. Then close ranks by shifting all cards into gaps at their left, for which purpose the right-hand end of the row above counts as being to the left of a row below. This brings all gaps to the bottom right. Fill them with cards turned from stock and repeat the process. Always eliminate all possible pairs before closing up.

RAYS (STAR) Played with a 32-card pack. Deal sixteen face up in the form of a star with two cards in each ray, and put the rest face down in the middle. At each turn face the top card and eliminate it together with any card of the same rank in the rays. If no match is possible, use it to fill any gap in the outermost circle of cards made by a previous elimination, otherwise the game is lost. When an outermost card is paired off, its space may only be filled with the top card of the centre pile. When an innermost card is paired off, fill its space by moving the corresponding outermost card inwards.

Totals

One pack
unless otherwise stated

Totals is a generic title for games in which the object is to eliminate all cards in pairs or larger groups whose combined face values make up a given total. For this purpose count Ace 1, Jack 11, Queen 12 and King 13 unless otherwise stated. The games are arranged in numerical order of required totals.

SEVEN UP (SEVENTH WONDER) Deal cards in a row from left to right. Eliminate all Sevens and any combination of cards which, in conjunction with the card just played, totals a multiple of seven. The game is bound to come out with proper play.

NINES Deal nine cards face up. Cover from stock (*a*) any Nine, (*b*) any pair of numerals totalling nine, (*c*) a Ten, Jack, Queen and King whenever all four appear simultaneously. In the initial deal cover combinations as soon as they appear – you need not wait until all nine are dealt. If you fail to place all fifty-two cards the game is lost. Otherwise it is still only half won, for you must then complete it by eliminating all top cards in the same way – i.e. Nines singly, pairs making nine, and higher cards in batches of four.

TENS Deal thirteen cards face up. Eliminate pairs totalling ten and courts in quartets of the same rank. Fill spaces from stock.

BLOCK TEN Deal nine cards face up. Cover from stock any exposed pair totalling ten, or a pair of Jacks, Queens or Kings. When a Ten turns up it blocks further play on the pile it heads. (Nasty!)

DECADE Deal cards in a row from left to right. Eliminate any two or more adjacent cards totalling ten, twenty or thirty, counting courts as ten each for this purpose. Win by eliminating all but one card. (Though similar to Seven Up, it rarely succeeds.)

ELEVENS Deal nine cards face up. Cover from stock any pair

totalling eleven and any single court card. (*Variant*: cover a Jack, Queen and King only when all three appear simultaneously.) If blocked, deal the next card face up to the centre pile. If this does not work the game is lost.

BLOCK ELEVEN Deal twelve cards face up. Eliminate courts and replace them from stock. (Do this whenever courts are subsequently dealt, so that the layout always consists of numerals only.) Cover from stock any pair totalling eleven. Show completion by crowning the twelve piles with the courts.

HADEN For two packs. Deal twelve piles of eight cards each face down and turn up the top cards. Put the rest face up to one side as a reserve. Eliminate pairs of exposed cards totalling eleven and turn up cards beneath. Eliminate one Jack, Queen and King whenever all three appear together. When stuck, pair off any numeral in the reserve that makes eleven with a top card, or one court if it makes a trio with any two exposed courts. Two courts may be taken from the reserve to go with an exposed third only if neither of them is duplicated on any of the piles.

BARONESS (FIVE PILES) Deal five cards face up. Eliminate Kings and any pair totalling thirteen. Deal five more, overlapping any that remain. Continue dealing in fives, after each deal pausing to play off exposed Kings and pairs totalling thirteen. The last two cards may be faced and used as grace cards to get the game going again if it blocks.

THIRTEENS (SIMPLE ADDITION) Deal ten cards face up. Eliminate Kings singly and pairs totalling thirteen. Fill spaces from stock.

PYRAMID (PILE OF TWENTY-EIGHT) Deal a pyramid of twenty-eight cards face up: one at the apex, overlapped by two side by side, these overlapped by three side by side, then four and so on to a base line of seven cards overlapping the six above. These seven are exposed and available. Every other card in the layout becomes available when both cards overlapping it are taken. The object is to demolish the pyramid from the bottom up. Remove exposed Kings singly and other available cards in pairs totalling thirteen, discarding them all face up to a single wastepile. An available card may be taken if it makes thirteen with the top of the wastepile. When stuck, deal the top card of the stock to the waste and see if this will pair with an available card from the pyramid. Win if you demolish the pyramid; lose if any of it is left when the last stock card has been played and no more pairings are possible.

FOURTEENS For two packs. Deal twenty-five cards face up in five rows of five. Eliminate pairs totalling fourteen, but only if both lie in the same row or column. Fill spaces from stock. You are allowed one grace per game: when stuck, exchange the positions of any two cards in the square. When the stock is empty and no more pairing can be done, fill gaps from left to right in the top row with cards taken from right to left in the bottom row, and so on until all gaps are shunted to the bottom right.

FIFTEENS Deal sixteen cards face up. Eliminate numerals in any combination of two or more totalling fifteen and fill spaces from stock. Tens, Jacks, Queens and Kings may only be eliminated in quartets of the same rank.

EIGHTEENS (FERRIS WHEEL, GRAND ROUND, WHEEL) For two packs. Deal twelve cards face up. Eliminate Aces singly and other cards in batches of four, each batch consisting of one court and any three *different* numerals totalling eighteen. Fill spaces from stock. (Alternative titles refer to a circular layout to which the Aces are discarded as 'spokes'.)

Abandon Hope

One pack
Even chances

Deal twenty-four cards face up and eliminate all the clubs. Shuffle the rest back in with the pack and do the same again. Repeat the process once more. Win if you have cast out all thirteen clubs by the end of the third deal.

HOPE DEFERRED (32 cards) The original game is played with a short pack, and all clubs are to be eliminated within three deals of fifteen.

Royal Flush
One pack
Odds against

The object of this torture is to extract, in the most roundabout way imaginable, the Ace, King, Queen, Jack and Ten of one suit. Call these cards 'royals'.

Deal five cards face down in a row, and keep doing so until you have five piles of varying heights. Take the left-hand pile, turn it upside down, and eliminate cards one by one until you come to a Ten or higher. This establishes the suit required and is therefore an automatic royal. If there is no such card in the first pile, eliminate it entirely and do the same with the second pile, and so on. As soon as you reach a royal, put that pile down with the royal on top and turn to the next pile. Do the same with each pile, eliminating cards until you either lose a whole pile or else reach a royal, at which point you leave it and turn to the next. This done, turn the piles face down, gather them up from right to left without disturbing the order of cards, and use this as a new stock. Now deal all cards face down to four piles, and, as before, upend each one in turn and go through it until you either reach a royal or eliminate it entirely. Gather them again and next time deal three piles, then two. Win if the final elimination leaves you with the royal flush and no other card.

Narcotic

Fours, Perpetual Motion
One pack
Odds against

Perpetual Motion is a good title for a game that is apt to go on for ever, but the older name better describes its stupefying effect.

Deal four cards face up in a row. If two or more are of the same rank, put duplicates on the leftmost of them. Then deal four more across, pause, and do the same. Keep going until you run out of cards. Gather the piles up from right to left, turn the whole pile upside down and start again. Whenever the four cards you deal are of the same rank, eliminate them. Win if you eventually succeed in eliminating all fifty-two. This may take years.

Aces Up

Drivel, Firing Squad
One pack
Odds against

In this game Ace ranks higher than King and the object is to finish up with all four in a row after eliminating the other forty-eight cards.

Keep dealing overlapping rows of four cards at a time. After each deal pause and see if any exposed cards are of the same suit. If so, eliminate all but the highest-ranking of them. Whenever a space is made by clearing out a pile or column you may fill it with any exposed card. This is the only way in which Aces can be made to unblock cards beneath them.

Cover Up
One pack
Odds against

Deal four cards face up in a row. If two or more are of the same suit, cover them with the next cards from stock. Keep covering duplicates in this way. Win if you build all fifty-two cards into the four piles; lose if ever the top four are of different suits.

Valentine
One pack
Odds against

Deal four cards face up in a row. If two or more are in suit and sequence, pile them together with the highest at the bottom and the lowest on the top. (Ace is low and not consecutive with King.) Turn the top card and see if it, too, can be placed in suit and sequence with a card or pile in the row. If so put it in place and turn the next. Keep going until you turn a card that will not match. Put this to one side as the first card of a new row of four, gather up the existing cards or piles from left to right, turn them face down and put them at the bottom of the stock. Deal three more cards to complete a row of four, and repeat the process. If you are lucky, and live long enough, you may finish with all fifty-two cards in suit and sequence. (The game will rarely come out, and it is difficult to tell at what point it becomes impossible.)

Accordion

Idle Year, Methuselah, Tower of Babel, etc.
One pack
Odds against

Accordion is the simplest and therefore the best of many games which differ from one another only in cosmetics. All operate at the absolute zero of intellectual temperature.

Deal cards face up in a row from left to right. Whenever a card turns up that is of the same suit as its left-hand neighbour or the third card along on the left (i.e. next-but-one to its neighbour), place it upon the matching card. Do the same whenever the same position arises as the result of piling cards up. Treat each pile as a single card and move or match it according to the card on top. Count a win for finishing with a single pile or half a win for finishing with two, and consider yourself lucky with three.

ROYAL MARRIAGE Put ♥K at the bottom of the pack and ♥Q face up to the left. Deal cards one by one in a row to the right of the Queen. Discard any card or two adjacent cards that lie between two cards of the same rank or suit (whether as the result of dealing or discarding) and close up the row. Win if you finish with the King side by side with the Queen. The consummation, though devoutly to be wished, rarely materializes.

PUSH-PIN This is the most interesting of several two-pack versions of Accordion. Deal cards face up from left to right. Eliminate one card or one pair of adjacent cards if it is sandwiched between two cards of the same rank or suit. (E.g. from ♣3–♥6–♣9–♣Q eliminate the Six and Nine.) If more than two are sandwiched in this way none may be taken unless they are all of the same suit, in which case they all go out. (E.g. from ♣3–♥6–♥K–♥4– followed by any club or Three, eliminate the hearts.) When all cards have been dealt and all eliminations made you are entitled to transpose any two cards, once only, to set the game going. Win by eliminating all but the last two matching cards. Similar games include Evicting and Halma.

REVERSI For two packs. Deal three rows of seven cards each, the second, fourth and sixth face down and others face up. Eliminate any reversi (down-card) if it is immediately flanked by two cards of the same rank, and eliminate the one on its right as well. Close ranks by shifting cards into gaps at their left. Deal three more rows of seven in the same way on top of the first layout, and eliminate reversis and their right-hand neighbours (or piles) in accordance with the same rule. When a row is reduced to three cards or piles, eliminate it entirely. Win by clearing the board, even if you have cards left undealt.

Hit or Miss

Harvest, Roll-Call, Talkative
One pack
Odds against

Deal cards face up to a wastepile counting as you go 'Ace, Two, Three . . .' and so on up to King, which is followed by Ace again. Whenever you turn a card corresponding to the rank you call, cast it out. When you run out of cards, turn the wastepile and use it as a new stock. Win if you eventually eliminate all cards. The game will fail if you get through two consecutive deals without hitting a correspondence.

Rondo

Eight-Day Clock, Perpetual Motion
One pack
Odds against

Deal four piles of thirteen cards face up. Mentally label them from Ace to King. Take the top card of the Ace pile (unless it is an Ace, in which case see below) and slip it under the Two pile, then slip the top of the Two pile under the Three, and so on. The top card of the King pile will go to the bottom of the Ace pile, and the sequence is repeated.

Whenever the top card of a pile is of the same rank as the pile itself, leave it where it is and ignore that pile, placing any card taken from an earlier pile under the next free pile ahead of it. As soon as the lifting of a card leaves all thirteen piles headed by cards of their corresponding ranks, discard those thirteen top cards and place the card you lifted at the bottom of the next pile along. Continue in this way. You win by eliminating three sequences of thirteen, as the fourth will automatically place itself in order.

Travellers

All Fours, Clock, Four of a Kind, Hidden Cards, Hunt, Sundial, Watch
One pack (52 or 32)
Odds against

This unusual game, of which Spoilt (below) is the short-pack version, introduces a rhythmical feature that might be called 'shuttling' – a term borrowed from the related game of Weavers.

Layout Deal twelve piles of four cards each face up, and a reserve of four face down.

Object To finish with thirteen piles, each containing all four cards of the same rank.

Play Imagine the piles to be labelled from Ace to Queen. (Some find it helpful to arrange them in a circle like a clockface, with Jack at 11 and Queen at 12, which accounts for some of the alternative titles.) Turn the top card of the reserve and start 'shuttling' as follows: put the turned card at the bottom of the pile corresponding to its rank or number, then take the top card of that pile and put it at the bottom of the pile corresponding to *its* own rank or number . . . and so on. When the top card of a pile proves to be a King, discard it to one side as a King pile, take the next card of the reserve, and start shuttling again.

Grace The game will fail if the fourth King appears before the other sets are built, but the variant called Watch allows you, in this event, to exchange the fourth King for any card that has not yet travelled to its proper pile.

SPOILT A short-pack (32) version of Travellers. Deal all cards face down in four rows of seven, and put the other four face down to one side as a reserve. Imagine the rows to be labelled spades, hearts, clubs, diamonds (in whatever order you find most memorable) and the columns to run from Eight at one end to Ace at the other. Thus every card higher than Seven has a specific place reserved for it in the layout. Now take the top reserve card and start shuttling – i.e. remove the down-card occupying its place, put the reserve card in position, then shift the turned up card to its proper place, and so on. When a Seven turns up, put it in position next to the Eight of its appropriate suit, turn up the next reserve and shuttle again. Keep going. If the last Seven turns up before the others are all in order, turn any down-card. If it is in its proper place turn another, and so until the game is won or 'spoilt'.

Part Two

HALF-OPEN GAMES

**presenting problems of increasing definition
to be solved by skill and judgement**

Builders

Builders are games in which the usual object is to divide the pack into suits and build each one up in numerical sequence without the aid of reverse sequences made by packing. The following games differ from Simple Builders in the following way. When as many cards as possible have been built from the initial layout, subsequent cards turned from stock are not discarded to a waste-pile but added to the layout. After each new deal of cards from stock you pause and build further, then deal more to the layout and repeat the process. Eventually a point is reached at which all unbuilt cards are visible, and the game can then either be solved by analysis or proved impossible by the same means. In other words, they start out as games of judgement but gradually become games of analytic skill. This category also includes games in which all cards are dealt to the initial layout, but some face down so that not all are yet known, and games which appear to be entirely open but in fact at a later stage require you to gather up the layout, shuffle and deal again. An aspect of skill most frequently called into play is that of making the best choice of play when confronted with alternative building possibilities, a feature well illustrated in the first game called Interregnum.

The following games are arranged in order of increasing number of cards dealt to the initial layout.

Interregnum

Constitution
Two packs
Odds in favour

Simple rules but opportunities for making winning (or losing) decisions make this another of my favourite patiences. The alternative title is not to be confused with a Packer of the same name. Similar games are Milton and Capuchin.

Layout Deal a row of eight cards (the 'indicators') at the top of the board. Leave room below it for another row of eight (not yet dealt), and below that deal a second row of eight. Allow room for the bottom row of cards to be extended in columns towards you. These constitute eight wastepiles.

Object To build eight suites in the middle row, in ascending sequence but regardless of suit. The base card of each suite, to be founded as and when it becomes available, is to be one rank higher than the indicator above it in the top row, and the indicator itself will subsequently be used to crown the suite to show that it has been completed. (*Example* Suppose the leftmost card of the top row is a Jack. When a Queen turns up, set her below the Jack as a base, and build K, A, 2 and so on. When the Ten is reached, crown that suite with the Jack and cease building.)

Play All cards in the bottom row are immediately available for founding as bases or building on any suite in the middle row. When all such moves have been made, deal the next eight cards of stock from left to right across the bottom row, filling vacancies from which previous cards have already been built. Where a card covers another, overlap them so that both are visible. Having dealt, pause and make any builds that may be possible. Each exposed card in the bottom row is available. When built, it releases the one below it for building. Continue in the same way, building as far as possible, then dealing eight across, then building again, and so on. There is no redeal.

Wheel of Fortune

Two separate packs
Even chances

The first half of this aptly named pictorial amounts to little more than a mechanical exercise, in which only your powers of observation are brought into play. And it may run around so swiftly and smoothly as to convince you that it must offer at least a hundred per cent chance of success. But when all the cards have been entered into play and you have to start thinking . . . that's when you may discover yourself to have been lulled into a false sense of security.

Layout and object From the first pack deal sixteen cards face up in a circle (if you want to be spaciously pictorial about it – otherwise two rows of eight will do). Take any Aces and Kings, arrange them tastefully in the middle of the wheel as bases, and fill the vacancies at once from stock. As they become available, found an Ace and a King of each suit and build them respectively upwards and downwards into thirteen-card suit-sequences.

Play Start building from the wheel if possible, and fill vacancies from stock. When stuck deal sixteen more cards in strict rotation around the wheel. Then pause and build what you can. The play of an exposed card releases the one beneath it, and any vacancy must at once be filled from stock. Continue alternately dealing and building in this way until both packs are exhausted.

If it proves impossible to complete the suites straight from the wheel, you may now exercise two modes of play. First, you may reverse cards between suites of the same suit if their top cards are in sequence. Second, any vacancy subsequently created in the wheel may be filled with any exposed card of the wheel.

Even then, the suites will not always reach completion.

Royal Parade

Financier, Hussars, Royal Procession, Three Up
Two packs
Odds against

We have here the original version of an unusual patience with several points of superior interest, spoilt only by the fact that success comes too rarely to render the game endearing, let alone popular. But it is worth describing in its own right as a forerunner of the more commendable Virginia Reel, which follows, rather than as a minor variant.

Layout and object Deal three rows of eight cards, none overlapping. The object is to get all the Twos into the top row as bases, and upon each to build upwards in suit by intervals of three to the Jack – i.e. 2–5–8–J. Similarly, all the Threes are to become bases in the middle row and to be built up to the Queen (3–6–9–Q), and the Fours to become bases in the bottom row for building up to the King (4–7–10–K). Aces play no active role and are rejected when they appear.

Play If there are any Aces in the layout, you may throw them away to make gaps. A gap may be filled at once with an available base card. (*Example* If there is an Ace in the top row and a Two in the second, remove the Ace and transfer the Two to that vacancy.) Throughout the game, no base card may be built upon until it is in its proper row, nor may a card in the layout be built upon a suite in a different row: it must first be moved into its proper row when a vacancy is created by the building of another card or by the rejection of Aces in the initial layout. Shift and build as many cards as possible. When stuck, deal a fourth row of eight cards face up from left to right to start a reserve. Reject any Aces, and replace them. These cards are available for building or filling gaps in the layout. A gap need not be filled by a card whose rank is appropriate to its row, but of course such a card will subsequently have to be shifted to a gap in its proper row before it can be built. When stuck again, deal another row of eight, overlapping any that may remain in the first row so that all are visible. The exposed cards are available, but not those beneath until released by the play of overlapping cards. There is no redeal, but a vacancy made in the reserve may be filled with any available card, and there is one grace. If, before you have finished dealing the bottom row, you discover an irreparable block in the reserve columns, you may pick up those so far dealt and redeal the row from right to left instead. This may only be done with the bottom row, and the privilege must be exercised before the last card is dealt to it.

Virginia Reel

Two packs
Odds against

This more frequently successful version of Royal Parade was devised by Morehead and Mott-Smith, and may be regarded as an improvement on it. Note the dance theme implied by the title – an American one, for a change of scenery.

Layout and object Take any Two, Three and Four and lay them in a column down the top left of the board – not overlapping, as they are bases. Deal seven cards face up in a row to the right of each. The object is to eventually get all the Twos into the top row and build each one up in suit and by intervals of three to the Jack; similarly, Threes are to be got into the middle row and built in suit by threes to the Queen, and Fours in the bottom row for building by threes to the King. (Summary: top row 2–5–8–J, middle row 3–6–9–Q, bottom row 4–7–10–K.)

Play Aces play no part, and may be rejected whenever the gaps they leave are most needed. First see if any building can be done, bearing in mind that a card may only ever be built when it is in its proper row, and is of the same suit as, but three ranks higher than, the card on which it is built. Any base card which is present, but in the wrong row, may at once be moved to a gap in its proper row left by the rejection of an Ace or by building. Furthermore, any two or three base cards in the wrong rows may be reciprocally interchanged provided that the result is to bring them all into their right rows. When stuck, deal a fourth row of eight cards face up to start the reserve, which will gradually get built up in columns towards you. Discard any Aces but do not replace them. These cards are available for building, but may not be used to fill gaps indiscriminately: only a base card (Two, Three or Four) in the reserve may be used to fill a gap, though not necessarily in its proper row. Build again. When stuck, deal another row of eight cards from left to right, overlapping them so that any beneath are visible. Exposed cards are available, and those beneath become available when released by the play of overlapping cards. A gap in the reserve may be filled only by the next deal. There is no redeal, but you are allowed one grace. When all cards are out, you may remove one card buried in the reserve, and count half a victory if this enables you to finish the game.

Tournament

Maréchal Saxe
Two packs
Odds against

An old game called Nivernaise or Napoleon's Flank, appended as a variant to this description, is quite interesting but somewhat spoilt by keeping so many cards concealed from the player. Morehead and Mott-Smith claim to have devised the variant called Tournament as an improved version of it offering more scope for skill, which they first published in 1938. Curiously, though, Tournament is identical with a game called Maréchal Saxe described by the pseudonymous Tarbart in his collection of 1905. I've no doubt that this is merely a coincidence consequent upon the proposition that great minds think alike. Tournament is certainly a better title.

Layout and object Deal a column of four non-overlapping cards down each side of the board. These eight form a reserve. Below the space between the two columns deal six columns of four overlapping cards each. The object is to found an Ace and a King of each suit in the space between the reserves and to build them respectively upwards and downwards in suit.

Play Found any Aces or Kings that may be exposed and replace them from stock. If there are none, remove one Ace and one King from the stock and found them, otherwise the game will not get started. The eight cards of the reserve and six exposed cards of the columns are available for building. A space in the reserve may be filled with any exposed card from the columns, either at once or whenever it seems best. The play of a card from a column releases the one beneath it. When an entire column is emptied, refill it at once with a column of four cards dealt from stock. When no further play is possible, deal another twenty-four cards to the columns, four to each, and resume play. If fewer than twenty-four remain, deal them in columns from the left as far as they will go.

Redeal When the stock is exhausted and no further play is possible, close the columns, gather them up in reverse order of dealing, and deal another six columns of four without turning the new stock upside down (so that the first card dealt was the one dealt last to the previous array). Two such redeals are allowed.

Grace Once in each of the three deals a card may be reversed between an Ace and a King suite in each suit.

NIVERNAISE (NAPOLEON'S FLANK) As Tournament, except that the twenty-four cards are dealt in six closed packets of four instead of columns. You may only inspect as many cards in a packet as there are gaps in the reserve. Only one reversal may be made at a time: further play must ensue before another is made. The packets may be gathered up and redealt once.

Hat

Two packs
Odds in favour

This somewhat static pictorial, based on a wildly unexciting theme, is structurally almost identical to Nivernaise. The only difference lies in the pattern, which is supposed to represent a top hat.

Layout and object Deal two columns of four cards, non-overlapping, with space enough between the columns to take eight base cards in two more columns. These form a reserve representing the sides of the hat. Deal twenty-four more cards in six rows of four, non-overlapping, to form a reserve representing the brim. The object is to found an Ace and a King of each suit as and when they become available, and to build the Aces up in suit to the Kings and the Kings down in suit to the Aces.

Play Available for founding and building are the eight cards of the side reserves, and the six outermost cards of the brim reserves. The play of a brim card releases for building the next one inwards from it. When a card is played from a side, its place is taken by an available brim card. This need not be done immediately. When an entire row of four brim cards is cleared out, deal four more from stock to take their place. Any number of cards may be reversed from suite to suite provided that they continue the suit-sequence. When stuck, deal twenty-four more cards to reform the brim reserve, covering any cards that still remain there. A covered card is not available until the one above it has been played, and the topmost card is not available unless it is the outermost card of its row of four. Wait until all twenty-four are dealt before continuing play.

Redeal Three redeals are allowed. In each case, gather up the brim reserves in reverse order from that in which they were dealt, and deal again. (You may shuffle them before redealing. Accounts vary on this point, but you should either shuffle them or not throughout the game – do not shuffle at one redeal but not another in the same game.) Cards in the side reserves stay in place during the redeal.

Sixes and Sevens

Two packs
Odds against

Though space-consuming, Sixes and Sevens may be commended for its unusual geometry and well-founded title.

Layout and object Deal sixteen cards in four rows of four, forming a centre square. Around it deal a frame of twenty cards (four parallel to each side and one at each corner), and around that an outer frame of twenty-eight to enclose the inner frame entirely. From the centre square, remove all cards which are not Aces or Kings, taking them from left to right and top to bottom as dealt, and place them face down to one side to form a reserve pile.

Object To eventually get all the Aces and Kings into the centre square as base cards, and to build the Aces up in suit to the Sixes, and the Kings down in suit to the Sevens.

Play All cards in the outer frame are immediately available for founding and building. The removal of an outer card releases for building that card of the inner frame which is adjacent to it edge by edge (not diagonally, for which reason the play of an outer corner card does not release an inner corner card). When stuck, deal cards from stock to fill gaps in the double frame, proceeding from left to right and from top to bottom. When the stock is exhausted and no more building can be done, turn up the cards of the reserve one by one and build them, pausing to build from the frame whenever possible. The cards of the reserve may not be used to fill gaps in the frames, and there is no redeal.

Lady of the Manor

La Châtelaine
Two packs
Odds against

A civilized title, a pleasing geometry and an unusual reserve combine to make this one of my favourites. As its 'closed' nature is not likely to appeal to modern tastes, I have devised the open version called Archway, to be described later, in which there is opportunity for planning ahead.

Layout and object Arrange the Aces in two rows of four to form bases. The object is to build each one up to a King, regardless of suit. Deal the next forty-eight cards face down in four packets of twelve each, then turn each packet face up so that only the top card is visible. Deal the remainder face upwards in twelve packets in the form of a crescent, or arch, spanning the three rows of four. Each packet is reserved for one rank, from Deuces on the left to Kings on the right, each card dealt being placed in its appropriate position or packet. Of course, there will not necessarily be the same number of cards in each packet, and some may be entirely vacant.

Play The top card of every packet is available for building, and its play releases the one below it for the same purpose. There is no redeal.

MY LADY'S The same, but although each pack is shuffled separately the two are not shuffled together.

Senior Wrangler
Mathematics
Two packs
Odds in favour

This is one of several patiences that like to make themselves sound more complicated than they really are, as the alternative title might suggest. The principle involved is a common enough one – simply that you are required to build suites up in different intervals, such as 2–4–6, 3–6–9, and so on. For similar games, see also Imaginary Thirteen, Calculation, Musical Patience. A wrangler, by the way, is one who wrangles, disputes, or otherwise argues learnedly. It was once the custom of Cambridge University to designate as Senior Wrangler the student who came first in the mathematics honours examination, followed by the Second Wrangler, and so on. (This will be no news to lovers of the limerick, one of which is devoted to a wrangler of Trinity Hall.)

Layout Deal a row of eight cards numbered from Ace to Eight inclusive. Below them leave space for a second row, on which the suites are to be built (not yet dealt), and below that deal the remaining cards, face down, in eight packets of twelve each. Then turn these packets face up so that only those on top are visible.

Object To found eight bases in the space between, as and when they appear, and to build them up to the Kings regardless of suit and by different intervals. The interval required for a given suite is prescribed by the card above it in the top row. Thus, below the Ace found a Two and continue 3–4–5– etc.; below the Two found a Four and continue 6–8–10–Q–A–3–5–7–9–J–K; below the Three found a Six and continue 9–Q–2–5–8–J–A–4–7–10–K; and so on. For this purpose each Jack counts 11, Queen 12, King 13, and any higher required number is met by a card representing 13 subtracted from it. (14 = A, 15 = 2, etc.)

Play The top card of a packet in the lower row is available for building, and its play releases the card beneath it for the same purpose. The top card of any suite is available for transfer to the top of another suite if necessary, provided that it follows sequence by the correct interval. When stuck, take up the first packet and deal the cards one by one across the lower row, placing the first in the space vacated. You are allowed to examine the bottom card of the packet, and elect whether to deal the packet from the top down or the bottom up. When stuck again, deal the second packet in the same way (upwards or downwards as preferred), then the third, and so on. If the game does not come out after the eighth packet is dealt, you should be ashamed of yourself.

DISTRIBUTION As above, but the rules state that any eight different numeral cards are set out to start with. Even this may be regarded as unnecessarily restrictive. As long as Kings do not appear in the top row you might as well deal eight cards at random, building up Jack suites by eleven and Queen suites by twelve. Nor does it matter if there are duplicates in the top row so that more than one suite is built up by the same interval.

Blockades

A small but distinctive branch of the Builder family is characterized by the fact that cards are not dealt overlapping one another, and that a card is only available for play if its lower edge (or sometimes also its upper edge) is 'free'. The effect of this feature will become immediately apparent from the play of either Labyrinth or Parallels, respectively the one-pack and two-pack simplest forms of the game.

The group takes its names from the original title of Parallels, namely 'British Blockade'. It is quite well descriptive, as a card which does not have its critical edge free is said to be 'blockaded' by the cards above and below it. Games with a similar positional aspect not included under this head include Quilt and Sixes-and-Sevens.

Labyrinth

One pack
Even chances

In the simplest of the Blockades, played with a single pack, a card may be taken for building on a suite if either its top or bottom edge is free. In effect this means that both the top and the bottom card of any column is available, instead of just the exposed card as is the case in packing games. For this reason Labyrinth can be dealt in overlapping rows, whereas most of this little family have to be dealt in separated rows. The point is made because it shows the relationship of Blockades to Packers quite clearly.

Layout and object Take the four Aces and put them at the top of the board. Build them up in suit to the Kings.

Play Deal the next eight cards face up in a row. Do any building that can be done and fill the spaces from stock. Keep building and filling until you can go no further. Then deal another row of eight overlapping the first, pause, and build again. From this row onwards do not fill vacancies except by the next deal, and always deal eight across before resuming play. After each deal the top and bottom cards of each column are available for building. The removal of either, of course, releases the next card above or below it. There is no redeal.

Parallels

The British Blockade
Two packs
Odds against

The alternative title served . to distinguish it from French Blockade, which itself is not a true blockading game.

Layout and object Take an Ace of each suit and put them in a column (not overlapping) down one side of the board, and put their corresponding Kings in a parallel column down the other side. Play to build the Aces up in suit to the Kings and the Kings down in suit to the Aces.

Play Deal ten cards face up in a row between the top Ace and King. Use these for building if possible and fill spaces from stock. When you can get no further, deal another row of ten beneath the first row, not overlapping it. Cards of both rows are available for building, and spaces must be filled from stock. When stuck, deal a third row beneath the second. From now on a card is only available for building if its upper or lower edge is free. Thus all the cards in the second row are blockaded by those above and below, until freed by the play of a perpendicularly adjacent card. When stuck, or earlier if preferred, fill all the spaces in order from left to right in the top row first and then in each succeeding row. Do not resume play until you have finished filling spaces. Whenever all the spaces have just been filled, you may deal another row of ten cards below the previous row, and must not resume play until the whole row is dealt. As before, the top and bottom card of each column is available, and cards between are blockaded until their upper or lower edge is free. Note: if you play with the stock face down, you may not look at the top card until all spaces are filled, and must, having looked at it, deal a fresh row.

Cards may be reversed between Ace and King suites when they are in sequence, but bases must be left intact.

Babette

Two packs
Odds against

The same theme is continued, but in a new variation whereby spaces are left unfilled.

Object To found an Ace and a King of each suit as they become available, and to build them respectively upwards and downwards into thirteen-card suit sequences.

Play Deal eight cards face up in a row. Build any that can be built, but do not replace them. Deal a second row beneath the first, not overlapping (at least, not until you are sufficiently experienced to keep track of available cards). Keep dealing rows of eight, pausing after each deal to build available cards. A card is available if its lower edge is free, either because it is at the near end of the column or because it lies immediately above a space. Never fill spaces.

Redeal Having dealt all cards into the game and built as much as possible, gather the columns up from left to right without disturbing the relative positions of the cards, consolidate them into a new stock and start dealing again. There is no further redeal. Cards in suit and sequence may be reversed from suite to suite if necessary, but leave bases intact.

Note (applying to Babette, Stag Party, Four Intruders, and any Blockade in which spaces are not filled): A query may arise in connection with these games that is not answered by any of the sources I have consulted. Suppose you deal the next row of cards and succeed in playing them all off, but are unable to build any of the others thereby unblocked in the row above. When you deal the next row, should you deal it directly under the previous row and so blockade any cards in it, or should you deal it under the vacant row (from which you have just played all the cards), in such a way as to leave all cards in the previous row available by virtue of lying above spaces? The latter strikes me as logically correct, though it would not surprise me to find that the inventor of the game intended otherwise.

STAG PARTY The title refers to the final effect, though the Queens play an important part as they are thrown one by one out of the game. Play as Babette, except that the object is to release all the Sixes for building up in suit to the Jacks, and all the Fives for building down in suit to the Kings (which go on the Aces). Discard Queens as they are dealt: their purpose is to create spaces. There is no redeal, but your chances of success are greater.

Four Intruders

Two packs
Odds in favour

The Blockades described above have all been equivalent to Simple Builders. Four Intruders and its variant, Triumph, are the Packers of the family. They are rather complicated.

Object Remove the eight Aces and found them in a row at the top of the board. The object is to build them up in suit to the Kings.

Layout Deal four cards face up in a column (not overlapping) down the left side of the board. The north-east corner of the top card should point diagonally to the south-west corner of the first Ace. These four start the tableau.

Deal eight cards face up in a row below the Aces to start the reserve.

Play Whenever the game blocks, or sooner if preferred, deal another row of cards to the reserve without overlapping the row above, and continue until only four cards remain in stock. Throughout play, any card of the reserve is available for building on a suite or packing on the tableau if its lower edge is free, either because it is the end card of a column or because it lies immediately above a space. Never fill spaces in the reserve.

Pack the tableau in suit and descending sequence, overlapping cards to form rows spreading to the left. Build from the tableau whenever possible, and consolidate two rows of the same suit when they join sequence with each other. Fill a vacancy in the tableau from the reserve, and do so before dealing another row.

When only four cards remain in hand, deal them into a column (not overlapping) down the right-hand side parallel to the tableau. These are the 'intruders'. They are not to be packed upon, but are themselves available for packing on the tableau or building on suites. Reserve cards may no longer be packed on the tableau, but can be used only for building on suites and filling vacancies among the intruders.

There is no redeal. See special note at end of Babette (above).

Triumph

Two packs
Odds in favour

Triumph is superficially similar to Four Intruders, and starts with the same layout. The chief differences are that reserve cards may not be packed in the tableau and that spaces in the reserve are filled before another row is dealt.

Object Found all eight Aces to start with and build them up in suit to the Kings.

Layout Deal eight cards in a row to start the reserve and four in a column to start the tableau (as for Four Intruders).

Play Tableau cards may be built on suites or packed on one another in suit and descending sequence. An entire packed sequence may be packed on a suitable card elsewhere in the tableau. A vacancy may be filled only from stock: in no circumstance may cards be played from the reserve to the tableau before the stock is exhausted.

Each card in the first row of the reserve is available for building, and is then replaced from stock. When no further play is possible and all spaces have been filled, deal another row of eight below the first, not overlapping. The lowest card of each column in the reserve is available only for building, not for packing, and its removal frees the one directly above it for the same purpose. When necessary, fill all spaces in the reserve from stock, dealing in order from left to right in each row from the highest downwards. After filling any space you may pause and play further, but you may not deal a new row of eight until all spaces have been filled.

If the game blocks when you have run out of stock, you may withdraw any four cards from the reserve. These may be built on suites or packed on the tableau (not more than one per tableau pile), either immediately or gradually. The card lying above each of the four vacancies thus created in the reserve may also be built or packed, but this privilege does not extend to the cards lying above them. Provided that all cards drawn for this purpose have in fact been built or packed, another four may be drawn for the same purpose. A third four-card draw is not permitted.

SENATE (CONGRESS) The same, but with one exception. Having started to fill spaces, you must fill them all before either playing further or dealing the next row of eight. This reduces the chance of success.

Planners

The Builders of this group call for considerable skill of a distinctive kind – that of pitting your wits against probabilities which are calculable in the long run but may work against you in the short.

The general procedure is this. You turn cards from the shuffled pack and build them in the usual way as far as possible. Cards which won't fit, however, you discard face up to any of several wastepiles. (The exact number varies from game to game, and the games in the following pages are arranged in order of increasing number of wastepiles.) At any stage in the game the top card of any wastepile may be taken for building if it fits, and its play releases the one beneath it for the same purpose. By the time you have played all cards from the stock the only way of finishing the game is to build off exposed cards of the wastepiles one by one, until either you complete the suites or the game blocks.

This is where the planning skill comes in. Each time you play an unbuildable card you must consider carefully which wastepile to place it on, so as not to block critical cards beneath. For example, if you are playing a one-pack game in which suites are to be built upwards in suit, you will avoid discarding (say) ♥7 to a pile which already contains ♥6 or lower; for the Seven can only be built on the Six, and the Six cannot be extricated before the Seven. And even if you get cards in the same suit the right way round, you must still avoid cross-blocks between different suits. For instance, you can safely discard ♥7 on ♣6 if another pile contains ♥6 on ♣7 (other things being equal), but not if the other contains ♣7 on ♥6. In such games it is nearly always advisable to hold one wastepile open (empty) for the receipt of Kings. As they do not come off for building until the very end they can be safely packed on but must not be allowed to block others.

It is, of course, not merely permissible but highly desirable to spread the cards of wastepiles towards you in columns so that all are visible, otherwise the whole point of the game – advance planning – is lost. It goes without saying that cards may not be shifted from one wastepile to another. The one game in which this is allowed to a limited extent (Shifting) seems to suggest that Packers may have evolved from Builders through games of this type.

'S'

Eights
Two packs
Odds against

A funny little game – it must take the prize for the shortest title.

Layout Take thirteen cards, one of each rank but regardless of suit, and arrange them in the form of a letter 'S' from Seven at one end to Six at the other, passing through Queen, King, Ace in the middle. These are bases.

Object To build cards in ascending sequence but regardless of suit upon each base until there are eight altogether. The thirteen completed suites will be surmounted by cards of different ranks ranging in order from Ace at one end to King at the other.

Play Turn cards from stock and build them if possible or else play them face up to either of two wastepiles, the top cards of which are always available for building. Cards may not be transferred from suite to suite or waste to waste. There is no redeal.

VARIANT In addition to the rules above, suits are also followed in rotation. Suppose you select the order spades, hearts, diamonds, clubs. Then start with all thirteen spades in the form of an 'S'. The next card built in sequence upon each one must be a heart, the next a diamond, and so on, so that the end result depicts all thirteen clubs. As this is much harder to achieve, you are allowed four wastepiles instead of two.

Rosamund

Rosamund's Bower
One pack
Odds in favour

Rosamund is a one-suite game like Robert, Golf and Black Hole. I should like to think it was named after Fair Rosamund (Henry II's mistress Rosamund Clifford), but in that case who is the Jack and who the King? At any rate, the game is equipped with enough redeals to render consummation of the affair a foregone conclusion.

Layout Take ♥Q, ♠K and ♣J. Put the Queen in the middle and deal eight cards around her: two above, two below and two each side. These eight represent the guards of the bower. Put the King up at the top right and deal a packet of seven cards face down beside him. These seven are a reserve of King's guards. Put the Jack down at the bottom left.

Object To build all the cards of the pack into a single pile by the ♣J, starting with a Ten, descending in sequence regardless of suit, passing from Ace to King as necessary, and finishing with ♠K followed by ♥Q. In story-line terms, the Knave's object is to dispatch all the guards and onlookers and find himself alone with the Queen of hearts.

Play Turn cards from stock and build them if possible or discard them to any of three wastepiles if not. Available for building on the single suite are the top card of stock, the top of each wastepile, and the eight guards of the bower. It is obligatory to build a guard of the bower as soon as possible, in preference to one from anywhere else, and to fill its space with the top card of the King's reserve. The ♠K is not to be taken till last, leaving the ♥Q to go off with her admirer.

Redeal When the stock is exhausted, gather up the wastepiles and start dealing again. Three redeals are allowed if you insist on a happy ending.

Matrimonial

One pack
Odds against

One of many games based on the theme of marrying off Kings and Queens, its low chance of succeeding is ironic in view of Rosamund's easy conquest (above). No doubt the Queen of hearts may be regarded as Henry II's wife Eleanor of Aquitaine, who lost two husbands but founded the Courts of Love.

Layout Take and found the Kings and Queens of hearts and spades as four bases.

Object To build four suites surmounted respectively by the King and Queen of diamonds and the King and Queen of clubs.

Building Each base King is to be followed by the Ace of its own suit, and that upwards in suit-sequence to the Jack, which is then crowned with the remaining Queen of opposite colour. Each base Queen is to be followed by the remaining Jack of opposite colour, and that built downwards in suit-sequence to the Ace, finally being crowned with the King.

Play Deal cards from stock and build them if possible or play them face up to any of three wastepiles if not. When the stock is exhausted, gather the wastepiles up into a single new stock and play again, but this time forming only one wastepile. The top card of each wastepile is available.

Redeal No further redeal is allowed, but (unless I am much mistaken) the game is so doomed to failure that you have my permission to either redeal once more or make the single redeal to two wastepiles instead of one.

Note In the first deal to three wastepiles, bear in mind the order in which the piles will be gathered up for the redeal, and, therefore, the order in which individual cards will again become available. It is vital to get them out again the right way round.

Display

Two packs
Odds in favour

A game for exhibitionists, requiring much table space, and featuring the unusual device of a two-dimensional building site.

Layout and object Deal the first card face up to the board in such a position as to represent the top left corner of a rectangle consisting of eight rows of thirteen cards, the building of which is the object of play.

Building Cards are not built on top of one another, but placed in position in the proposed rectangle. Each new card must be built adjacent to a card already in position (side to side, not diagonally). Each card must be one rank lower in sequence than the one immediately above it or to its left, and one rank higher in sequence than the one immediately below it or to its right. Building is carried out regardless of suit.

Play Turn cards from stock and build them if possible or play them face up to any of three wastepiles if not. When the pack is exhausted, gather the piles up into a new stock and run through it again, but this time deal to only one wastepile. The game should come out with careful play.

Sir Tommy

Old Patience, Try Again
One pack
Odds against

As hinted at by its alternative title, this has been claimed to be the ancestor of all patiences; but I do not know on what authority. Under the name 'Dictation' it makes an excellent competitive game for two or more players (as described later), and extensive experience of battle in that theatre enables me to assert with some confidence that the odds against bringing it to a successful conclusion lie between 12 and 15 to 1. Morehead and Mott-Smith put it at only 4–1, which makes them either geniuses or guessers, or just very lucky indeed.

Object To found four Aces as and when they become available, and to build each of them up in sequence to a King regardless of suit.

Play Turn cards from stock and build them if possible or play them face up to any of four wastepiles if not. No card may be transferred from one place to another except from the top of a wastepile to a suite, and there is no redeal. You may, however, examine the next card of stock before deciding whether or not to build a card from the wastepiles, but you must already have placed the previous card before doing so.

VARIANT One account states that you deal and place four cards from stock before pausing to build what you can, but this inelegant rule makes the game even harder to get out.

Shifting

One pack
Odds in favour

Evolutionists might regard Shifting as a good example of a 'missing link', representing a form transitional between the Planners represented by Sir Tommy and such Simple Packers as Single Rail.

Found the four Aces as they appear and build them up to the Kings regardless of suit. Turn cards one by one from stock and discard those that cannot be built to any of four wastepiles. These may be spread towards you in columns, and the uncovered card of each column is always available for building. So far the game is Sir Tommy, but now comes the addition of packing. The exposed card of any column may be shifted onto another which is next higher in rank, regardless of suit. A space made by clearing out a column may be filled only with an available King.

Puss in the Corner

One pack
Odds against

This slightly pictorial, thinly disguised variant of Sir Tommy introduces the rare feature of building suites in colour but not necessarily in suit.

Layout and object Arrange four Aces in a square at the centre of the board, and build each one up in colour to a King. Thus diamonds and hearts may be built on one another indiscriminately, and spades and clubs in like manner.

Play Turn cards from stock and build them if possible or play them face up to any of four wastepiles if not. To illustrate the title, each wastepile is placed with its longer edge lying diagonally against a corner of the central square of Ace suites.

Redeal There is one redeal. When the stock is exhausted, gather up the wastepiles into a new stock and play on.

VARIANTS One account permits you the following grace: every time a Seven is turned, you may, if you wish, place one wastepile as a whole on top of another, and then, also optionally, the third on top of the fourth. Another account states that you deal four cards at a time before building.

Alternate

One pack
Even chances

Another variation in the mode of building. (The title, I think, should be regarded as a verb, with the stress on the first syllable.)

Layout and object Found the two red Aces and two black Kings. Build the Aces in ascending sequence and alternating colour to the Kings, and the Kings in decending sequence and alternating colour to the Aces.

Play Turn cards from stock and build them if possible or play them face up to any of four wastepiles if not.

Redeal When the stock is exhausted, the wastepiles may be gathered up into a new stock and replayed once only.

Divorce

One pack
Even chances

This extension of the previous game might be regarded as a parody on all those patiences called Matrimony, Royal Marriage, and so on.

Object To found the four Aces and four Deuces as and when they become available, and to build suites upon them in alternating ascending sequence and alternating colour – i.e. A–3–5– etc. to the King, 2–4–6– etc. to the Queen, and simultaneously red on black, black on red.

Play Turn cards from stock and build them if possible or else play them face up to any of four wastepiles. The top card of each wastepile is available. There is no redeal.

Calculation

Broken Intervals, The Fairest
One or two packs
Odds against

Calculation is a more skill-demanding version of Musical Patience and Senior Wrangler, and is easily identified as another form of Sir Tommy – this time with suites built up in four different intervals. Calculation under its own name is played with one pack, but with two under the title Imaginary Thirteen.

Layout Take any Ace, Two, Three and Four, and put them in a row at the top of the board. These are the indicators.

Object To build four suites in a row below the indicators. Each base card is to be twice that of the indicator above it (2, 4, 6, 8) and is put into place when it turns up, and each suite is to be built upwards to the King, regardless of suit, by the interval prescribed by the indicator. For this purpose Jack = 11, Queen = 12, King = 13, and anything higher is thirteen less (i.e. 14 = Ace, 15 = Two, etc.). For example, the suite under the Four proceeds: 8–Q–3–7–J–2–6–10–A–5–9–K.

Play Turn cards from stock and build them if possible or play them face up to any of four wastepiles if not. There is no redeal.

IMAGINARY THIRTEEN Deal a row of eight indicators in order from Ace to Eight inclusive, regardless of suit. Below each one found a base card twice the value of the indicator above, and build it up to the King, regardless of suit, by the interval prescribed by the indicator. Play to four wastepiles, as above. (Compare Senior Wrangler.)

Above and Below

Two separate packs
Odds against

Although Sir Tommy would be virtually impossible to get out if you were required to build in suit, this two-pack variation makes just that requirement, but gives you an outside chance of succeeding. It is a well-balanced game.

Layout Shuffle each pack separately but do not mix them together. Turn up the first card and place it to one side of the board as an indicator. The other seven cards of the same rank will also be indicators, and are piled on top of the first as and when they appear.

Object To found, as and when they appear, the four cards one rank higher than indicators and the four cards one rank lower. These base cards are put in two rows of four, the higher ranks above, the lower ones below. The object is to build an ascending suit sequence of cards on each of the upper bases, and a descending suit sequence on each of the lower bases. When each suite contains twelve cards, it is completed by crowning with an indicator of the same suit.

Play Turn cards from stock and build them if possible or play them face up to any of four wastepiles if not. While the suites are being built it is permissible to transfer the top card of a suite to the top of the other of the same suit, if it fits and if it seems advantageous to do so. Do not forget to add cards of the same rank to the indicator pile.

Redeal When the stock is exhausted, gather up the wastepiles into a new stock and play through it once more only.

Jubilee

Two packs
Odds against

Another two-pack variation of Sir Tommy, invented in the golden year 1887. Those who experienced the more recent Silver Jubilee of 1977 will recall that Queen Elizabeth started a vogue for pronouncing this word with the stress on the last syllable.

Layout and Object Set out eight Kings and build them up in suit to the Queens in this complicated Victorian order: K–A–J–2–10–3–9–4–8–5–7–6–Q.

Play Turn cards from stock and build them if possible or play them face up to any of four wastepiles if not.

Redeal Two redeals are allowed. When the stock is exhausted, gather up the wastepiles into a new one and play on.

Note The unashamed complicatedness of the order is deliberately designed to make life difficult for the player. As Miss Whitmore Jones says, it is not the lot of every queen to have a golden jubilee.

Louisa

Two packs
Even chances

Like Jubilee, this one is also designed to drive you to your wits' end in trying to keep track of the sequences.

Object To found an Ace of each suit and a King of each suit as bases when they become available, and to build each base up in suit to the Seven in a special sequence as follows:

Ace   K–2–Q–3–J–4–10–5–9–6–8–7
King   A–Q–2–J–3–10–4–9–5–8–6–7

Play Turn cards from stock and build them if possible or play them face up to any of four wastepiles if not.

Redeal When the stock is exhausted, gather the wastepiles up from left to right and play through the consolidated heap once again. A second redeal is permitted, but unbuildable cards turned from stock may then only be played to a single wastepile.

Squaring the Circle

Two packs
Odds in favour

Once you get used to the deliberately confusing sequence required of the suites you will find this game somewhat easier than that of constructing a square exactly equal in area to a given circle, which the ancient Greeks showed to be impossible using straightedge and compasses alone. The sequence, indeed, should not be confusing at all when you realize that each suite consists of twenty-six cards arranged in the form of two interlocking sequences in opposite directions – exactly the same, in fact, as the 'Tweedledum-Tweedledee' variant of Gemini Patience described elsewhere, except that cards are built in one pile instead of two. One sequence proceeds A–2–3– etc. up to the King, the other K–Q–J– etc. down to the Ace, but the two must alternate, so that what you have to play is A–K–2–Q–3–J– etc. The two sequences automatically cross over when you reach the Sevens, and the whole suite concludes –J–3–Q–2–K–A. Easy, isn't it?

Layout Take an Ace of each suit and lay them face up in a square at the centre of the board. These are the bases. Deal the next twelve cards face up in a circle surrounding them. These form the reserve.

Object To build up a double, alternating suit-sequence of cards upon each Ace as described above, resulting in four 26-card suites surmounted by duplicate Aces.

Play Cards of the reserve may be built whenever possible, and are immediately replaced from stock during the initial period. When no more building is possible, start play proper by turning cards from the stock and building them if possible or playing them face up to any of four wastepiles if not. The top card of each wastepile is available for building, and whenever a card of the reserve is built its place must be filled at once by any available card from the wastepiles (or from stock if ever the wastepiles are all empty).

Redeal The stock exhausted, you may gather up the wastepiles in order, turn them to form a new stock, and play through it once more.

Higgledy Piggledy
Two packs
Odds against

A game of refreshing abandon.

Layout and object Shuffle the cards and scatter them face down all over the table. Make room in the middle for play to take place. Take any card and set it face up as the first base. The other seven cards of the same rank are to be set in line with it as they turn up. Build each base up in suit and sequence, turning from King to Ace where necessary, until it contains thirteen cards surmounted by a card one rank lower in value than the base.

Play Take up cards at random from the table and build them if possible or play them face up to any of four wastepiles if not. When all have been put in place, take up the leftmost pile and distribute the cards face up, one at a time, to the other three piles ad lib, building when possible. That done, take the leftmost pile again and distribute it to the other two, then the same again onto a single pile. If this cannot be built off, the game has failed.

Double Pyramid

Two packs
Odds in favour

Double Pyramid is a broadly similar game to Squaring the Circle, except that an extra nine cards are available from the reserve and the basic geometry is Ancient Egyptian rather than Ancient Greek. (Apparently the Egyptians were not as bright about geometry as the Greeks. Many are reported to have believed that if two plots of land had perimeters of the same length they must also have been equal in area. Real estate must have been a great business in those days.)

Layout Deal twenty-one cards face up in the form of an inverted V, with one at the top and ten down each side, overlapping to conserve space if necessary. These form a reserve called the 'pyramid'. Deal the next card face up inside and near the top of the pyramid. This is the first base. As the other seven of the same rank become available they are used to form more bases in the shape of a smaller pyramid inside the first, with three in its second row and four in its third.

Object To release the other bases when possible, and to build upon every base in suit and ascending sequence until it contains thirteen cards. Each sequence turns from King through Ace if necessary, and terminates with a card one rank lower than the base.

Play All cards of the reserve are available for building when possible, and are not replaced. Turn cards from stock and build them if possible or play them face up to any of four wastepiles if not, the wastepiles going to form the base of the pyramid while they last. There is no redeal. It is advisable to turn a completed suit face down to prevent yourself from absent-mindedly extending it.

Gemini

Two packs
Odds against

Not just twins, but Siamese twins, to make delivery even more difficult. Appropriately enough there are even two distinct forms of the game. The first one might be called Identical Twins, the second Tweedledum–Tweedledee.

Layout Deal the first four cards of different ranks that appear, and set them out as a row of bases. Leave enough space between them for each card's exact duplicate to be set at its right when it appears, forming another base.

Object These four bases, and the other four as they appear, are each to be built up into thirteen-card suit sequences (passing from King to Ace as necessary). But here's the catch: Each set of twins must be built up at exactly the same rate. For instance, having got the Two on the Ace of one spade suite, you can't build the Three until the other Ace of spades has been covered with its Two.

Play Turn cards from stock and build them if possible, or else play them face up to any of five wastepiles.

Redeal When the stock is exhausted, gather up the wastepiles from left to right and turn them upside down to form a new stock. This time, however, you may play them to only two wastepiles. And that's your last chance.

VARIANT The Tweedledum–Tweedledee method calls for a little more thought. Start as before, but this time build one twin upwards and one twin downwards in suit. (For example, a base of Seven builds upwards to the Six and downwards to the Eight.) Again, though, each pair must be built at the same rate. A convenient way of checking this is to remember that when two twinned suites are exactly level, their top cards total 14 (counting Jack 11, Queen 12, King 13). If ever they total less than 13 or more than 16 you will suddenly and unaccountably be turned into a pumpkin.

Fly

Reserve
Two packs
Odds against

Biologists and theologians may be surprised to learn that there are close relationships between the fly, the frog and the demon, but to Patience buffs they are all much alike.

Layout Take out the eight Aces and lay them in a row as bases. Then deal thirteen cards face down in a pile and turn up the top card. This forms the 'fly' (reserve).

Object To build each Ace up to the King regardless of suit, annihilating the fly in the process.

Play Turn cards from stock and build them if possible or play them face up to any of five wastepiles if not. The top card of the fly is available for building whenever possible, the one beneath it being turned up in its place. There is no redeal.

Frog

Toad, Toad-in-the-Hole
Two packs
Odds against

A close relative of the Fly (above) and second cousin to the Demon (elsewhere), Frog is also known as Toad, but of an entirely different species from its transatlantic namesake American Toad (which see). The significance of the name Fanny has not been vouchsafed.

Layout Deal thirteen cards face up; remove and replace any Aces among them; then square the pile and lay it face up as a reserve (the frog). Set an Ace in position as the first base.

Object To release the other Aces as they appear and build them all up in suit to the Kings.

Play Turn cards from stock and build them if possible or play them face up to any of five wastepiles if not. The top card of the frog is available for building. There is no redeal.

FANNY The same, except that all eight Aces are founded before play and the reserve contains only twelve cards. These should be dealt face down and squared up, with only the top card faced throughout play.

Colours
One pack
Odds against

This one is easier than Lady Betty in that suites are built merely in colour, not necessarily in suit, while the different numerical bases add a little spice to the concoction.

Object To found as bases, when they appear, a Two, a Three, a Four and a Five – the Two and Four to be of one colour (red or black, regardless of suit), the Three and Five to be of the other – and to build each one in colour and ascending sequence as far as the next rank lower than the base.

Play Turn cards from stock and build them if possible or play them face up to any of six wastepiles if not. There is no redeal.

Flip Flop
Eight Aces
Two packs
Odds in favour

Such an unusual procedure is demonstrated in this game that I have taken the liberty of renaming it in order to draw attention to its most interesting feature. 'Eight Aces' is colourless and confusing.

Layout and object Set out the eight Aces as a line of bases, and build each one up in sequence to a King regardless of suit.

Play Turn cards from stock and build them if possible or play them face up to any of six wastepiles if not.

Redeal When the stock is exhausted and all possible building done, take the exposed card of each wastepile and place it face down ('flip') at the bottom of the pile, releasing the next one for building. When stuck again, do the same. Continue until the face down cards have reached the top of their respective piles, turning them face up ('flop') as they surface and building if possible. No more transfers may be made, and the game fails if any card surfaces but fails to get built.

Missing Link

Blind, Mystery
One pack
Odds in favour

Victorian society was divided on the subject of evolution, particularly on that aspect which concerned itself with the question whether man was more closely related to apes or angels. As angels did not inhabit zoos and were therefore unavailable for studies in comparative anatomy, those who misunderstood the theory felt that all they needed was to dig up the fossil of a 'missing link' – some anthropoid exactly mid-way between man and ape – in order to confound their enemies. And that's only partly why I prefer 'Missing Link' to other titles. When you play the game you will find it to be the most descriptive term for the unseen card which has such an important part to play.

Layout and object Cut the pack and deal one card face down to one side of the board. This is the 'missing link'. The object of the game is to found the Aces as they appear and build them up in suit and sequence to the Kings.

Play Turn cards from stock and build them if possible or else play them face up to any of seven wastepiles. When stuck, turn up the missing link. If it enables you to complete the game you have proved the theory of evolution.

Grace When you build the last card of a wastepile you may fill the vacancy with any inconvenient exposed card you wish. My own view is that the game is easy enough without this grace, which must have been introduced by Huxley when no one was looking.

Lady Betty
One pack
Odds against

The lady is a close friend of Sir Tommy, or perhaps a relative.

Object To found each Ace as it appears and build it up in suit and sequence to the King.

Play Turn cards from stock and build them if possible or play them face up to any of six wastepiles if not. There is no redeal.

Strategy
One pack
Odds in favour

This superb game, one of my favourites, was invented by Morehead, or Mott-Smith, or both. It is a form of Sir Tommy, but with a sting in its tail. I believe the authors to overestimate its difficulty when they say 'Chances of success – one in five games'. Four in five would be a reasonable ambition.

Object To found the Aces as they appear, and eventually build them up in suit and sequence to the Kings.

Play Turn cards from stock and play them face up to any of eight wastepiles. Aces may be founded when they appear, but no other cards are to be built until the piles have been completed. With skilful packing, it should be possible to play off all forty-eight cards from the tops of the piles downwards.

Optional rule If you succeed, play the next game with only seven wastepiles, and keep reducing the number by one each time you succeed and increasing by one each time you fail. Regard success with only four wastepiles as a great victory.

Sly Fox
Twenty
Two packs
Odds in favour

These are improvements on their grandfather (see below) in that there is no single wastepile but a greater element of skill in playing to the reserve. My only source for the game called Twenty does not state whether extra cards are dealt to the reserve in strict rotation or in any order you please. If the former, it is a different game from Sly Fox, and inferior to it.

Layout Take an Ace of each suit and lay them in a column down the left side of the board as foundations, and do likewise with Kings on the right. Between the two columns deal twenty cards face up in four rows of five, forming the reserve.

Object To build the Aces up in suit to the Kings and the Kings down in suit to the Aces.

Play Build from the reserve as far as you can, filling spaces immediately from stock. When stuck, deal twenty more cards, one on each place in the reserve in any order you please. Use top cards of the reserve to build again as far as you can. The play of a top card releases the one below it for building if possible, but from now on do not replace cards from stock until you cannot (or will not) build any further. When that happens, deal another twenty cards as before. Keep playing in this way, replenishing the reserve not piecemeal but always twenty at a time, and not building until the deal is completed. (Of course, the last deal may comprise fewer than twenty.) Cards may not be reversed from suite to suite, and there is no redeal.

COLORADO Play as Sly Fox but with these differences. Do not start by picking out Aces and Kings for foundations, but wait until they turn up in the play before founding them as bases. Deal the layout in two rows of ten, then found and build as far as possible, filling spaces from stock as soon as they occur. When stuck, turn cards from stock one by one and either build if possible or play them face up to any depot if not – in effect, the depots are wastepiles. It is not permitted to examine the next card of stock before settling the position of the present one. There is no redeal.

Grandfather's

Two packs
Even chances

Grandfather's Patience is held by some to be the oldest one known, which, if true, makes it the grandaddy of all patiences. (The same is claimed for Sir Tommy, but as the two are obviously related they can share the honours equally.) The point of Grandfather's is that you have to build in suit, unlike Sir Tommy, and you are given twenty wastepiles to make it a bit easier – but not without strings attached, as we shall see.

Layout Deal twenty cards face up in two rows of ten, forming a reserve.

Object To found an Ace and a King of each suit as and when they appear, and to build the Aces up in suit to the Kings, the Kings down in suit to the Aces.

Play If there are any Aces or Kings in the layout, found them and start building on them if other exposed cards fit. When stuck, fill empty gaps from stock and continue building, refilling again as necessary. When no more building is possible, turn cards from stock and build them if possible. If not, either play them face up to form a single wastepile, or put them on top of cards of the reserve. No place in the reserve, however, may ever contain more than two cards at a time, and only the uppermost is immediately available.

Redeal The single wastepile may be turned and dealt through once more.

DOUBLE LINE In this variant there is no redeal, but there is a grace. Whenever all the places are full (two cards each), you may shift the top card of stock to the bottom, whether it is playable or not. Five such shifts may be made in all.

Grandmother's

Two packs
Odds in favour

This one is obviously related, by marriage, to Grandfather's. We now have a 22-card reserve instead of twenty, and another reserve of four cards to boot. Consequently, in the words of Miss Whitmore Jones, 'The failures are to the successes as one is to ten.'

Layout Deal twenty-two cards face up in two rows of eleven, forming the main reserve. Deal the next card face up at the top left of the board, forming the first base.

Object To found seven more bases as and when they become available, and to build them all into thirteen-card suit sequences. Three of these will be of the same rank as the first base, all four being of different suits, and are to be built in descending sequence. The other four must be of different suits and one rank higher than the first base, and are to be built in ascending sequence. (*Example* If the first base is a Seven, the upper row will be of Sevens built downwards to the Eights, and the lower row of Eights to be built upwards to the Sevens. King and Ace, of course, rank consecutively.)

Play Build from the reserve as far as you can, filling each vacancy at once from stock. When stuck, turn cards from stock and build them if possible or play them to the reserve if not. No place, however, may ever contain more than two cards, and only the uppermost is immediately available for building. There is no single wastepile to be formed as at Grandfather's, but up to four otherwise unplayable cards may be laid face up to one side as a secondary reserve. All these are simultaneously available for building when possible, thereby creating temporary vacancies for other unplayable cards turned from stock. Cards may not be reversed from suite to suite, and there is no redeal.

Poker Patience

Poker Squares
One pack

Poker Patience is the solitaire version of Poker Squares. which is a good game for any number of players. Although it does not fall into the usual run of 'building' patiences, it calls for exactly the same type of thinking as the Planners described on previous pages.

Turn twenty-five cards from a shuffled pack one by one, and place each on the table in such a way as to build up a square of $5 \times 5 = 25$ cards. A card once placed may not be moved to alter its position relative to any other placed card. The next card of the stock may not be looked at until the one just turned has been placed. The object is to make the best possible Poker hands in the resultant ten rows and columns.

There are two scoring systems: English and American. Treating each row or column as a Poker hand, count for it as follows:

	English	*American*
straight flush	30	75 (100 if 'royal')
four of a kind	16	50
straight	12	15
full house	10	25
three of a kind	6	10
flush	5	20
two pair	3	5
one pair	1	2

The English score is based on the relative difficulty of forming the various combinations in this particular game, while the American is based on their relative ranking in the game of Poker. Consider yourself to have won if you make 75 English or 200 American points.

(A straight flush is five cards in suit and sequence, counting Ace low (A–2–3–4–5) or high (10–J–Q–K–A) as preferred. An Ace-high straight flush is called a royal flush in American practice. A straight is five cards in sequence (Ace high or low ad lib) but not all of the same suit, and a flush is five of the same suit but not all in sequence. Four or three of a kind means four or three of the same rank, the other card or cards being unmatched. Full house is three of a kind plus a pair, a pair is a pair of cards of the same rank with the other three unmatched, and two pair is self-explanatory, with one odd card.)

Cribbage Square

One pack

This game is the equivalent of Poker Patience for Cribbage fans. Cribbage combinations are shorter and sharper than those of Poker, and score as follows:

> Fifteen = 2 (two or more cards whose face values, regardless of suit, total fifteen. Ace counts one, others face value, courts ten each.)
> Pair = 2 (two cards of the same rank)
> Prial = 6 (three cards of the same rank)
> Double pair royal = 12 (four cards of the same rank)
> Run = 1 per card (three or more cards in sequence, regardless of suit)
> Flush = 1 per card (hand of cards of same suit)

Play as at Poker Patience, turning up sixteen cards one by one and building a square of 4 × 4 = 16 cards. Turn the seventeenth card as the 'starter'. Score for each row and column of the square as if it were a Cribbage hand, including the starter as its fifth card. A flush is valid only if all four in a line are of the same suit, whether or not of the same suit as the starter. Count 'one for his nob' if you placed the Jack of the same suit as the starter, or 'two for his heels' if the starter is a Jack. Consider yourself to have won if you make 61 points in all. (Note: Unlike Poker combinations, cards in a Cribbage combination may be counted more than once provided that they form part of distinct combinations each time. For example, a hand containing 7–7–7–8–9 counts twelve for the double pair royal – i.e. two for each pair that can be made out of it – plus two for each of the three 7–8 combinations totalling fifteen, plus three for each of the 7–8–9 runs, for a total of 27 points.)

Packers

Packers are games in which you build cards into main suit sequences in one place and assist this process by building other cards in reverse sequence in another place called the tableau. In the Simple or Closed Packers (covered earlier) unplayable cards are thrown to a wastepile. In the Open Packers (covered later) all cards are dealt face up to start with and nothing remains hidden. Half-open Packers, as the name suggests, lie half-way between the two.

In these games a point is eventually reached at which all cards are lying face up on the table for you to examine, and the task of bringing the game to a successful conclusion (or proving that a blockage is inevitable) depends entirely upon your powers of analysis. There are several ways in which this turning point may be approached. In most games, for example, you deal some of the pack face up and play as far as you can, then deal more cards into the layout, and so on until they have all been entered. Such games are not fully open because while you are playing at an early stage you cannot foresee how later cards are going to fall. In others, such as Intelligence, all cards are dealt face up, but at a later stage they are gathered up, shuffled and redealt. Again, this makes it impossible to play the first stages in such a way as to accommodate the second, and it is only in the last stage that the game is fully open. Yet a third type is represented by Stonewall, in which all cards are dealt to start with and there is no redeal, but some of them are dealt face down, and it is not until the downcards are all turned up that the point of openness is reached.

The following games are arranged in order of increasing number of tableau columns.

Merry-go-round

Two packs
Odds in favour

Like Great Wheel, which it superficially resembles, Merry-go-round is all fuss and glitter.

Layout and object Take all the courts from both packs. Radiate the Queens from the centre so that their inner short edges delineate an octagon (see illustration): these are the 'supports'. Against the outer short edge of each one place the long edge of a King of the same suit: these are the 'horses'. Outside each King put a Jack of the same suit: these represent the boys wanting a ride on the merry-go-round, which they cannot do until they have paid the 'fare'. This is represented by building suit sequences on the Jacks. Each suite when completed is paid to an imaginary 'till' at the centre of the array, enabling the Jack to be placed on its kingly horse and so achieving the object of the game.

Play Shuffle the remainder of both packs and deal cards in pairs to each of three wastepiles in rotation. The upper card of each pair is immediately available for building or packing, as is the top card of any wastepile at any time.

Building Two suites are built on each Jack, one based on an Ace and ascending in suit and sequence to the Five, the other on a Ten and descending in the same suit to the Six. When both are complete, the fare (presumably five-and-sixpence old style, which is even more exorbitant than sixty-five pence new style) is paid to the centre and the Jack placed on the King. A Five may temporarily be placed on an adjacent Six if it turns up before the Four, or a Six on its neighbouring Five if it turns up before the Seven.

Packing The top cards of the wastepiles are not only available for building but may also be packed on one another in ascending or descending sequence regardless of suit.

Redeal When the stock is exhausted the wastepiles may be

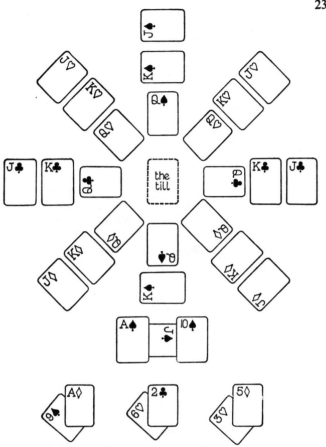

deal in pairs to three wastepiles: the top card
of each may be built or packed

MERRY-GO-ROUND   Each Jack is to be covered with its Ace and Ten
as they become available (as shown here in spades). The Aces are to be
built up in suit to the Fives and the Tens down in suit to the Sixes.
Completed suites are paid into the till, allowing the Jacks they uncover
to mount their horses (Kings). In this diagram ♦A can be founded on
♦J and ♠9 then built on ♠10.

gathered up, shuffled together and dealt again as a new stock. Only one such redeal is allowed.

Ladies' Battle

One pack
Odds in favour

Miss Jones describes this as 'a brisk and amusing little game', which does it more than justice, and adds 'there is no particular skill required in it', which is an understatement. In case you should think otherwise from the rather silly theme, it might be worth pointing out that Women's Lib began in Victorian times in all but name, even though certain persons of the present epoch seem to think they invented it.

Layout Take out the four Jacks and throw three of them away. Put the fourth at the top of the board as the apex of a triangle, and set the four Queens out in a row as its base. Complete the triangle by dealing three cards diagonally down each side. These six form the tableau, while the Queens are bases.

Object To see which Queen wins the Jack by beguiling him to her suite first. Upon each Queen base build upwards in suit and sequence, starting with the King and then proceeding from Ace to Ten. Whichever suite reaches the Ten first is crowned with the Jack.

Play Pack cards on the tableau in descending sequence and alternating colour, moving only one card at a time. Fill vacancies from the stock. When you can get no further, deal six more cards round the tableau to cover the previously exposed cards, and then see if any more packing can be done. You must deal all six before packing, and you must always deal them in the same order – top to bottom of the left side first, then top to bottom of the right. If the stock is exhausted before a Queen suite wins the Jack, gather up the tableau piles in the same order as dealt, consolidate them into a new stock and start again. Two such redeals are allowed. If this fails to make one of the Queens happy you should be taken out and beheaded.

Note No favouritism is allowed. If two or more available cards form a suit-sequence, you must play them all off before turning to another suit. This is particularly important when bystanders are betting on the result.

Stonewall

One pack
Odds against

It is the face-down cards which are likely to stonewall progress at this often aggravating little game.

Layout Deal six overlapping rows of six cards each, the first, third and fifth row face down and the others face up. Regard the result as six columns of six. Deal the remainder face up in a row, forming a reserve.

Object To release the Aces and build them up in suit to the Kings.

Play The sixteen cards of the reserve are all available for building or packing as the opportunity arises, and are not replaced. On the exposed cards of the tableau pack in descending sequence and alternating colour. When a down-card is exposed turn it face up. Any length of properly packed sequence may be shifted to another column provided that the join follows the rule. A space made by clearing out a column may be filled at any time with any available card or packed sequence.

Agnes (Sorel)

One pack
Odds against

There are two similar patiences called Agnes, one with an unusual packing rule and one with a reserve, and both stand somewhere mid-way between Klondike and Miss Milligan. By way of distinction I have given them family names borrowed from two historical Agneses. Agnes Sorel, the mistress of Charles VII, is thought to be the lady referred to as Rachel where she appears on the Queen of diamonds or clubs in some patterns of French 'named' playing cards.

Layout Deal overlapping rows of cards face up with seven in the first, then six, five and so on down to one. Regard the triangular result as consisting of seven columns varying in length from seven to one cards in that order. These form the tableau. Deal the next card face up to the top of the board as the first base.

Object To found the other three cards of the same rank as the first base as and when they become available, and to build them all up into thirteen-card suit-sequences, turning from King to Ace as necessary.

Play Pack the tableau in descending sequence and following colour, i.e. red on red and black on black, not necessarily in suit. Packed sequences of the same suit must be moved as a whole onto an exposed card of the same colour, not individually or in part-sequences. A space made by clearing out a column must not yet be filled. When you can get no further, deal seven more cards from stock, one to each column starting with the one that originally held seven, and then pause to pack again. All seven must be dealt before further play takes place. Gaps are only to be filled by each redeal. Only exposed cards on the tableau may be built on suites. When there are only two cards left in stock you may look at them before playing from the previous deal, and they must be dealt on the first two columns in the usual way. There is no redeal.

Agnes (Bernauer)

One pack
Odds against

Agnes Bernauer, after whom I have named the second of two
games called Agnes, was a commoner who married a duke at a
time when such things were deplored for their interference in
dynastic aspirations. She was drowned in the Danube 'for witch-
craft' in 1435 (12 October, if you like to commemorate these
things), but survives as the Bavarian folk-heroine known as the
Angel of Augsburg.

Layout and object Deal cards face up to a triangle of seven rows
and columns as in the previous game, but after dealing the first
base deal another row of seven cards below the tableau. These
form a reserve.

Play Cards may only be built onto suites from the tableau. Pack
the tableau in descending sequence and alternating colour, taking
cards from the reserve for this purpose whenever you can and
wish. Do not fill spaces in the reserve (yet). A space in the tableau
may be filled only with a card next lower in rank than the base. A
strict rule of packing is that properly packed sequences must be
shifted as a whole, not in part or by individual cards; but some
accounts of the game treat this as optional. When you can get no
further, deal another row of seven cards to the reserve, covering
any that may still be left and filling spaces where others have
already been taken. After dealing all seven, pause and play again.
The play of an exposed card in the reserve frees the one beneath
it. There is no redeal.

Yukon

One pack
Odds against

A more open variant of Klondike – and commemorating another gold-rush – Yukon has an unusual packing rule that relates it to the Spider family.

Layout Deal, face down, seven overlapping rows of cards with seven in the first row, six in the second, and so on down to one in the seventh. On the exposed ends of the first six columns only (ignoring the odd card at the end) deal four more cards face up, exhausting the pack.

Object To found the Aces as they become available and build them up in suit to the Kings.

Play Any faced card in the tableau may be packed on an exposed card in another column which is of opposite colour and next higher in rank. Any and all cards lying on the faced card are moved bodily with it. When a down-card is exposed, turn it face up. A space made by clearing out a column may be filled only with a King, plus any and all cards lying on it.

Carlton

Two packs
Odds against

CARLTON is a minor variant of both forms of Agnes. Deal eight columns of from one to eight cards in a triangular array, face up. Found Aces as they become available and build them up in suit to the Kings. Pack the tableau in descending sequence and alternating colour, shifting individual cards or any length of packed sequence as a whole, and filling spaces with any available card or packed sequence from the tableau. When stuck, deal eight more cards across the exposed ends of the tableau and then resume play.

MILLIGAN HARP, a cross between Harp and Miss Milligan, amounts in effect to a minor variant of Carlton, from which it differs only as follows: deal all cards face down, and turn the eight exposed cards face up. Face down-cards as they become exposed during play.

Cone

Two packs
Odds in favour

Slight points of interest are the shape of the layout and the building of four double suites.

Layout Deal seven cards face up in a row, then five across and overlapping the middle five, three across the middle five, and one across the middle three. This makes a cone-shaped tableau consisting of seven columns containing respectively 1, 2, 3, 4, 3, 2 and 1 cards.

Object To found an Ace of each suit when possible and to build them up in suit and sequence to form four double suites of twenty-six cards, the second Ace being built on the first King.

Play Exposed cards of the tableau are available for building or may be packed on one another in descending sequence and alternating colour. Cards may be shifted from column to column singly or in any length of properly packed sequence, provided that the join follows the rule. Fill a space with any exposed card or sequence, not from stock. When necessary, deal seven more cards from stock across the tableau, one per column, and resume play. When only four cards remain in stock, deal them face up to one side as a reserve. They are all simultaneously available for building or packing, but may not be packed upon and are not replaced when taken. There is no redeal.

Miss Milligan

Two packs
Odds against

A classic game, which one writer among my sources categorically refers to as 'the best patience' without further qualification, Miss Milligan seems to stick in many English people's minds as the archetypal patience of which all else are pale imitations. I cannot explain why, especially for a game that has been estimated to have a one in twenty chance of succeeding. Nor do I know the identity of the original lady, who has always evoked in my mind the spiky image of a Victorian schoolmarm. Incidentally, I suppose the title should nowadays be written 'Ms' Milligan.

Object To found all eight Aces as and when they appear and build them up in suit to the Kings.

Play Deal eight cards face up in a row. Extract any Aces and cards that may be built upon them. Do any packing that may be possible, in descending sequence and alternating colour. Cards may be moved singly or in any length of packed sequence. A space may be filled only with a King, either singly or at the base of a packed sequence. When stuck, deal eight more cards across the ends of the columns or spaces, then pause and play further. Continue until all cards have been entered into the game.

Waiving When no more cards remain in stock, and if the game gets completely blocked, you are permitted a privilege variously called waving, waiving or weaving. This entitles you to take any exposed card and hold it out as a reserve while you proceed with further building and packing among the cards thereby released. You must then properly pack the reserve on an exposed card of opposite colour and next higher in rank – if unable to do so, and still stuck, you have failed. This privilege may be taken as often as may be necessary to get the game out. In some accounts of the game, especially those which refer to the process as 'weaving', you may hold out an entire packed sequence as a reserve, of which all cards are simultaneously available. (I think 'waiving' is the best word for it.)

GIANT This close relative of *la* Milligan was said, in the 1890s, to be especially popular with the Emperor's Guards at Berlin. (The Hohenzollerns did not last long after that.) It differs from the above in two respects. First, a space in the tableau may be filled with any available card or packed sequence in whole or part. Second, the privilege that may be taken after the stock is exhausted and whenever the game blocks is to worry back cards from the suites into the tableau, provided that they pack properly. A third difference is that the chances of bringing Giant out successfully are probably in favour of the player.

Muggins

Two packs
Even chances

Muggins is an unusual and infuriating game which, when it fails, tends not to do so until the very last minute, just when you think it is going to come out right in the end. It bears some relation to a Victorian round card game called (Joe) Muggins, one of several played by Mr Pooter in the Grossmith Brothers' classic *Diary of a Nobody*.

Layout and object Deal eight cards face up in a row to start a tableau. Turn the ninth and place it in position above the tableau, forming the first base. As the other cards of the same rank become available, found them alternately below and above the tableau as bases. Build on the upper bases in ascending sequence regardless of suit, and on the lower bases in descending sequence regardless of suit, until each pile contains thirteen cards. (King and Ace are consecutive in either direction.) It is useful to project the bases slightly from the suites to act as a warning when to stop building.

Play If any of the first eight cards of the tableau are bases, or can be built on a base, put them in place and refill the gaps from stock. Then turn cards one by one from stock and deal them from left to right across the tableau to form eight piles. Normally, deal one card in turn to each pile. But whenever you turn two or more cards that are consecutive in rank, regardless of suit, keep building them on the same pile, and only pass on to the next when the sequence breaks. The sequence may go up and down ad lib, and Kings are consecutive with Aces. At any time throughout play you may take exposed cards for building on the suites, with the proviso that the base card of each of the eight piles must not be taken or moved.

Packing When you have dealt all the cards out, you may start packing on the tableau by transferring one exposed card at a time and placing it on another that is consecutive in rank. Pack and build as far as you can, but do not move the eight base cards of the tableau. Only when the game blocks may you pack or build one of them, and if that sets the game going you must wait until it blocks again before moving another. It is advisable to turn the top cards of a completed suite face down to show that it is finished. There is no redeal.

Note You are permitted to look through the tableau piles to see what they contain, and may therefore wish to arrange the layout differently so as to spread the tableau piles towards you in columns where all are visible.

New York

Two packs
Even chances

It is not always advisable to pack cards just because you can. Skill lies not only in deciding which of three wastepiles to discard to, but also in knowing when to discard rather than pack. The wastepiles may be spread towards you in columns so that all cards are visible. (The game is a hybrid between the Packers and the Planners.)

Layout and object Deal eight cards face up in a row to start the tableau, which will consist of columns spread towards you. Deal the ninth face up above this row as a base. As the other cards of the same rank as the first base turn up, put them in a row alongside it and build them all into thirteen-card ascending sequences of the same suit, turning from King to Ace as necessary.

Play Tableau cards are available for building on suites or packing on one another. Pack in descending sequence (turning from Ace to King as necessary) and alternating colour, moving only one card at a time. A vacancy made by emptying a tableau column may be filled with a top card from stock or waste.

Turn cards from stock and build or pack them if possible and desirable. If not, discard them face up to any of three wastepiles, of which each top card is always available. There is no redeal.

Algerian

Two packs
Odds against

Not to be confused with Algerine, Algerian is an interesting but difficult game. The chances of success may not be inherently against the player when enough experience has been gained, but it is certainly a tough nut to crack at first attempt.

Layout Deal eight cards face up in a row to start a tableau, and a reserve consisting of six packets of four cards each. These also are dealt face up and may be spread so that the contents of each packet are visible.

Object To found an Ace and a King of each suit as they become available, and to build them respectively upwards and downwards into thirteen-card suit sequences.

Play Do not deal any cards from the stock until you have played as far as you can and will from the initial layout. The exposed cards of the tableau and reserves (fourteen in all) are available for founding or building on suites and for packing on the tableau.

On the tableau pack cards one at a time in suit and sequence. For this purpose King and Ace are consecutive, and any exposed card may be played on any consecutive card of the same suit. A space in the tableau may be filled with any available card. In the reserve, no packing takes place and a space made by clearing out a reserve packet is not refilled. The top card of the stock is not available for play.

Whenever no further play is possible (or desirable) on the existing layout, deal two more cards face up on the exposed end of each reserve packet, then pause and resume play. Continue in this way until only eight cards remain in stock, then deal them across the tableau, one per column (regardless of whether or not they pack properly).

Continue play until the game succeeds or blocks.

Optional rule When all cards have been entered into the game and none remain in hand, a space in the reserves may be filled with a single available card until it can be built on a suite.

Unlucky Thirteen

Two packs
Odds in favour

Don't be misled by the title – this elaborate hybrid is strictly for people who can't bear unhappy endings. The rules of play are so lax that once you have set it going it will play itself through to a successful conclusion while you get on with the housework.

Layout Deal thirteen cards face up in a row to form a reserve. Below it, deal three overlapping rows of eight and regard this tableau as eight columns of three. Deal the next card face up above the row of thirteen as the first base.

Object To found the other seven cards of the same rank as the first base as they become available, and to build them all up into thirteen-card suit sequences, turning from King to Ace as necessary.

Play All cards of the reserve are simultaneously available for building on suites or packing on the tableau, and are replaced at once from stock.

Exposed cards of the tableau are available for building on suites or packing on one another in descending sequence regardless of suit, turning from Ace to King as necessary. Packed sequences may be shifted as a whole if there is a suitable card to receive them, and a space made by clearing out a column may be filled with any available card or packed sequence headed by one.

Turn cards from stock and use them for building or packing if possible. If not, discard them face up to any of eight wastepiles, of which each exposed card is available for building or packing.

As if this were not enough, the wastepiles may be gathered up and dealt again. Count a double victory if you contrive to block the game deliberately so that no further play is possible.

Senate

Congress
Two packs
Odds against

A plain and even austere game, of which Kingsdown Eights (see below) is a more palatable version.

Layout and object Take out the Aces and build them up in suit to the Kings. Below the row of Aces deal eight cards face up to start the reserve. To the right of this deal a column of four cards to start the tableau. These must not overlap, and should be dealt sideways so that when packed they extend columns towards the edge of the board.

Play Any exposed card in the reserve or tableau may be built on a suite. Pack the tableau in suit and descending sequence, using cards taken from the reserve or elsewhere in the tableau. A sequence may be packed as a whole on a suitable card. A space in the tableau must be filled at once from the reserve, but a space in the reserve must be left for the time being.

When you can or will play no further, deal another row of eight cards across the reserve in the same order as the original deal, filling vacancies or covering existing cards as the case may be. Do not resume play until all eight have been dealt.

When all cards are in play continue packing and building until the game either comes out or fails.

Kingsdown Eights

Two packs
Odds in favour

The title of this straightforward member of the Half-open Packers sounds like a cross between a dance and a horse race, but I can't vouch for either.

Layout At the top of the board deal four overlapping rows of eight cards and regard them as eight columns of four. These form a reserve. The next eight cards are to be dealt in two perpendicular rows of four each to the right and left of the space below the reserve, orientated sideways so that each can be packed into a column extending towards the edge of the board. These form the tableau.

Object To found the eight Aces in the space below the reserve as they become available and build them up in suit to the Kings.

Play The exposed cards of the reserve and tableau are available for building on suites or for packing on the tableau. Pack in descending sequence and alternating colour, moving only one card at a time. A space in the tableau may be filled with any available card at any time. No packing takes place on the reserve, and when a reserve column is cleared out it is not refilled except by the next deal. When the game blocks, or sooner if you prefer, deal four more rows of eight cards across the reserve before resuming play.

A third deal of four rows of eight to the reserve will eventually consume the rest of the pack, and if the game blocks after that it is lost.

Cicely
Two packs
Odds against

Cicely (surname unknown) is a back-to-front version of Kingsdown Eights, in that fresh cards are dealt to the tableau instead of to the reserve.

Layout Deal four overlapping rows of eight cards, and regard the tableau as eight columns of four. Deal a separate row of eight cards as a reserve.

Object To found, as they become available, an Ace of each suit down one side of the board and a King of each suit down the other, and to build the Aces up in suit to the Kings and the Kings down in suit to the Aces.

Play The exposed cards of the tableau and all those of the reserve are available for building on suites or for packing on the tableau. Pack in suit and sequence up or down ad lib, moving only one card at a time. Changes of direction are permitted in the same line of packing, but King and Ace are not consecutive. A space made in the tableau by clearing out a column must be filled by dealing into it a fresh column of four cards from stock. No packing takes place on the reserve, but when a card is played from it the space may be filled with an exposed card from the tableau (not from the stock). When stuck, or sooner if you prefer, deal four more rows of eight across the reserve and then resume play. A third deal will eventually consume the rest of the pack.

Grace Cards may be reversed between Ace and King suites if necessary, but Ace and King bases must be left intact. If the game blocks after the last deal you may (once only) take any buildable card buried in the tableau to set it going again.

Bristol

One pack
Odds against

The invention of Morehead and Mott-Smith, Bristol amounts to a hybrid of several games – or rather (I hasten to add) of the best elements of several other good games. No explanation of its title is vouchsafed.

Layout and object Deal eight fans of three cards each to start the tableau (which may be regarded as eight columns of three, if preferred). If any of them are Kings, shift them to the bottom of their fans. The object is to found the Aces as and when they become available and build them up to the Kings regardless of suit.

Play Turn cards from stock three at a time and place them one on each of three wastepiles in order from left to right. Exposed cards of the fans and wastepiles are available for building on suites or packing on the tableau. Pack in descending sequence regardless of suit, moving only one card at a time. A vacancy made by clearing off a fan is never refilled, and there is no redeal.

Note The wastepiles may be spread towards you in columns. The authors do not specifically allow this, but neither do they condone the sort of memory game it would become by keeping the piles strictly squared up.

Mount Olympus

Two packs
Odds in favour

An interesting member of the family, Mount Olympus takes its name from the traditional pictorial layout aptly representing an arc of Kings and Queens surmounting a tableau in the form of a mountain. To save space you may prefer to arrange the base cards in two rows of eight and the tableau as a row of nine below, which makes it easier to pack in columns.

Layout Extract all the Aces and Twos and arrange them in an arc at the top of the board. Alternate Aces with Twos and couple them in suits. Below, deal nine non-overlapping cards face up in the shape of a triangle (an apex, a row of three, then a row of five).

Object To build the Aces up in suit and alternating sequence (odd numbers) to the Kings and the Twos in alternating sequence (even numbers) to the Queens.

Play Pack on the nine tableau cards in suit and descending, alternating sequence, filling spaces immediately from stock. A packed sequence may be shifted in whole or part. When stuck, deal nine more cards over the tableau and play on. There is no escape if the game blocks once the stock is exhausted.

Note Another way of making a representational layout is to arrange the sixteen base cards in the form of a mountain, with one at the apex and rows of three, five and seven below. Then deal the nine cards of the tableau in an arc above this, and pack them outwards like rays. In this version the arc disappears and you are left with the mountain, instead of vice versa as described above.

Adela

Two packs
Odds against

This difficult game is similar to Herring-bone, and can be laid out in much the same pictorial fashion.

Layout Deal a tableau of nine cards face up, strictly in the form of a 3 × 3 square, but more conveniently in a row.

Object To found the Jacks as and when they become available, and build them in suit and descending sequence to the Ace. Kings and Queens act as blocks until they can be matched with their Jacks.

Play Whenever a Jack is exposed on the tableau take it as a base, arranging all eight in a line down one side of the board. One King and one Queen may be taken from the tableau for each Jack of the same suit that has been founded, and either discarded or arranged decoratively around the Jack. (See Herring-bone, page 90.) Cards in the tableau are to be packed in suit and ascending sequence, for which purpose they may be shifted singly or in whole or part sequences. Fill spaces from stock as soon as they occur. When no more packing or building can be done, deal nine more cards across the tableau and play on. There is no escape if the game blocks when the stock is exhausted.

Note The rules do not specifically state what happens to Kings and Queens in the tableau which cannot be taken because there is no spare Jack of their suit, but it would seem logical to pack an exposed King on his exposed mate when the opportunity arises.

Hammer of Thor

Two packs
Odds against

Underneath its heavy disguise, Hammer of Thor differs only in minor respects from Adela.

The object is to found the Aces as and when they appear, arranging them in the form of a hammer-of-Thor (i.e. swastika), and to build them up in suit and sequence as far as the Nines. Deal a tableau of nine cards and pack them in descending sequence regardless of suit, filling spaces from stock or with any exposed card. When stuck, deal nine more cards on the tableau. When all have been entered, and the game blocks, gather the piles or columns of the tableau to form a new stock and repeat the whole process, except that the tableau must now consist of only six cards instead of nine. Play again until you succeed or fail. Cards higher than Nine serve no purpose other than to make life difficult.

Vacuum

Two separate packs
Odds against

Very few patiences are named after anything with a remotely scientific connotation, but this is one of them. It has enough interest to compensate for the perhaps one in ten chance of succeeding, which some players may find they naturally abhor. Similar to Vacuum and its close relatives is Russian Patience, described in the following section.

Layout Take the Aces and Kings from one pack and lay the Aces out in a row at the top left of the board. Deal a row of eleven cards, of which the first four lie directly below the Aces. Place the Kings in a row above the last four, in the same order of suits as the Aces. The space of three cards width between Aces and Kings is the 'vacuum'.

Object To build the Aces up in suit to the Kings, and the Kings down in suit to the Aces.

Play If any of the first or last four cards can be built upon the Ace or King immediately in line above it, make that build and fill the space from stock. Any of the three cards beneath the vacuum may be built on an Ace or King suite regardless of position, and its space filled from stock.

When you can get no further, start dealing cards from the remainder of the first pack and then from the whole of the second pack in overlapping rows of eleven from left to right, forming the tableau into columns. Whenever a card is turned that can be built on the suite directly in line above it, or, if it is below the vacuum, on any Ace or King suite, build it instead of dealing it and turn the next card for that place. Whenever an exposed card becomes buildable in accordance with the same positional rule it may be taken, but is not replaced.

When both packs are exhausted the rules are relaxed, and any exposed card may be built on a suite regardless of position. You may also pack the tableau up and down in suit, and reverse cards between Ace and King suites if this will help the game. (Base cards, however, must be left intact.) A vacancy made by clearing a column may be filled with any exposed card or sequence from another column.

Redeal If the game blocks, gather up the first column without shuffling and place it on the second, then both on the third, and so on until you have a new stock. Turning this face down, deal and play again in the same way, remembering that some cards are restricted from building by their positions until all have been dealt. A second such redeal is permitted, but if the game blocks again you are defeated.

Note It is unclear whether or not sequences may change direction in the same line of packing. It seems right to permit such changes, but to prohibit the transfer of a mixed sequence to another column.

HOBBLED PATIENCE follows similar principles. The object is to release an Ace and a King of each suit and build them respectively upwards and downwards in suit sequences. Shuffle the two packs together and start dealing cards in overlapping rows of eleven. Before covering the first row you may extract and replace any bases and cards that can be built upon them, and fill spaces from stock. From the second row onwards, however, a card turned from stock may only be built if it is due to fall into the first, second, tenth or eleventh position in the row, and its place in the row must be taken by the next card turned (unless that can also be built, and so on). A card once placed in a row cannot be taken.

When the stock is exhausted the rules change. The tableau may be packed in suit and sequence regardless of direction, but only by one card at a time. A space made by clearing a column may be filled with any exposed card. Any exposed card may be taken for building on a suite.

If the game does not come out, gather up the columns in order from left to right, consolidate them into a new stock, and start again. Exactly the same rules apply as to the first deal, and the same relaxations ensue when all cards have been dealt. A second such redeal is permitted, but no more.

REFORM This game seems to be a corruption of Hobbled. It professes the odd rule that a turned card may only be built if it is due to fall into the first, tenth or eleventh positions in the row, ignoring the second, though I think this is due to a misinterpretation of the original rules. It allows two deals instead of three, and restricts suite-to-suite reversals to one card only per deal. In short, it seems even more hobbled than Hobbled.

Royal Family

One pack
Odds in favour

Both Royal Family and The Indefatigable (a curious title: it sounds more like a symphony by Nielsen) belong to that awkward and old-fashioned tradition by which cards are dealt face up into squared-up piles or packets. Since we can see them all when we are dealing, and since no patience is intended to be a memory game unless otherwise stated, we might as well deal them into spread columns so that all are visible throughout play.

Layout and object Found the four Kings as bases and deal the remainder into four overlapping columns of twelve each, making twelve columns of four. Build the Kings down in suit to the Aces. (Arrange the court cards of each suit, when in position, in some sort of pictorial effect to justify the title.)

Play Pack the tableau in ascending or descending sequence and alternating colour. Only one card may be moved at a time, but sequences may change direction in one column. Fill a vacancy with any available card. If and when blocked, gather up the columns in order and redeal in the same way as at first. No further redeal is permitted, or, indeed, should be necessary.

THE INDEFATIGABLE Found the four Aces as bases and deal the remainder into four overlapping columns of twelve each, making twelve columns of four. Play to build the Aces up in suit to the Kings. Pack the tableau in accordance with the same rules as above, but in suit instead of in alternating colour. Gather up and redeal as often as necessary. The game is lost only if a deal produces no playable exposed card.

Four Corners
Two packs
Even chances

This old favourite is one of the simplest and neatest of the positional patiences, in which cards may only be taken if they occupy required positions or specified alignments. The classic game in the series is St Helena, which we shall arrive at shortly.

Layout Imagine a square of $4 \times 4 = 16$ cards, with another card placed diagonally against each corner. Deal a tableau of twelve cards in the following order: top left corner, four down the left-hand side (not overlapping), bottom left corner; then the same on the right: top corner, side of four, bottom corner. This establishes a rotation for the rest of the game. If any Aces or Kings turn up in the deal, found them as bases in the two central columns of the square (as described below), and fill their places in the tableau from stock.

Object To found an Ace and a King of each suit as and when they appear, and to build them respectively up and down into thirteen-card suit sequences. The Aces are to form one column down the centre of the board and the Kings another, and each pair of adjacent bases must be of the same suit. These columns are to be formed from the top downwards, each new suit as it appears going beneath the pair of the previous suit.

Play Continue dealing cards from stock in exactly the same rotation to each of the twelve positions. Any Ace or King that

FOUR CORNERS Each round of twelve cards must be dealt in the order shown, any Aces or Kings being taken as bases and replaced. Each Ace-King pair must be of the same suit and founded from the top downwards. Cards dealt to the corners (1, 6, 7, 12) may be built as dealt if possible, but those to the sides only if horizontally aligned with the appropriate suit.

turns up may be taken as a base. A card turned from stock which is due to fall on a corner may instead be built on any suite it may fit. A card turned from stock may also be built if it is due to fall in the same horizontal row as the suite it fits, but not in any other. Whenever a card is taken in any of these ways, fill the position it would have occupied with the next unplayable card turned from stock. A card once in position on the tableau may not be taken (yet).

When the stock is exhausted the rules change. All exposed

cards may be taken for building, regardless of position. They may also be packed on one another, one at a time, in ascending or descending sequence regardless of suit, turning the corner between King and Ace and changing direction as much as may be necessary. A vacancy may be filled with any available card.

Redeal When the game blocks (which, surprisingly in view of the lax rules of play, it often does), gather up the twelve tableau piles in proper rotation and consolidate them into a new stock. Play through this again, following the same restrictive rules as in the original deal until all have been dealt, then packing and building in accordance with the relaxed rules. A second redeal is permitted.

VARIANT In Mary Whitmore Jones's account the four King bases are to occupy the top two pairs of the base columns and the four Ace bases the lower two pairs, with each group of four arranged in the same pattern of suits. If you get used to the game in one form, the other may renew the challenge.

CORNER-STONES The version of the game described by Morehead and Mott-Smith under this title differs in two respects from the original. First, it permits top cards of the central suites to be reversed onto one another when possible and desired, though Aces and Kings must be left intact. Second, it does not allow for any redeal. It is hard to determine whether these differences are deliberate or accidental, but as one is a relaxation and the other a restriction they probably cancel each other out.

St Helena

Napoleon's Favourite, Washington's Favourite
Two packs
Odds in favour

Yet another game with Napoleonic artificial flavouring, St Helena exhibits the range of alternative formats and titles that one associates with especial popularity. Oddly enough, the title most descriptive of the layout is 'Spider,' which bears no particular relationship to the family of spiders inhabiting another part of this collection.

Layout and object Put a King of each suit in a row and an Ace of each suit in a row beneath them. These are the bases. The object is to build the Aces up in suit to the Kings and vice versa.

Play Turn cards from stock and deal them in rotation as if to form a frame around the two rows, starting above the top-left King and proceeding in a clockwise direction – four above the Kings, two in a column at the right, four below the Aces, and two in a column at the left. Keep going until the stock is exhausted. But: If a turned card due to fall in the top row can be built on a King suite, build it. Similarly, a card due for the bottom row may instead be built on an Ace suite if it fits. A card due for any of the four lateral positions may be built on any suitable suite regardless of position. After building a card, fill the position it would have occupied with the next unplayable card turned from stock.

When the stock is exhausted the rules change. Any exposed card may be built, regardless of its position. You may also pack single exposed cards on one another if they are of the same suit and consecutive in value. (Ace and King are not consecutive.) A vacancy may be filled with any available card.

Redeal If the game blocks, gather up the tableau piles in reverse order of dealing, consolidate them into a new stock, turn it face down and start playing again. The positional restrictions apply again until all have been dealt, when the rules are relaxed and packing takes place again. Two such redeals are allowed in all.

VARIANTS Older accounts suggest that the two packs should not be shuffled into each other at the start of play, but this is of no great significance. One modern account declares packing to take place regardless of suit. This seems very lax for a game with two redeals.

BOX KITE The same, but with a variant rule which gets round the inconvenience of having to gather up the piles for a redeal.

When all the cards have been entered into the game, packing may take place in circular sequence – i.e. turning the corner from Ace to King or vice versa as required. To counterbalance the greater likelihood of bringing the game out (St Helena itself succeeds far more often than not) there is a restriction to the effect that a vacancy in the tableau may not be refilled. It is not a very harsh restriction.

I should add that my only source for this game merely says 'deal out the pack as in St Helena'. I assume this means in accordance with the same positional restriction on the building of cards turned from stock. If not, it is a variant of Louis, not of St Helena.

SPIDER is a similar game of which I think it would be true to say that St Helena is the variant rather than the other way round. It is presumably named from the fact that when the surrounding piles are spread out into columns, so that all are visible, eight of them look like legs. (What the other four may represent of a spider's anatomy is beyond my ability to suggest.) During the deal, pause after each fresh batch of twelve and build what you can to the suites, bearing in mind that those in line with King suites may not be built on Ace suites and vice versa. Do not replace cards taken in this way, except by the next deal around. When all cards have been entered, positional restrictions cease and exposed cards of the tableau may be packed on one another in suit and sequence. A space may be filled only with an Ace or King. Two redeals are allowed.

ONE-PACK VARIANTS All these games can be played with a single pack. The four bases consist of two red Kings in the top row and two black Aces in the bottom. There are eight tableau piles instead of twelve: two in line with Kings, two in line with Aces, and two at each end. The one-pack version of Spider is called Little Spider, but, since it has the correct number of legs, it would seem proper to refer to it as Spider and to regard the two-pack version as a Spider and a half.

Louis

St Louis, Newport
Two packs
Odds in favour

'Who's Louis?' – 'My uncle. He *was* mad.'

If this repartee fails to strike a lost chord in your memory, you will have to consult your elders and betters. Nor is it inappropriate, for the game of Louis has been somewhat madly dealt with. It is usually described as a variant of St Helena, but as it lacks the positional element which is that game's most distinguishing feature it legitimately calls for a heading of its own. Various copyists have garbled the rules in the course of transmission. Those which follow are of the earliest account to hand.

Layout and object Take an Ace and a King of each suit and put them in two rows of bases. Build them respectively upwards and downwards in suit.

Play Deal cards face up into twelve piles around them starting at top left and proceeding in clockwise order (as at St Helena). If a turned card can be built on any suite, build it and deal the next card to the next position. Once you have dealt a card to its position on the perimeter, you must leave it there until the stock is exhausted.

When the stock is exhausted, you may pack on the tableau upwards and downwards in suit, moving only one card at a time. Changes of direction are permitted in the same pile, but the sequence is not continuous between Ace and King. Fill a vacancy with any exposed card.

When stuck, gather up the piles in reverse order of dealing, turn them into a new face down stock, and deal again. Two such redeals are permitted.

Notes Modern accounts state that Louis is played like St Helena to the extent that cards may only be built during the deal if they fall in the correct position relative to the top or bottom row.

There is no such rule in the earliest account I know, which dates from about 1860, though it is not an excessively harsh one if taken by itself.

But it is usually reported in conjunction with another restriction to the effect that cards may not be built during the deal in any circumstance: they must be put into position and left there until all have been dealt around. Such a conjunction of restrictions makes the game almost impossible to bring out. I rather suspect that someone has misinterpreted an original line of copy which is admittedly rather ambiguous.

The 1860 book (by Blanccœur) says of cards in the tableau: 'When they have once been laid down, (they) cannot be made use of in the play until the whole of the cards have been dealt out.' But does this mean that turned cards must be laid down instead of being built if possible? In his 1920 translation of the German edition of this account, Hoffman adds an explanatory footnote to this rule as follows: 'Any card turned up in the course of play may at once be played (if its suit and value permit) to a given foundation. But if it is not so played, and another card is dealt, the first then ceases to be playable until the whole are distributed.' I am quite sure that Hoffman's interpretation is the right one, and that conflicting modern accounts are wrong on this point.

Also in the *Illustrated Book of Patience Games* referred to above is an interesting rule that seems to have got lost in later copies. Suppose you have an Ace suite built up to the Seven and its corresponding King suite to the Nine, and you turn up the Eight. You may now put this Eight to one side in abeyance until you turn up either the other Seven or the other Nine, at which point you must immediately build it in conjunction with the Eight. In effect, this is a limited form of suite-to-suite reversal.

It would appear from this that Louis might be the older form, and St Helena a derivative made by introducing the restriction about building according to position, but compensated by permitting the player to pack regardless of suit.

On the other hand, it is possible that the Comtesse de Blanccœur is wrong, and simply failed to grasp or at least perpetuate the positional rule. In favour of this possibility is the fact that without the positional element there is no point in dealing cards around the bases in a frame: the tableau might just as well consist of twelve columns of cards spread towards the player.

French Blockade

Two packs
Odds against

French differs from British Blockade in that it is not a true blockade in the sense explained in the introduction to the Blockade family. In fact, it is no more than a slightly elaborated packer. The purpose of keeping rows separate instead of overlapping is to show quite clearly where spaces are to be filled before a new row is dealt. The following description is based on the intelligible portions (few in number) of several conflicting accounts.

Object To found the eight Aces as they become available and build them up in suit to the Kings.

Play Deal a row of twelve cards face up from left to right. These are available for founding, building, or packing on one another in suit and descending sequence. Fill vacancies from stock. Play and fill again as often as you can and wish.

At any time when all vacancies have been filled, deal another row of twelve cards below the first. Do not overlap the first row, and do not resume play until all twelve are in place. Play the second row in the same way as the first. A space made in the new row releases the card immediately above it for building, or for packing in conjunction with any exposed and released card, but when such a space is refilled it again blocks the card above. At any desired stage in the proceedings, fill all spaces from stock in order from left to right and from the top row down. You may then resume play or else deal a new row of twelve, but you must always refill all spaces before dealing a new row. There is no redeal.

Notes Except in the case of the first row, you must finish filling spaces before resuming play. If a card dealt to a new row is of the same suit and one lower in rank than the one immediately above it in the next row you may pack it to create a vacancy, but the privilege does not hold whenever the lower card is blocked by one below it. When a 'lane' is created by the removal of all cards in a column you may fill the vacancy in the top row with any exposed card that is not blocked. Cards may only be packed one at a time. When playing from a packed sequence you are not obliged to build all the constituent cards.

BLOCKADE The game described by Morehead and Mott-Smith under this name is superficially similar, but (a) packed sequences may be shifted *en bloc* and (b) spaces are not refilled, but when a whole tableau column is cleared out it is restarted with the top top card of stock. For this reason the rows are piled up instead of being dealt separately. The game described under the same title by Hoffman (from *Le Livre Illustré des Patiences*) is essentially French Blockade, except that 'lanes' must be refilled from stock.

Algerine

Three or more packs
Odds against

Algerine is to Algiers as tangerine is to Tangiers – except that a tangerine is a delicious fruit and an algerine is a sort of archaic pirate. A sumptuous space-and-time consuming game, supposed to be played with at least four packs and up to six, it was evidently designed for shipwreckees.

Layout Start with a single complete pack and shuffle the others together. Deal the shuffled single pack face upwards in four rows of thirteen, with no cards overlapping. Regard the tableau as consisting of thirteen columns.

Object To found the Aces of all the packs as they become available, and build them up in suit and sequence to the Kings.

Play In each of the thirteen columns only the lowest card (the one nearest you) is available for building a suite. When taken, it releases the next one above it in the same column for the same purpose.

Any uncovered card in the tableau may be packed on another which is next higher in rank and of opposite colour, but only if it is in the same or a higher row. No card may be packed on one in a lower row. When all the cards of a column are taken, the vacancy may be filled with a single (unpacked) card taken from the lowest position of another column. It may not be filled from stock.

Having played as far as you can, turn cards from stock and build or pack them if possible or else discard them face up to any of three wastepiles. The top card of each wastepile is always available for building or packing, but not for restarting a vacant column.

There is no redeal.

Drop

Two separate packs
Odds against

This game starts off like blank verse. When it begins to rhyme, resemblances will be found to such 'fan' games as Belle Lucie and House on the Hill.

Layout Take the first pack and 'drop' out of it thirteen packets of cards, face down, with at least three and at most six cards in each packet. Turn the exposed cards of each packet face up. These form the tableau.

Object To found all eight Aces (eventually) and build them up in suit to the Kings.

Play Exposed cards of the tableau may be taken for building or else packed on one another in descending sequence of the same suit. Throughout the game, only one card may be moved at a time. Down-cards are turned face up when they become exposed. Fill a space with any exposed card to restore the number of packets to thirteen.

When no further play is possible, take the second pack and deal all cards from it, one at a time, face up to any or all of the thirteen packets in any order you choose. That done, resume play as before, but this time do not refill a space made by clearing out all the cards of a packet. There is no redeal.

Note Whitmore Jones does not explicitly state that all cards of the second pack must be distributed before any further building takes place, but this restriction is assumed in order to make a more interesting and skilful game.

Kaiser Bill

Two packs
Odds in favour

Space-consuming patiences that force you to pack cards in piles rather than columns have gradually lost out in popularity stakes. But this particular example has become a great favourite of mine, and I can assure you it is well worth the effort of sorting through piles of cards to see what can be done. You will nearly always break through to the delight of discovering that an apparently hopeless position yields, on closer examination, what Chess pundits call a 'winning resource'.

Layout Deal three rows of nine cards face up, starting at the top row and dealing from left to right. Do not overlap any, but space them out as much as you can. These form the tableau.

Object To found the Aces as and when they become available, and build them up in suit and sequence to the Kings.

Play Throughout the game cards may only be founded and built that come from the lowest position in a column. Thus at the start of play an Ace and any cards buildable upon it may only come from the lowest of the three rows. However, the removal of a card in that row frees the one above it, and if this should also be taken for building it frees in turn the corresponding card in the top row. Do not yet fill any spaces made by building or packing.

Cards on the tableau may be taken for packing on one another in descending sequence of the same suit. Any exposed card or packed sequence of cards (in whole or part) may be packed on a suitable exposed card anywhere in the layout, not necessarily in the same row or column.

When stuck, or sooner if you prefer, deal another twenty-seven cards over the tableau in the same order as the original deal, placing them upon vacancies or packings as the case may be. Do not start playing again until the deal is complete. Remember that cards may only be built from the bottom of a column, so that a card in the top row is only buildable when both lower positions are vacant.

Two more deals take place in the same way, the second of which will exhaust the pack and peter out along the bottom row. The game is then entirely open to analysis and there is no way out if it blocks completely. With proper play, however, it will rarely fail.

Note If you find success going to your head, have a go at Tramp instead (page 279). It is much the same, but harder.

Martha

One pack
Odds in favour

A suitably relaxing little game to play after a hard day's work, Martha may be regarded as belonging to the same circle as Miss Milligan.

Layout and object Extract the Aces and play to build them up in suit and sequence to the Kings. Deal the remaining cards out in four overlapping rows of twelve, the first and third face up and the others face down. Regard the result as twelve columns of four.

Play Exposed cards are available for building. Pack the tableau in descending sequence and alternating colour, moving one card at a time or any length of properly packed sequence. When a down-card is exposed turn it face up. A vacancy in the tableau may be filled only with a single available card. There is no redeal.

Burleigh

One pack
Even chances

This is one of the few patiences intended to be played as an exercise of memory. You can evade this by spreading the piles of cards towards you so that all are visible, but there is no point in doing so as the game offers little else by way of interest. Which of many Burleighs it might be named after is open to suggestion.

Layout and object Deal twelve cards face up to start the tableau. The object is to found the Aces as and when they appear and to build them up in suit to the Kings.

Play Do any founding and building that may be possible from the layout, and fill gaps from stock. Cards in the layout may also be packed on one another in suit and sequence, forming piles with the lowest number on top and the highest underneath. A card may be placed on top of a pile if it is next lower in rank than the previous top card, or slipped beneath the pile if it is next higher than the previous bottom card. You must, however, remember what the bottom card is: all the piles must be kept squared up to prevent direct knowledge of their contents. A pile may be placed on top of another, provided that it follows the suit-sequence at the join.

When you have packed and built as far as possible and filled all the spaces, turn cards one by one from the top of the stock, and place each one on top of or at the bottom of an appropriate pile. When you reach a card that will not fit, put it to one side face up and start dealing cards off the bottom of the pack. (Or, if you are already doing so for the same reason, start dealing again from the top.) Pack the card held in reserve as soon as you can, for if a second unplayable card turns up before the first is placed the game has failed.

By the time you have run out of cards you should be able to build all the suites to completion by running down the piles on the tableau. If you are unable to run through a pile because the sequence is broken you have lost the game through lapse of memory.

Boomerang

Two short packs
Even chances

Morehead and Mott-Smith devised these two intriguing games to fill a gap caused by under-exploitation of themes in certain areas of patient endeavour. The aptly titled Boomerang is designed for play with a Bézique pack – that is, a 64-card double pack that counts Ace high and omits all cards lower than Seven. Sudden Death, which is descriptive of how the game ends if you fail to get it out, is a version designed for play with a Pinochle pack – a double pack lacking all ranks lower than Nine.

Layout Deal a tableau of twelve cards in three rows of four, none overlapping.

Object To found one Seven of each suit as it appears, and to build each up in the following suit-sequence: 7–8–9–10–J–Q–K–A–K–Q–J–10–9–8–7–A.

Play Any exposed card in the tableau may be taken as a base or built on a suite, and if its removal leaves a space fill it immediately with the next card from stock. Exposed cards may also be packed on one another in suit and either ascending or descending sequence, but not both in the same pile. (Thus an Ace may be packed only on a King, and terminates an ascending sequence; but a King or a Seven may be packed on a lone Ace to start a descending or ascending sequence respectively.)

All cards must be played one at a time. You lose the game if and when you turn a card that cannot be placed.

SUDDEN DEATH The same, but played with a 48-card pack. Deal a tableau of only ten cards. The required suites run 9–10–J–Q–K–A–K–Q–J–10–9–A.

Castles in Spain

One pack
Odds in favour

This is an easy little game similar to Martha. The title is vaguely pictorial.

Layout and object Deal thirteen packets of four cards each face down, and turn the top cards face up. Found Aces as and when they appear and build them up in suit to the Kings.

Play Top cards of the piles are available for building suites or packing on one another in descending sequence and alternating colour. Only one card may be moved at a time. When a down-card is exposed turn it face up. A vacancy made by clearing out a pile may be refilled with any exposed card.

Note The piles may be spread towards you in columns in order to give you something to think about, but then it will hardly ever fail to come out. If you leave them in squared-up packets you at least have the challenge of a memory test, as in Burleigh. A completely open version of the same game is Spanish Patience.

Heads and Tails

Regiment
Two packs
Even chances

An enjoyable and well-named game, rather like Kaiser Bill but with an element of risk.

Layout and object Deal eight cards in a row face up (the heads), then below and in line with them eight packets of eleven cards each, all face down except the uppermost cards (the reserves), and below them a final row of eight cards face up (the tails). The object is to found an Ace and a King of each suit when possible and to build them respectively upwards and downwards into thirteen-card suit sequences.

Play The heads and tails form a tableau of sixteen cards, which are available for building on suites or packing on one another one at a time. Pack in suit and sequence, ascending or descending ad lib and with changes of direction permitted. (Spread the heads into upward and tails into downward columns for convenience.) A vacancy in the tableau must be filled by turning the top card of the reserve packet immediately in line with it and laying it face up in position. If there is no packet aligned with it (all the cards of the packet having been absorbed) take instead the top of the nearest packet on its left if any, or furthest on its right if not. There is no redeal.

Intelligence

Two packs
Odds against

Despite its title, Intelligence is a less intelligent version of House on the Hill and its variants. Whereas these are fully open games, Intelligence starts with only half the pack revealed.

Layout Deal eighteen fans of three cards each, face up. If any Aces appear, put them to one side as bases and replace them from stock. The object is to found all the Aces and build them up in suit to the Kings.

Play Exposed cards of the fans may be taken one at a time for building, or for packing on one another in ascending or descending sequence of the same suit. Aces and Kings are not consecutive. When the last card of a fan is taken, deal three cards from stock to form a new one. If the game blocks, or when no cards remain in stock, gather up all cards except those built in suites, shuffle them together, and deal them all out in fans of three again. (The last 'fan' may have only one or two cards.) Two such redeals are allowed.

Rainbow

Two packs
Odds against

This attractive but recalcitrant game is the packers' version of Crescent.

Layout and object Take one Ace and one King of each suit and found them as bases. The object is to build them respectively upwards and downwards into thirteen-card sequences. Then deal sixty cards in twenty fans of three arching over the bases in representation of a rainbow. These constitute the tableau.

Play Exposed cards of the tableau are available for building on suites or packing on one another. Pack upwards or downwards in suit, changing direction if necessary but not regarding Ace and King as consecutive. Move only one card at a time. A space made by clearing out a fan is refilled with a new three-card fan dealt from the stock. Cards of the same suit may be reversed from suite to suite when consecutive in rank, but base cards must be left intact.

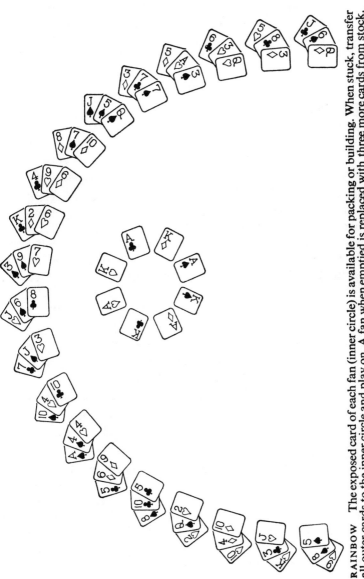

RAINBOW The exposed card of each fan (inner circle) is available for packing or building. When stuck, transfer all outer cards to the inner circle and play on. A fan when emptied is replaced with three more cards from stock. In this diagram, ♥K down to the Four, ♠A can be built up to the Four. ♥K down to the Jack, and two Queens (diamonds and spades) played to their respective Kings. There are also several opportunities for packing, such as ♥6 to ♥7 (releasing ♦2 for building) and the left-hand ♦10 to ♦9, permitting diamonds to be built up to the Four.

When play ceases, transfer the bottom card of each fan to the top, thus exposing it for further play. This process may be repeated twice more.

Zodiac

Two packs
Odds against

This tough but excellent game is described in the volume by Lady Cadogan which is one of the earliest of patience books in English, but has rarely appeared in later collections. A probable reason is that successive compilers have taken one look at the space-consuming layout and assumed that such apparent elaboration could not possibly conceal anything worthy of serious attention. My suggestion that the odds are against success is frankly based on my own failure to bring it out, but I feel uncomfortably sure that an expert player would beat the pack more often than not.

Layout Deal eight cards in a row face up to form a reserve called the 'equator'. Deal twenty-four more cards face up in a circle around the equator to form a tableau called the 'zodiac'. (Or, to save space, deal them in three rows of eight below the reserve.)

Object The eventual object is to build four Ace-King and four King-Ace suit sequences, but, as no building is done until all cards are in position, the real object is to enter and pack cards in such a way that they will finally come off in the right order.

Play The twenty-four cards of the zodiac-tableau cannot be taken or moved until the end of the game. They can only be packed upon, and the cards packed on them are also non-transferable once in position.

Any card in the equator may be packed on an exposed card of the zodiac if it is of the same suit and consecutive in rank. Changes of direction are permitted on the same pile, but King and Ace are not consecutive. Vacancies in the equator are filled from the top of the waste pile, or, when this is empty, from stock.

Turn cards from stock one by one and pack them on the zodiac if possible. If not, discard them face up to a single waste-pile, the top of which is always available for packing or filling vacancies.

Turn the wastepile as often as may be necessary and deal through it again until all cards have been entered into the layout. (If they cannot all be entered, you have already failed.) When all have been entered, build four different suit sequences from Ace up to King and four others from King down to Ace, taking for this purpose successively exposed cards of the zodiac and those of the equator. Suite-to suite reversal is not permitted.

Robin Post

Two packs
Odds in favour

Robin Post is a superb positional patience invented by Col. G. H. Latham and first published in George Hervey's *Card Games for One*. How would you set about arranging fifty-two cards in the form of a regular hexagon? It was the brilliance of this design that first attracted my attention.

Layout From the shuffled double pack deal the first fifty-two cards in the form of a regular hexagon – i.e. a top row of four cards with a card's width between each pair; below that a row of five cards, of which the three central ones lie immediately below the spaces in the top row, and such that all cards lie diagonally or point-to-point with one another; then similarly rows of six, seven, eight, seven, six, five and four. (See illustration.)

Object To found an Ace and a King of each suit as they become available, and to build them respectively upwards and down-wards into thirteen-card suit-sequences.

Play A card whose four corners are touching the corners of four other cards is blocked, and may be neither moved nor packed

ROBIN POST   Fifty-two cards are dealt face up in the form of a regular hexagon – an outstanding *tour de force* in the geometry of Patience!

upon. A card with two or more corners free may be taken for building or packing. A card with one corner free may not be moved but may be packed upon in ascending or descending sequence and alternating colour. A sequence may not change direction in the same pile, but may be taken as a whole (not in part) and either reversed onto a single unblocked card (not another sequence) of the proper rank and colour, or packed without reversal onto any unblocked card or sequence of the proper rank and colour.

Cards may be reversed between Ace and King suites of the same suit whenever possible, but Ace and King bases must be left intact.

When blocked, or earlier if preferred, deal the remaining fifty-two cards over the whole array, one to each position on top of vacancies, single cards or sequences as the case may be in the same order as the original deal. Continue play as before until the game succeeds or fails.

Note The rules as published refer to whole-sequence reversal onto individual unblocked cards in the tableau, but say nothing either for or against shifting whole packed sequences without reversal. As nothing is said to the contrary, we must assume (as above) that customary rules apply. The rules also fail to state whether a card with two or more corners free may be packed upon, or whether it is only available to be taken. I would assume the latter to be the case.

Tramp

Two packs
Odds against

So called from its ragged appearance, observes Miss Jones in a brilliant flash of guesswork, Tramp is the more soul-destroying version of Kaiser Bill. Count half a victory for completing as many as four suites.

Layout and object Deal thirty-six cards in four rows of nine, none of them overlapping and with plenty of space between them. Lay the thirty-seventh card face down to one side as a reserve. Found all eight Aces as they become available and build them up in suit to the Kings.

Play Any exposed card in the bottom row is available for founding or building on a suite. A vacancy made in the bottom row frees the card in the row immediately above it for building; if both positions are vacant the third card up is freed, and a card in the top row is only free when there are three vacancies below it.
 Cards in the tableau are available for packing on one another in suit and descending sequence, either singly or in whole packed sequences. A card or sequence may be packed on any suitable card either in the same row or anywhere in a lower row, but may not be moved upwards into a higher row. Vacancies are not to be filled except by the deal.

When stuck, or earlier if preferred, deal the next thirty-six cards over the tableau in the same order as before, filling vacancies or covering cards as the case may be. Lay the next card face down to one side as a second reserve card.

When blocked again, deal enough cards to cover the top three rows (twenty-seven in all). There will be three left over. These are to be added to the reserve, which is now turned face up, and of which all five cards are simultaneously available for packing and building.

Belle Lucie

Alexander the Great, Clover Leaf, Fair Lucy, Midnight Oil
One pack
Odds against

Imitation being the sincerest form of flattery, the original 'fair Lucy' must have been a vision of loveliness if we may judge by the number of imitators surrounding her. I had intended to put all these and the two-pack versions into a separate section entitled 'Fans' from the way the cards of the tableau are laid out, but closer examination showed that the games are not sufficiently distinct from one another to merit such attention. Visually, they share a distinctively attractive feature. In each case the tableau consists of cards dealt face up in groups or sweeps of three at a time, forming what look like fans rather than columns. (The name 'fan' is emphasized by the related game of that name, in which all the fans are arranged in the form of a single large fan, as illustrated.) The exposed card of each fan is available for packing or building exactly as would be the case if the groups of three were dealt in columns. When dealing these games out, allow plenty of room for packing to take place in a sideways direction from each fan. Similar games include Fan, Bristol, Intelligence, Rainbow and House on the Hill.

Layout and object Deal all the cards face up in eighteen fans, seventeen of three cards and one left over (or, if preferred, in sixteen of three cards and two of two). Play to release the Aces and build them up in suit to the Kings.

Play Uncovered cards are available for building on suites or for packing on one another in suit and descending sequence. Move only one card at a time. Do not refill a vacancy made by clearing off a fan. There may never be more than eighteen fans.

Redeals When stuck, gather up the cards of the tableau, shuffle them and redeal again in as many fans of three as possible (plus an odd fan of one or two cards if necessary). Two such redeals are allowed.

TREFOIL (Les Fleurons) is the same as Belle Lucie, except that the Aces are taken out and founded to start with, and the rest dealt in sixteen fans of three.

DEMON FAN is similar to Belle Lucie, but the fans are dealt face down and only the top card of each is exposed. Packing takes place in alternating colours. Six redeals are allowed. It is a silly game.

SUPER FLOWER GARDEN is the same as Belle Lucie, except that packing takes place regardless of suit, which puts it rather more in favour of the player. (Its title seems to have undergone confusion with another game in the course of oral transmission.)

Spiders

Small in number but distinctive in habits are Half-open Packers that exhibit the following remarkable feature: that you are not required to release certain base cards and build suites on them away from the tableau, but instead do all your building within the tableau itself. As soon as you have completed a thirteen-card suit sequence, or whatever else the particular rules of the game may specify, you simply take it out of the tableau and carry on with the rest. In this way, if successful, you gradually eliminate the whole pack in built suites, one at a time.

The archetypal game of this family is called Spider (though not identical with the eight-limbed patience of that name described by Cavendish and others – see Index). It was the happy thought of Morehead and Mott-Smith, some time during the 1930s, to retitle similar games with names recalling the arachnid relationship, such as Spiderette and Scorpion. This excellent idea has unfortunately not been pursued by subsequent inventors, but I do recommend the practice to others who may follow with compositions of their own.

One or two examples of this procedure are entirely 'open' or analytical games and will be found among the Open Packers: see Curds and Whey and Mrs Mop.

German Patience

Two packs
Odds against

This rarely recorded patience looks ridiculously easy at first sight, but turns out to be cunning in its deceptiveness. It is one of my favourites.

Layout and object Deal eight cards face up. Each of them may act as a base, and the object is to build upon a base in ascending sequence regardless of suit until it contains thirteen cards (ranking continuously via King, Ace etc.). The end product is therefore eight piles of thirteen cards.

Play Before turning any cards from stock, you may build as far as you can and will amongst cards on the table, filling the vacancies they leave with cards turned from stock so that there are always eight bases. When you can or will proceed no further, turn cards from stock and build them if possible or discard them face up to a single wastepile if not. Throughout the game, the top card of any suite may be built upon the top of any other if it fits. In this way it is sometimes possible to whittle a pile far enough down to receive the top card of the wastepile, or to clear one out entirely so that its space may be occupied by a new base turned from stock or taken from the top of the wastepile. It is important to keep track of each suite, and to turn it face down as soon as it reaches its full complement of thirteen, after which it goes out of play. No redeal is allowed. Every effort must therefore be made to deplete the wastepile by the judicious transfer of available cards in the layout.

Simple Simon

One pack
Odds against

If Simple Simon must be retitled to bring it into line with other members of the family, I suppose we should call it 'Little Ms Muffet'.

Layout Deal all cards face up in overlapping rows, with ten in the first row, nine in the second, and so on down to three in the eighth. Regard the tableau as consisting of ten columns of diminishing length.

Object To build four thirteen-card sequences from King to Ace in the tableau.

Play Exposed cards in the tableau are available for packing on one another in descending sequence regardless of suit. Available cards must be moved one at a time, but a packed sequence of cards of the same suit – note the proviso – headed by an exposed card may be lifted as a whole and packed on a suitable card. A space made by clearing out a column may be filled with any available card or suit sequence. There is no redeal.

SPIDERETTE Deal twenty-eight cards in seven packets face down, with seven in the first packet, six in the second, and so on down to one in the last. Turn the top cards face up. These form the tableau. The object is to build four suit sequences in the tableau, each one being eliminated upon completion. Play as described above (Simple Simon), turning down-cards face up when they are exposed. When stuck, deal seven more cards across the tableau from the stock, then play on. The last deal will be of only three cards, which must be distributed in the same order as the first three of each previous deal.

WILL O' THE WISP A variant of Spiderette (by Morehead and Mott-Smith) whereby the chances of success are improved from about 1 in 20 to 1 in 4. The only difference is that the layout consists of three overlapping rows of seven cards, the first two face down and the third face up, making seven columns of three.

Spider

Two packs
Odds against

The patriarch of the spider family is more amenable than most of his relatives, chances of success being of the order of one in three according to those who have worked it all out. The game is said to have been a particular favourite of Franklin D. Roosevelt.

Layout Deal fifty-four cards face down in ten piles, with six in each of the first four and five in the others. Turn the top cards face up.

Object To build eight thirteen-card suit sequences from King to Ace in the tableau, eliminating them one by one from the game when they start to get in the way. You need not discard them as soon as you can, but you must eventually discard them all.

Play Exposed cards are available for packing on one another in descending sequence regardless of suit. When a down-card is exposed, turn it face up. A packed sequence of cards may, provided they are all of the same suit, be shifted as a whole so long as the join follows the rule (descending but not necessarily in suit). Fill a vacancy with any exposed card plus any suit-sequence properly packed on it. When stuck, or earlier if preferred, deal ten more cards across the tableau, one to each column in the same order as dealt, and then resume play.

Microbe

Two separate packs
Odds against

Microbes do not belong to the arachnidae, but the Victorians were not very good at taxonomy. Perhaps they thought microbes looked like stripy caterpillars.

Layout Deal four overlapping rows of eleven cards each, the first and third rows face down and the others face up. Regard the tableau as eleven columns of four. Shuffle the odd eight cards into the second pack.

Object To build eight thirteen-card sequences running not in suit but in alternating colour (red Queen on black King, black Jack on red Queen etc.). A completed sequence is called a microbe, and is removed from the tableau.

Play Pack the tableau in descending sequence and alternating colour, facing down-cards as they become exposed. Any length of properly packed sequence may be shifted as a whole. Fill a vacancy with any exposed card together with any packed sequence it may head. When stuck, or earlier if preferred, deal another card face up to the end of each column and resume play. When all the cards have been entered there is a restriction on play: you may no longer fill any vacancy made by clearing out a column.

King Edward

Two packs
Odds against

This one sounds more like a potato than a spider. Perhaps, by way of correction, it should be renamed after, say, Robert the Bruce. It is my favourite member of the family, though I have not yet succeeded in winning.

Object To build a tableau of eight columns, each of which is headed by a King and runs in descending sequence and alternating colour to an Ace.

Play Deal eight cards face up in a row. Start any packing that may be possible, in descending sequence and alternating colour. Remove any Aces and put them to one side: they need not be entered until the end of the game. You may also remove a Two if there is no Three to pack it on, but may not at any time hold out two of the same suit. Do not fill vacancies except by the next deal.

Having packed as far as you can, deal another row of eight cards overlapping the first row, then pause and play again. Both Aces and one Two of each suit may be put to one side as before. Pack only one card at a time, and do not fill vacancies except by the next deal. Continue alternately dealing and packing until all cards have been entered.

Now the rules change (for the better). The top *and* bottom cards of each column are available for packing, together with any length of properly packed sequence attached to them. Any end card and attached sequence may be shifted as a whole to the top or bottom of any column, always provided that the join follows the rule of packing and that cards always descend in sequence from the covered to the exposed end. If a vacancy is created it may be filled with any available card or sequence, but when a suite is completed from King to Ace it is not removed from the table and therefore does not create another vacancy. The Twos and Aces may be added at any time. (Ace and King are not to be treated as consecutive in rank.)

Note The rules given by Whitmore Jones fail to state whether or not it is permissible *before* all cards are dealt to shift whole sequences instead of individual cards or to fill a vacancy with an exposed card or sequence. The game is so difficult without either possibility that we may be justified in assuming such licence.

Scorpion

One pack
Odds against

Scorpion is rather more subtle than your average spider, and is aptly named (by Morehead and Mott-Smith, who fail to identify the original) for the sting in its tail represented by the few cards dealt face down.

Layout Deal forty-nine cards in seven overlapping rows of seven, the first four cards in each of the first three rows face down and all the others face up. Regard the tableau as seven columns of seven. Put the odd three cards face down to one side as a reserve.

Object To build four thirteen-card suit sequences from King to Ace in the tableau and eliminate them.

Play Exposed cards in the tableau may be packed upon in suit and descending sequence. (A King may not be built on an Ace.) Any up-card in the tableau may be taken for this purpose, even if partly covered, but all cards above it up to and including the exposed one must be taken with it and packed as a whole in the appropriate place. Whenever a down-card is uncovered, turn it face up. A space made by clearing out a column may be filled only by a King, together with any and all cards that may be covering it. When stuck, deal the three reserve cards face up across the exposed ends of the first three columns and continue play.

Note Need it be assumed that play must come to a standstill before we are permitted to deal out the reserve cards? If not, an additional element of skill and judgement is brought out in deciding at what point to make use of the reserve.

Rouge et Noir

Two packs
Odds against

The invention of Charles Jewell, this game is a combination of several themes. Strictly speaking it is only half a spider – a four-legged one perhaps? – and is unfortunate in its choice of title, which has already been used for several different games. To compensate, however, it was never more appropriate.

Layout Deal nine overlapping rows of cards face down, with nine in the first, eight in the second, and so on down to one in the ninth. Regard the triangular tableau as consisting of nine columns of decreasing length, and turn the uncovered card of each column face up.

Object The object is twofold. First, to release any two black Aces and any two red ones as they become available, to make bases of them and build them up in colour (not necessarily in suit) to the Kings. Simultaneously, to build within the tableau four thirteen-card sequences descending from King to Ace in alternate colours. (These must necessarily be founded on two red and two black Kings.)

Play Pack the tableau in descending sequence and alternating colour. When a down-card is uncovered, turn it face up. Move one card at a time, together with any length of properly packed sequence that may be attached to it. Exposed cards are available for starting and building Ace suites, which are to be built in colour – that is, red on red and black on black but otherwise regardless of suit. When a King suite is completed, remove it from the tableau. A vacancy made by clearing out a column may be filled only with a King – either one that is itself exposed, or which lies at one end of a properly packed sequence with an exposed card at the other. The tableau may contain up to ten columns at any given time, and should therefore be regarded as containing a vacancy at the start of play.

When you can proceed no further, deal one more card face up to the end of each column or vacancy as the case may be. That will be ten cards in all, except on the last deal, when there will be only nine.

It is not compulsory to discard a King suite as soon as you can, but all four must be discarded before the game is won.

Part Three

OPEN GAMES

**presenting definite problems
to be solved by positional analysis**

Open Builders

Builders are games in which you build cards into suit sequences without the assistance of packing in reverse sequence. The distinguishing feature of Open Builders is that all cards are dealt face upwards at the start of play, presenting you with the same sort of open, positional or 'definite' problem as may be encountered in Chess or similar board games. All you have to do is study the position and work out the most effective order in which cards must be taken up to complete the building of the suites. They are undoubtedly thinking rather than doing games, and for this reason tend to require more time.

It does not follow that perfect play will always lead to a successful conclusion, because in any game it is always possible for the distribution to fall against you. The shuffling of cards may produce a particular position in which a kink or blockage can never be overcome. This need not be held to negate the skill factor. Before play, examine the position and decide whether or not it will come out. If not, count half a moral victory for gathering up the cards and reshuffling, thereby effecting a tactical advance to the rear and proving that discretion is the better part of valour. Once you have started play, however, you should feel duty bound to go on to the sweet or bitter end, and count a double defeat for failing to bring it out.

As a general rule, always look ahead to the consequences of any move you are about to make, and never build anything just because you can. There may sometimes be an advantage in holding back. Remember that although perfect play will not secure a win against a blockage in the deal, a single false move can lead to the loss of an otherwise winnable game.

294

Stalactites

Old Mole, Grampus
One pack
Odds in favour

This open Builder has a clearly descriptive title, but is not quite as straightforward as it looks.

Layout Deal the first four cards face up in a row as bases at the top of the board. It is advisable to orientate them horizontally rather than vertically, so that you will be able to see what the bases are when you subsequently build on them. Deal the remainder face up in eight columns of six.

Object To build the bases up into thirteen-card suit sequences, turning the corner from King to Ace as necessary, building either consecutively or in twos.

Play Decide whether to build consecutively (e.g. J–Q–K–A–2–3– etc.) or in twos (J–K–2–4– etc.). Whichever you choose must apply to all suites. All eight exposed cards are available for building. You are allowed a two-card reserve during play – up to two cards at any time may be taken from anywhere in the layout and held out until they can be built. (It is not clear if they can then be replaced, but the working of my source seems to imply this.) A space made by emptying a column is not refilled.

Archway

Two packs
Odds against

Archway is my open adaptation of one of my favourite 'closed' patiences, Lady of the Manor. Even opening the game up does not greatly improve your chances of success, though it increases the skill factor.

Layout Remove an Ace and a King of each suit. Deal forty-eight cards face up in four columns of eight. Deal the remainder face up in thirteen packets forming a semi-circle arching over the columns, each packet consisting of all the cards left over of a

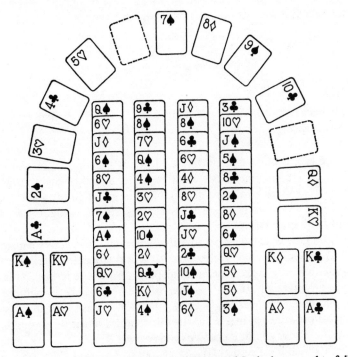

ARCHWAY In this particular deal all Sixes and Jacks happened to fall in the central columns, leaving two stones of the arch unfilled (dotted lines).

given rank – i.e. a packet of Aces, then Twos, then Threes and so on. There will be different numbers in different packets, and some ranks may not be represented at all.

Object On either side of the columns arrange a square of four bases (two Aces and two Kings, with each King lying above the Ace of the same suit). Build Aces and Kings respectively upwards and downwards into thirteen-card suit sequences.

Play The exposed card of each column and all the cards in the arch are available for building on suites. Cards may be reversed between Ace and King suites of the same suit when they meet, but bases must be left intact. A space made by clearing out a column may be filled with one available card in order to unblock others, but only one card may occupy one space at a time.

Salic Law

Two packs
Even chances

There is a group of distinctive and popular patiences of which Salic Law is the chief representative. Their most obvious characteristics are that cards are dealt into columns of varying lengths and that the final result usually displays all the Kings, Queens and Jacks in three rows.

Salic Law is so called because the Queens take no active part in the proceedings, but are exalted to a lofty position (or, some would say, are kicked upstairs) to play a purely decorative role. The original Salic Law was that of the Franks, by which the crown could not pass to a female heir. It achieved greater historical prominence in the fourteenth century, when the question arose whether or not it could pass *through* a female heir to a male successor. If so, Edward III of England had a good claim on the French crown when the last of the Capetians died without a male heir. But the lawyers of Philip of Valois came to the carefully considered foregone conclusion that it could not. So Philip became the VI of France, and the Hundred Years War kicked off soon after.

Altogether, a most instructive patience. With careful play it should succeed as often as not.

Layout and object Found a King near the top of the board and start dealing cards face up on it in a column spreading towards you. When another King turns up, put it next to the first one and start another column in the same way, so that by the time all the Kings are out you will have eight columns of varying length. As the Aces appear, place them in a row above the Kings. Build these up in sequence to the Jacks, regardless of suit, using cards turned up in the deal whenever they will fit. As the Queens appear, put them in a row above the Ace suites. The object is to finish with a row of Queens, a row of Jacks, and a row of Kings.

Play When all cards have been entered continue building by taking exposed cards of the tableau one at a time. No packing is carried out, but when a King is uncovered it may be treated as a temporary space for the packing of any single card taken from the end of another column.

KING AND QUEEN This variant is virtually identical, but when a King is cleared it may temporarily hold up to three cards taken from the exposed ends of other columns.

INTRIGUE (GLENCOE, LAGGARD LADY) As Salic Law, but with the following differences. Start with a Queen and begin a new column every time another Queen appears. As the Sixes appear, place them in a row above the Queens and build them upwards in sequence as far as the Jacks, regardless of suit. As the Fives appear, put them in a row above the Sixes and build them downwards in sequence to the Aces, surmounting the Aces with the Kings, also regardless of suit. Build as much as you can while you are dealing. After that, try to complete the suites by playing from the exposed cards of the Queen columns. An exposed Queen may be temporarily covered with a single card from the end of a column. The game is harder to get out than Salic Law.

Strictly speaking, and to justify the title, Fives should be founded above the Queens and Sixes below, and subsequent cards dealt on the Queens in piles, so that the end product displays a line of Queens sandwiched between the Kings and Jacks. But this prevents piled cards from remaining open to view.

In Laggard Lady, bases may not be founded faster than Queens. For example, if a fourth Five or Six turns up before the fourth Queen it must be dealt to the tableau. In Glencoe, a base may only be founded above a Queen of its own suit. For example, if

♥5 or ♥6 turns up before either ♥Q, or before the second if the first has already engendered the same base, it must be dealt to the tableau.

Capuchin

Primrose, As You Like It
Two packs
Odds against

The original of this game, under any of its varied and inexplicable titles, is a slightly inferior form of the excellent Interregnum. Although sources differ in minor details, they all agree that ninety-six cards are dealt in eight squared-up packets of twelve, with the effect that only the eight top cards are visible. As described below, however, the game is much improved (and no easier to conclude) if they are spread in columns towards you so that all are visible.

Why the game should be named after an order of hooded monks or a Shakespearian play is beyond me. As for the alternative 'Primrose', here is Mary Whitmore Jones (*c.* 1898) on the subject: 'The attempt is occasionally made to divide England into sharply defined and hostile camps – the masses against the classes. It is the special mission of the Primrose League to endeavour to counteract this, and draw all ranks together in a chain of friendship. The game of patience under notice is intended to illustrate the efforts of the League. The classes are represented by an upper row of single cards, the masses by packets below them. The aim of the player is to elevate the lower row and amalgamate it with the upper one . . .'

For other examples of thematic bosh, see Amazons (Women's Lib), Exit (Gay Lib), Salic Law (male chauvinism), and Hemispheres (racism).

Layout Deal eight cards in a row at the top of the board as bases, and below them deal the remainder of the cards face up in twelve overlapping rows of eight cards each. Regard the result as eight columns of twelve.

Object To build each base card up into a thirteen-card sequence regardless of suit, turning from King to Ace as necessary.

Play It is advisable to leave the bases projecting slightly so that you will know when to stop building, the last card of each suite being exactly one rank lower than the base. Use exposed cards from the columns to build on the bases. When you can get no further, or sooner if you prefer, square up the leftmost column, turn it face down, then deal all the cards from it face up across the ends of the columns, starting with the second and returning to the first position after covering the eighth. When all have been distributed, play further. When next stuck, square up the second column and again deal cards in rotation across the columns from left to right, filling spaces where columns may have been emptied out. Continue in this way, redistributing the other six columns one by one. You lose the game if you fail to finish all eight suites after the eighth redeal.

Note If there are too many duplicated ranks among the eight bases you may prefer to shuffle them back in and deal again, otherwise the odds are not in favour of success. Whitmore Jones, in a desperate effort to amalgamate the masses with the classes insists that the eight base cards should deliberately be made to consist of different ranks.

Crescent

Two packs
Odds in favour

Crescent is one of those problematic old games in which cards are dealt in packets face up. By spreading the packets so that all are visible it becomes an open and hence more skilful game.

Layout and object Take an Ace and a King of each suit and make bases of them, the object being to build them respectively into ascending and descending thirteen-card suit-sequences. Deal the other ninety-six face up in sixteen packets of six each, spread slightly so that all are visible. (These sixteen should be arranged in the form of a crescent to justify the title.)

Play Exposed cards of the packets are available for building on suites. When you can get no further, cease building and transfer the bottom card of each packet to the top, then resume play. 'The transfer of the undermost cards to the top of their respective heaps may be thrice repeated,' says Professor Hoffman in his translation of the original. 'If by that time you have not attained the desired object, you have lost the game.' It should be noted that suite-to-suite reversal is not permitted – a card once built may not be moved. There is a relaxation of this rule in the original account, but if you play with all cards visible you don't need to take advantage of it.

Black Hole

One pack
Odds in favour

That recently discovered cosmological phenomenon, the Black Hole, is a type of degenerate star, which, like a cannibal, swallows up all matter that may chance to fall within its gravitational reach. This game of my own invention (but derived from Golf and similar 'one-up' games) shows you how.

Layout Put the Ace of spades in the middle of the board as the base or 'black hole'. Deal all the other cards face up in seventeen fans of three, orbiting the black hole.

Object To build the whole pack into a single suite based on the black hole.

Play The exposed card of each fan is available for building. Build in ascending or descending sequence regardless of suit,

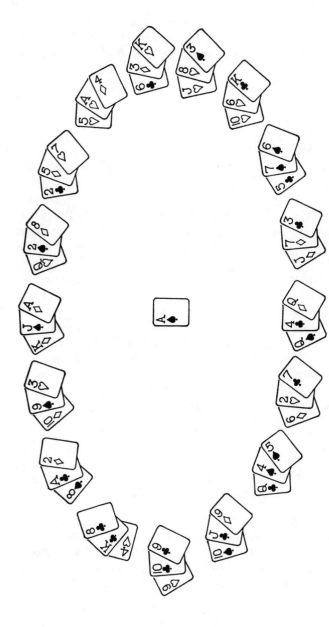

BLACK HOLE   This deal was brought to a successful conclusion without once changing direction in the building of the central suite.

going up or down ad lib and changing direction as often as necessary. Ranking is continuous between Ace and King. For example, a start might be made as follows: A–K–Q–K–A–2–3– 4–3– and so on.

Buffalo Bill

Two packs
Odds in favour

Mary Whitmore Jones describes a game called Little Billee, which she says is American, affords little scope for skill, and fails to come out more often than it succeeds ... Well, on all points except its origin I must, for once, beg to contradict the lady. If you deal the packets in fans so that all cards are visible, the game is an open one and cannot fail to invite skill – and even Miss Jones allows you to look through the packets to decide on the best course of play, so why not? And again, if you take proper advantage of the two redeals, I think you will find Little Billee coming out more often than not. The only trouble is those redeals. They interrupt the flow of the game and flaunt an element of blind chance that spoils the open, rugged honesty of the basic plan. So here, first, is my fully open adaptation, named after a Mr Cody of Wild West fame.

Layout and object Deal all the cards out in twenty-six fans of four each. The object is to found an Ace and a King of each suit as they become available, and to build them respectively upwards and downwards into thirteen-card suit sequences.

Play The exposed card of each fan is available for founding or building on a suite. An exposed card may alternatively be transferred to a reserve, from which it can (eventually) only be taken for building, not returned to the fans. Up to eight cards may be held in reserve at any one time. There is no redeal.

LITTLE BILLEE Deal eight cards to a reserve and the rest in

twenty-four fans of four cards each. The object is the same as above. A reserve card is only available for building on a suite, and may be replaced with an exposed card from a fan. The exposed card of a fan may be taken for building or for filling a vacancy in the reserve. When stuck, gather up the fans in reverse order of dealing (leaving the reserve and partly built suites untouched) and deal them out again in fours as far as they will go. Two such redeals are allowed.

Heap
Two packs
Odds in favour

Heap is reminiscent of 'S', but, played open, gives you more to think about.

Layout Make a row of thirteen cards running in sequence and alternating colour from Seven at one end to Six at the other, passing from King to Ace in the middle. These are bases. Deal the rest face up in twenty-two fans of four cards each and one of three.

Object To build each base into an ascending sequence of thirteen cards, passing from King to Ace as necessary. All suites are to be built in colour (red on red, black on black) except the one based on Six, which is to be built in alternating colour.

Play Exposed cards are available for building. When stuck, gather all the fans up, shuffle, and redeal in as many fans of four as possible, with one smaller fan if there are any left over at the end. There is no second redeal.

Open Packers

In these packing games, all the cards are dealt face up on the table for you to examine before starting play, and you should often spend more time analysing the possibilities of the position than actually shifting cards about.

It would not be true to say that every game will come to a successful conclusion given perfect play. In some cases it is possible that the initial deal may produce an entirely fortuitous blockage. You could almost count half a victory for deciding that a particular layout is impossible, and abandoning it before touching a card. To be fair, however, you should counter this by acknowledging a double defeat if you once embark upon a game and then fail to carry it through.

The games are presented, as usual, in increasing order of numerical complexity.

Thirty

One short pack (*32*)
Odds against

Try this by way of introduction to the general principles of 'open' games. Whether it comes out or not is largely a matter of luck, because if the cards happen to fall in a favourable distribution (which rarely happens in my case, but I'm born like that) it requires little effort to work out how to play them.

Layout Deal six overlapping rows of five cards each and regard the tableau as five columns of six. Hold the other two out as a reserve.

Object To found the Aces and build them up in suit to the Kings. (Ace is followed by 7, 8 etc.)

Play Both reserve cards are available for packing or building, but once used are not replaced. Pack the tableau in descending sequence regardless of suit, moving one card or any length of packed sequence at a time. Fill a vacancy with any exposed card or sequence.

Bouquet

Flower Garden, Garden, Parterre
One pack
Even chances

A pleasant game, well known to all Patience lovers.

Layout Deal six overlapping rows of six cards each and regard the tableau (the 'flower garden') as six columns of six. The other sixteen cards form a reserve (the 'bouquet') which is held in hand so that all are visible.

Object To found the Aces when they become available and build them up in suit to the Kings.

Play Pack the tableau in descending sequence regardless of suit, moving only one card at a time. Fill a vacancy with any available card. All exposed cards and all those of the tableau are simultaneously available for packing and building. Cards of the bouquet are not replaced when used.

BRIGADE Much the same, but starting with seven columns of five ('the columns') and a reserve of thirteen ('the reserve') after founding the four Aces. As if this modification did not already make the game easier to bring out, a grace is permitted when the game blocks. This entitles you to take an exposed card of the tableau and pack it on a reserve card which is next higher or lower in rank. The grace may be taken once only.

Penguin

One pack
Odds in favour

One of my own inventions, Penguin is a variation on Eight Off or Baker's Game. Most games of that type strike me as being either too easy or too hard. I think Penguin balances quite well. It should come out rather more often than not with careful play, but you must give each new layout very careful thought before taking the plunge.

Layout Deal cards face up in seven overlapping rows of seven to make a tableau of seven columns. The first card dealt from the pack is the 'penguin' – it will lie at one corner of the finished tableau at the buried end of the first column. As you deal, take out and found as bases the other three cards of the same rank as the penguin.

Object To free the penguin as the fourth base card, and to build all bases up into thirteen-card ascending suit sequences, turning from King to Ace as necessary.

Play Exposed cards are available for building or packing. Pack the tableau in suit and descending sequence, turning from Ace to King as necessary. A properly packed sequence headed by an exposed card may be shifted as a whole provided that the join follows the rule. A space made by clearing out a column may be filled only with a card one rank lower than the bases, either alone or at the bottom of a packed sequence headed by an exposed card.

During play any exposed card may be moved into a reserve called the 'flipper', which at any time may contain a maximum of seven cards. All cards in the flipper are available at any time for building on suites or packing back on the tableau, or for filling spaces in accordance with the appropriate rule. (It is therefore possible, though rarely desirable, to free the penguin in the first six moves.)

Grace If the game blocks when the flipper is full, you may remove from it a card which is one rank lower than the bases and put it in position to start an eighth column of packing (counting half a victory if you then win) or a ninth as the case may be (for a quarter-win). A blocked game is lost, however, if the flipper contains no such card.

Fission

One pack
Odds in favour

Another of the few games with an aptly 'scientific' flavour is this remarkably original invention of Morehead and/or Mott-Smith.

Layout Deal seven overlapping rows of seven cards each and regard the result as seven columns of seven. These constitute the reserve. Deal the remaining three to one side in a non-overlapping column to start the tableau.

Object To build four ascending suit-sequences of thirteen cards each, turning the corner from King to Ace as necessary, but not necessarily built on base cards of the same rank.

Play Cards in the tableau are to be packed in rows (not columns) so as not to interfere with one another. The packing is to take place in suit but regardless of rank or sequence. Although there are only three cards in the tableau to start with, it may contain up to four at any one time, and a vacancy may be filled with any available card from the reserve.

Exposed cards of the reserve are available for packing on the tableau. When the first card of a reserve column has been taken, pull the remaining six apart into two separate columns of three, each of whose exposed cards is thus made available. When the exposed card of a three-column has been taken, separate the remaining two. These two then become bases, each of which is to be built in suit and ascending sequence with the aid of exposed cards from the tableau and the reserve. Two or more sequences should be consolidated when they run together, so as to save space and record progress clearly.

Picture Gallery

Intrigue
Two packs (or one)
Odds in favour

These are versions of Salic Law but with packing on the tableau – an additional feature that brings them to a successful conclusion more often. Both can be played with one pack instead of two, building four suites instead of eight.

Object The ultimate objective is to finish with three rows of cards; the top row displaying eight Queens, the bottom row eight Kings, and between them a row of eight suites built upwards in alternating colour from Aces to Jacks.

Layout Take a King and put it in position as the first card of the eventual King row to start a tableau. Starting from the King, deal a column of overlapping cards extending towards you. Take out any Aces that turn up and lay them in a row above the King as bases. When another King turns up, place it to the right of the first King and deal a column of cards on it in the same way. Continue this procedure, taking out Aces as dealt, until you have eight columns (of varying lengths) all headed by Kings.

Play Exposed cards may be packed on one another in ascending or descending sequence and alternating colour. Only one card may be moved at a time, but changes of direction are permitted in the same line of packing. Exposed Queens are taken and put in a row above the Aces. Build cards in alternating colour upwards on the Aces and downwards on the Queens. When the top card of a Queen suite is in sequence with the top card of any Ace suite, any or all of the cards built on the Queen may be reversed onto the Ace suite. All the Queens must eventually be cleared and the Aces built up to the Jacks for the game to succeed. Kings may not be moved or packed on, except as provided below.

Grace Once only during a game, an exposed red card may be packed on an exposed black King; and, once only, an exposed black card may be packed on an exposed red King. Packing may then take place on the moved cards in the usual way.

EIGHT AWAY An irrelevant title, not to be confused with Eight Off. Deal all cards face up in eight columns of irregular length headed by Kings (as for Picture Gallery, but leaving Aces where they fall). The object is to release the Aces, found them in a row above the Kings, and build them up in suit to the Queens. Pack the tableau in suit and descending sequence, moving cards singly or in any length of packed sequence. Queens may be packed on exposed Kings. Exposed cards may be taken and held out in reserve. Up to eight may be reserved at any time, and all are available for building or for packing back into the tableau.

FAERIE QUEEN This is the sort of title that gets Patience a bad name. Deal eight columns of irregular length headed by Kings, as for Picture Gallery, and take out the Aces as they turn up. Put them in a row above the Kings. Having dealt, play to build the Aces up in suit to the Queens. Pack the tableau in descending sequence regardless of suit, moving only one card at a time. An uncovered King is equivalent to a space: any card may be packed on it.

ROYAL PATIENCE As Eight Off, but with these differences: Pack the tableau in descending sequence and alternating colour. Move only one card at a time. Only Queens may be packed on Kings. Not more than seven cards may be held in reserve simultaneously.

Zingara

Two short packs
Odds against

Morehead and Mott-Smith devised these short-pack patiences evidently under the influence of Salic Law. Zingara uses the double-32 or Bézique pack with no cards lower than Seven, Xerxes the double-24 or Pinochle pack with nothing lower than Nine.

Layout Put a Seven at the top left as a base. Below it, start dealing a column of overlapping cards. You may hold out and build an Eight on the Seven and a Nine on the Eight if they turn up, regardless of suit, but may not build any further as yet. When the next Seven turns up, put it next to the first one and deal a second column in the same way. Keep going until you have eight columns of various lengths. During the deal you may build on any or all of the suites as far as the Nine.

Object To build eight sequences of eight cards running 7–8–9–10– J–Q–K–A, regardless of suit.

Play Continue building by taking exposed cards from the tableau. A vacancy made by clearing out a column may be filled with any exposed card. No packing takes place.

XERXES The same, but with a 48-card pack and using the Nines as base cards. No building may take place on the Nines until all cards have been dealt.

Grandfather's Clock

One pack
Odds in favour

The clock theme ticks on in yet another branch of the patience family – this time with all its innards exposed to view. This makes for a game of skill, though it is not a difficult one to keep going once you have properly wound it up. (The same title, incidentally, has been used for various related clockwork games, which is a pity.)

Layout Take the following cards and found them as bases, putting the first at the top of the board in twelve o'clock position and arranging the others in a clockwise direction from it to form a circle representing the clock face: ♦9–♠10–♥J–♣Q–♦K–♠2–♥3–♣4–♦5–♠6–♥7–♣8. Deal the rest in five overlapping columns of eight cards each, and regard this tableau as eight columns of five.

Object To build on each base in ascending suit-sequence until the top card shows the number corresponding to its position on a clock face. (This will absorb all cards from the tableau.)

Play Exposed cards of the tableau are available for packing and building. Pack in descending sequence regardless of suit, moving only one card at a time. Fill a vacancy with any available card.

Eight Off

Eight Away
One pack
Odds in favour

Eight Off boasts the rare distinction of having formed a subject of discussion and problemism in Martin Gardner's column in *Scientific American*, where it appeared (June 1968) in a slightly harsher version named after a mathematician, C. L. Baker, who drew it to his (Gardner's) attention. I don't think there is any intrinsic reason why it should have been so singled out from many other fully open patiences, or games of 'perfect information' as they are called in the trade. It is a straightforward fully open packer with a replenishable reserve, and can be made easier or harder to get out by varying the number of cards the reserve may be permitted to hold. In this connection, see also Penguin.

Layout and object Deal six overlapping rows of eight cards each and regard the tableau as eight columns of six. Deal the last four face up to start a reserve. Play to release the Aces and build them up in suit to the Kings.

Play Exposed cards of the tableau are available for building or for packing on one another. Pack in suit and descending sequence, moving only one card at a time. A vacancy in the tableau may be filled only with an available King. Cards of the reserve may not be packed upon, but are themselves individually available for packing or building. An exposed card of the tableau may be moved into reserve whenever there is a vacancy for it. The reserve may hold up to eight cards at a time, so that when play begins it consists of four cards and four vacancies.

BAKER'S GAME The same, except that (*a*) the last four cards are dealt to the first four columns, and (*b*) the reserve – empty to start with – may hold a maximum of four cards at a time. This version is much harder to get out than Eight Off, which itself is generally too easy.

PRISON Baker (see above) inherited the game from his father, who was shown it by an Englishman in the 1920s. An evident forerunner is the vaguely pictorial Prison described by Whitmore Jones in the 1890s. Deal the first card as a base, and put the other three of the same rank in line with it as they turn up during the deal. The object is to build them into thirteen-card suit sequences, turning the corner between Ace and King as necessary. Deal the remainder into ten columns of four and a reserve of eight called the 'prison'. Decide whether to build the bases in ascending or descending sequence, whichever seems more likely to be successful according to the initial distribution. All must be built in the same direction. Whichever it is, cards on the tableau are to be packed in suit and sequence of the opposite direction. Play as for Eight Off, using the prison as a reserve for single cards.

Beleaguered Castle
Laying Siege, Sham Battle
One pack
Odds against

Another classic patience is indicated by the alternative titles and methods of play.

Layout and object Put the four Aces in a non-overlapping column down the centre of the board, and play to build them up in suit to the Kings. On either side of each Ace deal a row of six over-lapping cards from the centre of the board outwards.

Play The exposed or outer card of each row is available for build-ing, or for packing on the exposed card of another row in des-cending sequence regardless of suit. Only one card may be moved at a time. A vacancy made by clearing out an entire row may be filled with any available card.

STREETS AND ALLEYS The same, but shuffle the Aces in with the pack and deal seven cards to each of the top four rows. The Aces must be freed by careful packing. This reduces the chances of success from about 1 in 3 to 1 in 4.

CHESSBOARD (FIVES) As Fortress, but, immediately after dealing, you may choose which rank to select for the four bases according to how the cards happen to lie. Build these into thirteen-card suit-sequences, turning the corner from King to Ace as necessary. In packing, turn the corner from Ace to King as necessary. Easier than Fortress, harder than Streets and Alleys.

CITADEL Keep the Aces in. Object and play are as for Be-leaguered Castle, but the deal differs. Produce the same eight rows, but deal cards in columns to achieve that effect. Whenever you turn an Ace or a card that can be built on a suite already commenced, put it in place instead of dealing it to the tableau, and leave its place in the tableau unfilled. A card once placed may not be moved until the deal is complete. When play begins, the eight rows will be of varying lengths.

FORTRESS (FORT) Keep the Aces shuffled in the pack and deal ten rows, five down each side of the board: the first two contain six cards and the others five. The object, as above, is to release the Aces and build them up in suit, but packing on the tableau must also take place in suit, though it may be in ascending or descending sequence (not both in the same row). An ascending packed sequence can obviously not be built into a suite as it stands, but it can be reversed by shunting one card at a time when a vacancy occurs. Chances of success are considerably against the player. Fort is the same, except that two Aces are founded to start with and the rest dealt 10 by 10. If the game blocks, the grace may be taken (once only) of transferring any exposed card to the far end of its row. These changes slightly improve the chances of success.

Canister

One pack
Odds in favour

The older patiences tend to have one-word titles preceded by 'the', and those which remain popular usually acquire new names. The Canister sounds as if it ought to be pictorial – but it isn't and it hasn't changed its name.

Layout and object Deal (by overlapping rows) four columns of seven cards and four of six. Play to release the Aces and build them up in suit to the Kings.

Play Exposed cards are available for building suites or packing on one another. Pack in descending sequence and alternating colour, moving only one card at a time. A vacancy in the tableau may be filled only with an available King.

Pendulum

One pack
Odds against

Out of the ordinary run of patience games is this wickedly ingenious and aptly titled strain on your mental resources and power of judgement. It was invented either by Ernest Bergholt or by his colleague Margaretta Byrd.

Layout Take out the Aces and deal the other forty-eight cards in six rows of eight, not overlapping. Regard the tableau as eight columns of six.

Object To build a thirteen-card ascending suit sequence from each Ace, the interval of the sequence being the same for all suites but as chosen by the player after examining the layout. For example, if you decide to build by intervals of five, each suite will run A–6–J–3–8–K–5–10–2–7–Q–4–9.

Play The bottom card of each column may be built on a suite or packed on the card immediately above, provided that the latter is of the same suit and next higher in rank by the required interval. (Example: If building by fives, place a Five on its Ten, or a Ten on its Two; and so on.) Two or more cards packed in this way may always be packed on the card immediately above if it properly continues the sequence. Any card or packed sequence at the bottom of a column may be packed on the card at either end of the top row, provided that it properly continues the sequence.

When a vacancy is made by clearing out a column, it must be filled with a card of the rank required to crown a suite (e.g. a Nine if the interval is five) as soon as one becomes available.

When the game blocks, set it going again by 'swinging the pendulum' as follows: Move all the cards in the bottom row up to the right, without altering their relative positions, so that all gaps in that row lie consecutively to the left. Do the same with each row above it in turn until you come to a row without gaps; then stop. Never swing the top row, even if it has a gap. This procedure realigns the cards in vertical relation to one another and should yield more play. Next time the game blocks, swing all rows with gaps (except the top one) to the left. Continue playing and swinging alternately right and left until the game either comes out or stalls.

Notes Assume that a space in the top row may be filled with a card of the suite-crowning rank even if it has other cards properly packed upon it. Since you have the choice of interval by which to build sequences, there is no reason why you should not also have the free choice whether to build by this interval in ascending or descending sequence, packing, of course, in the opposite direction. This can hardly make the game more mind-contorting than it is already, and can only increase the chances of success, given superhumanly accurate play.

Sixty-four Square

Two 32-card packs
Odds in favour

Another game to play with a 64-card Bézique pack, containing no ranks lower than Seven.

Layout and object Deal all cards face up in a square, making eight columns of eight. The object is to found the eight Aces as they become available and build them up in suit to the Kings (starting A, 7, 8 etc.).

Play You may choose either the cards in the top row or those in the bottom row to be considered 'exposed', and, having chosen, must play by that rule throughout. If playing downwards, of course, the removal of an exposed card releases the one below it, and so on. Pack exposed cards of the tableau on one another in descending sequence and alternating colour, moving only one card at a time. A space made by clearing out a column may be filled with any available card. A ninth column may be started by moving any exposed card into the nearest or furthest position in it (depending on whether you are playing downwards or upwards), and then packing. There is no redeal.

PERSIAN (BÉZIQUE, EIGHT BY EIGHT, STRATA) Deal eight overlapping rows of eight. Only the bottom card of each column is exposed. Free Aces, build them up in suit to Kings, pack one at a time downwards in alternating colour, fill a space with any available card. No ninth column is started. When the game blocks, gather the cards up, shuffle and redeal. Two redeals are allowed and there is a grace: in each deal you may once take an exposed card and exchange its position with any buried card required for building. (The different titles refer to slightly differing versions, of which the account given here is a composite.)

Kings

Two packs
Odds in favour

Few of the oldest patiences are fully open or otherwise skill-demanding, but this is one of them. For all that, it is not particularly difficult if you keep your eyes open.

Layout and object Lay the eight Aces out in two columns down the centre of the board, and aim to build them up in sequence to the Kings regardless of suit. Deal a card to the right of each right-hand Ace from the top down, and a card to the left of each left-hand Ace from the bottom up. Continue dealing cards in the same rotation, overlapping cards of the same horizontal row in order to conserve space. If in the course of the deal you turn up a Two, you may build it on either of the Aces in the same row, and so on with a Three, Four etc. provided always that such cards are built only on suites lying in the same horizontal row as the positions to which they would otherwise have been dealt. When a card is built in this way, do not fill its intended place in the tableau, but proceed to the next row in rotation.

Play When all cards are out, linear restrictions cease and all eight exposed cards are available for building on any of the eight suites. They may also be packed on one another in ascending or descending sequence regardless of suit, and a space may be filled with any available card. Sequences may change direction in the same row. There is no redeal.

Somerset

One pack
Odds against

These three triangular games go together as differing from one another only in degree of difficulty. Somerset seems the least likely to come out, while King Albert and Raglan give you an escape route in the form of a reserve from which to draw cards when in difficulty.

Layout Deal eight overlapping rows of cards, with ten in the top row, then nine, eight and so on down to three. Regard the resultant triangular tableau as consisting of ten columns varying in length from eight cards to one.

Object To release the Aces and build them up in suit to the Kings.

Play Exposed cards of the tableau are available for building or packing. Pack in descending sequence and alternating colour, moving only one card at a time. Fill a vacancy with any available card. You may, if need be, worry back cards from suites into the tableau.

KING ALBERT The same, but deal nine columns varying in length from nine cards down to one, and lay the remaining seven to one side as the ('Belgian') reserve. Do not pack on the reserve or fill vacancies in it, but all cards in it are simultaneously available for packing or building as the opportunity arises.

RAGLAN The same as King Albert, but the first three columns contain seven cards each (followed by six down to one) and the reserve contains six.

Nationale

Two packs
Odds in favour

These three games go together by similarity of structure: they are all based on a tableau of 12 by 8, build suites upwards and downwards, pack in suit, and allow of a limited amount of building during the deal. They are also fully open to view, but Capricieuse and Russian introduce an element of chance by virtue of the redeal when play reaches a halt. No doubt this accounts for the capriciousness alluded to in one of the titles; as to the others, it is hard to see what is generally nationalistic of one or particularly Russian of the other.

Object Found an Ace and a King of each suit to start with. Build the Aces up in suit to the Kings and the Kings down in suit to the Aces.

Layout Deal cards *in columns* (not in rows) of eight, overlapping one another to save space. If you turn a card that can be built on an Ace or King suite, build it, but do not fill its place in the column with the next card. Each column will therefore contain eight cards or as many fewer as have been built, and there will be twelve columns in all. (It is advisable to count from one to eight out loud when dealing a column, so as to keep track in case some are built.) Once a card has been dealt and covered it cannot be taken until the deal is complete; but a card at the exposed end of a column is always available for building during the deal.

Play After dealing, pack the tableau in suit and sequence, moving only one exposed card at a time. Sequences may ascend or descend and change direction in the same column. A vacancy may be filled with any exposed card. There is no redeal. (The original rules allow a vacancy to be filled with any length of packed sequence taken as a whole and without reversal. I think this is a mistake.)

CAPRICIEUSE As above, but deal cards in up to eight overlapping rows of twelve each. A turned card may be built if possible, and its place in the tableau must be filled with the next unplayable card turned. A card once dealt cannot be taken until the deal is complete. Play as described above. When the game blocks, gather up the columns from left to right in order and deal and play again. A second such redeal is permitted.

RUSSIAN PATIENCE has the redealing element of Capricieuse and the curious positional elements of Vacuum and related games. Deal all cards face up in eight overlapping rows of twelve cards each. The object is to found an Ace and a King of each suit and to build them respectively upwards and downwards in suit. Pause after dealing the first row, and take out any Aces, Kings, Twos, Queens and so on capable of starting or building suites, filling their places at once from stock. When you can get no further, continue dealing rows of twelve. As other required base cards turn up they may be founded and their places in the tableau filled with the next cards turned, but other cards may only be built on the suites if, when turned, they were due to fall in either the first or the last (twelfth) position in the row. When such a card is built, fill its position with the next unplayable card turned. A card once placed in position cannot be taken until the deal is complete.

Play consists in packing exposed cards, one at a time, in ascending or descending suit sequence, changes of direction being permitted in the same column. Fill a vacancy with any exposed card. When stuck, gather up the columns in order, consolidate them into a new stock, and deal again. The same restrictions apply during this deal: cards may only be built that come from the top row or either outside column. A second redeal is permitted.

Baker's Dozen

One pack
Odds in favour

There is nothing out of the ordinary about these closely related one-pack open games, except perhaps their classic and un-pretentious simplicity.

Layout and object Deal the whole pack face up in four overlapping rows of thirteen, and regard them as thirteen columns of four. Transfer the four Kings to the bottom of their columns. The object is to release the Aces and build them up in suit to the Kings.

Play Pack the tableau in descending sequence regardless of suit, moving only one card at a time. Do not fill any vacancies.

GOOD MEASURE A slightly harder one to get out. Deal the pack in five overlapping rows of ten and regard the result as ten columns of five. Put the first two Aces that turn up to one side as bases; the others are not founded until they become available after the deal.

SPANISH PATIENCE Deal thirteen columns of four, as for Baker's Dozen, but build and pack regardless of suit. (The original rules state that Aces are founded to start with and the tableau is to consist of twelve squared-up packets of four cards each. If this is interpreted to mean that lower cards may not be known until they are exposed, then the game is, in effect, Castles in Spain.)

BISLEY Put the four Aces in a row at top left, leaving room above them for their corresponding Kings. Deal a row of nine cards to the right of the Aces. Below these cards deal three more rows of thirteen. Cards may be overlapped into thirteen columns, but keep the Aces clear. The object is to build on them in ascending suit sequence, and, at the same time, to release the four Kings as they become available, found them in a row above the four Aces, and build on them in descending suit sequence. The game ends when all cards have been absorbed from the tableau into the eight suites. Pack the tableau in suit and sequence, ascending or descending as required, and moving only one card at a time. Do not fill any vacancies.

Reversible Sequences

One pack
Odds against

After much study and experimentation I think I have managed to de-garble the original account of a game which requires an extraordinary amount of analysis before any move can be made with safety. The accurate but unprepossessing title fairly reflects the nature of the task.

Layout Deal the whole pack into four rows of thirteen, with no overlapping.

Object To release either an Ace or a King of each suit, and to build on these four bases either upwards or downwards in suit as the case may be.

Play Only cards in the bottom row are available for founding as bases and building on suites. When a card is taken for either purpose, the one perpendicularly above it is moved down into the space to become available in its turn.

Examine the layout and decide for each suit whether to start with a King and build downwards, or with an Ace and build upwards. You may build up in some suits and down in others, or all in the same direction if you prefer, but you may only build in one direction per suit.

Start play by removing any bases there may be in the bottom row and cards that may be built on them, remembering to move cards down into the spaces they originally occupied.

When no more building can be done, a limited degree of packing may be carried out. If there are two cards in the bottom row of the same suit and consecutive in sequence, you may take either one of them and place it either upon or beneath the other to make a couple. Which one you move will depend upon which will bring the most useful card into the bottom row to take its place; whether you put it on or under the other depends on whether you are building upwards or downwards. (However, as the title implies, you are allowed to reverse the sequence of a couple if it proves necessary, so this positional aspect is not important except to perfectionists.) Not more than two cards may be packed together in this way at any time.

My only source for this game does not state whether a vacancy made by clearing out a column may be filled. If not, the game hardly ever comes out. It would therefore seem reasonable to permit a vacancy to be filled with any card or couple already occupying the bottom row. In this event the game seems to come out more often than not, though never without a struggle to get it going in the first place.

Curds and Whey

One pack
Odds against

This game of my invention is an open member of the Spider family and introduces a rare form of packing, that of rank on rank. This leads to a good deal of breaking up and reforming of packed lines, which somehow puts me in mind of spooning curds and whey (nowadays represented by junket). It proves to be a very busy game that always looks as if it is going to come out but often lets you down at the last minute. Perhaps you will have more success than the inventor.

Layout Deal all cards face up in four overlapping rows of thirteen, making thirteen columns of four.

Object To build within the tableau four descending suit sequences from King to Ace.

Play Exposed cards are available for packing on one another in descending suit sequence ('whey') or rank on rank ('curds'). For example, ♥5 can be packed on ♥6 or any other Five. Any length of packed sequence may be shifted for packing provided that the join follows either rule, as may any packed number of cards of the same rank. For example, you could take ♥5–4–3 and pack it on ♥6 or any Five, or you could take ♥5–♣5–♠5 and pack it on ♥6 or ♦5. But you may not take a whole batch of cards which combines a sequence with a group – for instance, you could not shift as a whole ♥6–♥5–♥4–♦4–♣4, though you could shift any number of Fours in one or more moves and then shift the whole heart sequence on the next. A space made by clearing out a column may be filled only with a King, together with any length of properly packed sequence or group of Kings that it may head. It is always permissible to pack a card of the same rank as the exposed card of a sequence headed by a King, but of course it will have to be moved off again before the game can be got out.

Mrs Mop

Two packs
Odds against

Another open member of the Spider family, and the invention of Charles Jewell, Mrs Mop is named after an ITMA character possibly for the necessity for 'mopping up' completed suites in order to keep the game from blocking.

Layout Deal the whole pack face up in eight overlapping rows of thirteen cards each and regard the tableau as thirteen columns of eight.

Object To build eight thirteen-card suit sequences from King down to Ace and eliminate them from the tableau one by one.

Play Pack the tableau in descending sequence regardless of suit. Move one exposed card at a time, together with any ascending sequence of cards attached to it provided that the cards of the sequence are all of the same suit. A vacancy made by clearing out a column may be filled with any exposed card or packed sequence.

Quinzaine

Fifteen in a Row
Two packs
Odds against

The baldly numerical title sounds rather dull when translated into English. Quinzaine is also the French for 'fortnight', which will give you some idea of the time to set aside for embarking upon it. The game itself is essentially a version of Baker's Dozen scaled up for two packs, which does not so much double the difficulty as square or even cube it.

Layout and object Deal all the cards face up in seven overlapping rows of fifteen cards each (the last row will be one short). Regard the result as fifteen columns. Play to release an Ace and a King of each suit, and to build them respectively upwards and downwards into thirteen-card sequences.

Play If there are no base cards in the bottom row take any there may be in the row above it. Thereafter only the exposed card of each column is available for building or packing. Pack the tableau in suit and sequence, ascending or descending as required A vacancy may be filled with any available card, but not with a sequence lifted *en bloc* (though it may be reversed into the space).

A vacancy may also be filled in the following way, which virtually amounts to a grace: you may take all the exposed cards of a given suit, and pack them into the vacancy in either ascending or descending numerical order even though they may not all be consecutive. The grace may also be taken, once only, of lifting an exposed card and taking the one beneath it for packing or building. There is no redeal.

Chequers

Two packs
Odds in favour

The proper way of laying out Chequers is, as the name implies, in the form of a chequered square – that is, a square of 4 × 4 packets enclosing a square of 3 × 3 so that packets meet only at the corners. But as it is essential to see lower cards in the packets and to allow room for packing, they would more usefully be dealt out as twenty-five columns of four, or even as fans. Apart from this rigmarole, the mechanics of play are quite ordinary, and Chequers might be regarded as an easier variant of Quinzaine. (In fact it is the two-pack version of Chessboard, which was described earlier without reference to its chequered layout.)

Layout and object Deal all the cards face upwards in twenty-five packets, columns or fans of four each, and lay the odd four face down as a squared-up reserve. Play to release an Ace and a King of each suit, and to build them respectively upwards and downwards into thirteen-card suit sequences.

Play Pack on the tableau, moving only one card at a time, in suit and ascending or descending sequence as required. When a vacancy occurs, fill it with the top card of the reserve. When the reserve cards have been entered, fill a vacancy with any exposed card. There is no redeal.

Fan

One pack
Odds against

These closely related games are the fully open equivalents of Belle Lucie and her half-open 'fan' club. See next entry for the two-pack versions.

Layout Deal all cards face up in seventeen fans of three cards and one of one card (or sixteen of three and two of two). If you have room, arrange them in a representation of a large fan (whence the name of the game) with the odd one-card 'fan' as its handle.

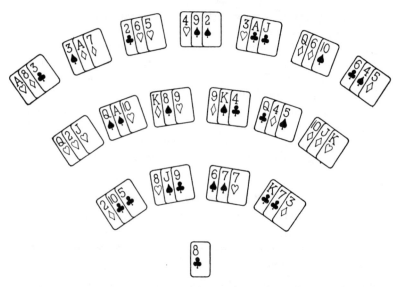

FAN Available for building and packing are the exposed card of each three-card fan and the single card representing the handle of the entire fan pattern.

Object To release the Aces and build them up in suit to the Kings.

Play The exposed card of each fan is available for packing and building. Pack downwards in suit, moving only one card at a time. A space made by clearing out a fan may be refilled only with an exposed King. There is no grace or redeal.

SHAMROCKS (THREE-CARD FAN) is a harder version of Fan. The layout and object are the same. After the deal, move all Kings to the bottom of their respective fans. Pack on the fans up or down ad lib and regardless of suit, but no fan may ever contain more than three cards at a time. Obviously, it will not come out unless at least one Ace is exposed in the initial layout and its removal uncovers a card that can be packed on. If not, to save redealing, you may draw any Ace to set the game going. The variant called Three-card Fan has even harsher rules, in that packing may only take place in descending sequence.

SCOTCH PATIENCE is not usually spoken of in the same breath as Fan, but is one of those older games in which cards are supposed to be dealt face up in squared-up packets. Since you are allowed to examine covered cards, you might as well deal them in fans so that all are visible. Deal eighteen such fans as described above. The object is to release the Aces and build them up to the Kings in alternating colours. Pack on the fans in descending sequence regardless of suit, moving only one card at a time.

House on the Hill

Two packs
Odds in favour

These are the two-pack versions of Fan or Belle Lucie. Similar but only half-open games are Intelligence and Rainbow (and, with one pack, Bristol).

Layout and object Deal all the cards face up in thirty-four fans of three cards each and two odd ones. each of which may become a fan by subsequent packing. Play to release the Aces and build them up in suit to the Kings.

Play Exposed cards are available for building on suites or packing on one another downwards in suit. Move only one card at a time. There may never be more than thirty-four fans, and a vacancy made by playing the last card of a fan is not to be refilled. There is no redeal.

HOUSE IN THE WOOD The same, but play to release an Ace and a King of each suit, and build them respectively up and down. Packing may take place in ascending or descending sequence with changes of direction on the same fan. Cards may not be reversed from suite to suite.

CROMWELL This tightening up of the games above was effected by Charles Jewell. Deal all cards out in twenty-six fans of four each. Play to release the Aces and build them up in suit to the Kings. Pack in suit and descending sequence, moving either a single exposed card or a packed sequence in its entirety. A space made by clearing off a fan is not to be refilled. There is no redeal, but there is one grace: at any point in the game, you may exchange the positions of any two cards whether they are covered or exposed. (If the deal produces not a single example of a King at the bottom of a fan, the grace must be used to create such a position, otherwise the game is bound to fail.)

Open Non-Builders

A few of the minority of games that do not involve building or packing are entirely open to view. All except the unusual but excellent Maze are games described earlier as Eliminators, in which the object is to gradually eliminate all the cards of the pack in matched pairs. There seems to be plenty of scope for the development of new members of this small family, and I have added two of my own by way of encouragement.

Nestor

Matrimony
One pack
Odds against

Nestor was once a wise and eloquent Greek king and is today a genus of parrots. The game is old enough to have been named after the king, though its one-to-one repetitiveness will probably bring parrots to mind. Warning: it is not as easy as it looks. Score half a victory for examining the layout and giving it up without moving, and a double defeat for starting play and failing.

Layout Deal cards face up in six overlapping rows of eight. Avoid getting duplicates in the same column: if a turned card is of the same rank as one immediately above it, slip it to the bottom of the pack and deal the next in its place. Lay the odd four face up to one side as a reserve.

Object To eliminate all cards in pairs of the same rank.

Play Eliminate exposed cards in pairs of the same rank. All four cards of the reserve are available for pairing with exposed cards in the columns, but may not pair off together unless three or four of the same rank are in the reserve.

VERTICAL This variant starts with seven columns of six and a reserve of ten.

Striptease

One pack
Odds against

This unclassifiable game of my own invention is somewhat tantalizing, as the title may suggest. Although the odds seem to be against success in the form described below, it can nearly always be got out by slightly increasing the number of wastepiles. At time of writing I have not yet done it with fewer than five. But four is undoubtedly the proper number, if propriety may be said to come into it at all.

Layout Put the four Queens in a row at the top of the board. Deal four cards face down in a row, overlapping the Queens. Deal the rest of the cards face up in successive overlapping rows of four until you finish with a tableau containing four columns of thirteen.

Object To strip the Queens of their covering cards.

Play Take exposed cards one by one and use them to start and build four wastepiles. Each wastepile must be built in consecutive sequence, up and down ad lib and regardless of suit. For this purpose Kings are consecutive with both Jacks and Aces. (E.g. part of a sequence might run –10–J–K–A–2–A–K–etc.)

Now for the tricky bit. Not one of the down-cards may be faced and taken until all four have been uncovered. If they cannot then all be properly built on one or more of the wastepiles the game has failed.

Fourteen Out

One pack (*version for two*)
Odds in favour

In Fourteen Out and its two-pack variant, Juvenile, Jack counts 11, Queen 12 and King 13.

Layout Deal cards face up in four overlapping rows of twelve. Regard the result as twelve columns of four and deal the remaining cards one each to the ends of the first four columns.

Object To eliminate all cards in pairs totalling fourteen.

Play Eliminate exposed cards in pairs whose face values total fourteen.

JUVENILE Deal all cards face up in sixteen columns of six and two of four. Eliminate exposed cards in pairs whose face values total fourteen. (In the original version it seems that the two odd batches of four give eight cards simultaneously available for pairing, but this makes the game too easy.)

Exit

Gay Gordons
One pack
Odds in favour

This is my 'open' adaptation of Elevens and similar eliminators.

Layout Deal all cards face up in five overlapping rows of ten and a reserve of two, one overlapping the other. If any of the resultant ten columns contains exactly three Jacks, exchange the middle one for the upper card of the reserve.

Object To eliminate all cards in pairs.

Play Throw out exposed cards two at a time as follows. Eliminate any two numerals that total eleven, such as A + 10 etc. Marry off Kings and Queens in couples, each couple being of two different suits to avoid inbreeding. Jacks (Gordons) pair off and exit (or exeunt) together.

Triplets

Triple Alliance
One or two packs
Odds in favour

Whitmore Jones describes two similar patiences under different names, one of which is playable with one or two packs. It would be convenient to record Triplets as the one-pack game and Triple Alliance as its two-pack alternative.

Layout Deal all cards face up in sixteen fans of three and two of two (if playing with one pack. If two, sixteen of six and two of four.)

Object To eliminate all cards in sequences of three.

Play Eliminate exposed cards in sequences of three, regardless of suit and counting Queen–King–Ace–Two etc. as sequential. There will be one odd card left over from the one-pack game, two from the two-pack game. For additional skill aim to make the two odd cards consecutive, or the one odd card as high ranking as possible (King highest).

Maze
One pack
Odds in favour

These few games are quite unrelated to the normal run of patiences; in fact, they are more like sliding block puzzles than anything else. The classic example is the one known as Spaces, or Gaps, but this has the demerit of being only half open: when the game blocks, you gather up the non-ordered cards, shuffle them and deal again. The fully open members of the family are Maze and Spaces-and-Aces. They, for their merits, come first.

Layout Deal two rows of eight cards each, face up and not overlapping, followed by four rows of nine. Discard the four Aces, which have no further part to play. Regard the result as a rectangle of $6 \times 9 = 54$ positions, of which forty-eight are occupied by cards and the other six are gaps or spaces (four by the removal of Aces, plus two by the dealing of two short rows).

Object To order the cards into four consecutive suit sequences, starting with the Two of any suit at the top left corner, followed by all the cards of its suit to the King, followed by the Two of another suit and its whole sequence to the King, and so on. The entire forty-eight card sequence 'reads', like a printed page, from left to right in each row, and from the top row downwards. It does not matter in what order the four suits occur.

Play At each move take up a card, thus creating a fresh space, and use it to fill an existing space. It may only be moved, however, if in its new position it is either of the same suit as the card on its left and next higher in rank, or of the same suit as the card on its right and next lower in rank. (Example: the space in the sequence ♥6–o–♣Q can only be filled by ♥7 or ♣J.) For this purpose a space at the end of a row is considered to be flanked by the card next to it and by the card at the opposite end of the row in sequence to it. Similarly, the top left-hand card is in sequence to the bottom right-hand card. Where two spaces are consecutive, only one card is capable of filling either, and where three or more are consecutive those in the middle cannot be occupied. You may play a Two to the right of a King of different suit, but may not play a King to the left of a Two (unless, of course, also to the right of its Queen).

Notes It is always possible to shunt complete sequences into their required final positions without contravening the rules of movement, and to all intents and purposes you may consider the game won when you have all forty-eight in proper sequence. (Don't stop at forty-seven: the last one may not be as easy as you think.) My source for this game starts by removing the Kings, but I have changed this to Aces to bring it into line with its relatives. My own preference is for retaining Aces and Kings and rejecting Jacks, so that Ten and Queen are in sequence.

SPACES AND ACES is the open version of an old one called Spaces, and was devised by magician Robert Harbin for the curious reason that he found the original game 'impossible to handle' (see Select Bibliography). I'm not sure what this means, but the result is certainly an improvement.

Deal four rows of thirteen cards face up, with no overlaps. The object is to convert them into four thirteen-card suit-sequences running from Ace (left) to King (right) in each row. Start by taking the four Aces from their dealt positions and placing one at the left end of each row. This determines the suit to be built in that row, and, as the Aces may not be moved once in place, their exact positioning is of some importance to the success of the game. Their transference results in $4 \times 14 = 56$ positions, four of which are spaces. At each move take up any card other than an Ace, thus creating a fresh space, and move it into an existing space, provided that in its new position it is of the same suit as the card on its left and higher in rank, though not necessarily in sequence. It follows that a space to the right of a King cannot be filled, and success depends largely on correct management of the Kings.

SPACES (GAPS) Deal four rows of thirteen and discard the Aces to produce four spaces. The object is to convert each row into a sequence of cards running in suit from Two (left) to King (right). At each move, fill a space with a card of the same suit as the one at its left and next higher in rank. Nothing may be played to the right of a King, but the sequence of rows is not continuous and a space at the extreme left of a row must be filled with a Two. When the game blocks (all spaces being to the right of Kings) gather up all cards that are not in proper sequence with their initially-placed Twos and shuffle them thoroughly. Deal them out again from left to right and top to bottom to bring each row up to its full complement of cards. If a row starts with a Two, leave a space behind it or the last card properly in sequence to it, and deal the first new card of the row to the right of that space. If not, deal the first new card of a row immediately to the right of the first space in it. (This enables a Two to be placed in position as soon as the deal is complete.) Play on as before. A second such redeal is allowed if the game blocks again, but not a third.

HOUSE OF COMMONS This apparent forerunner of Spaces is played in exactly the same way, except that the court cards are not used and each row is to be built in suit from the Two to the Ten. There is only one redeal. In true Victorian fashion, everything about it is twisted into representationalism. The courts, which play no active part, are the House of Lords, being placed apart 'to meditate, perchance, on the chances of the game'. The four Aces represent the Speaker, his Deputy, the Clerk to the House, and the Serjeant-at-Arms. The Twos are the leaders, and succeeding numerals the rank and file. If the game fails to come out, 'the motion before the House is blocked and indefinitely shelved'.

Part Four

COMPETITIVE PATIENCES

**presenting games of skill and judgement
for two or more players**

Patience for Two or More Players

There are various ways in which forms of Patience can be played by more than one player. The simplest is the straightforward competitive, in which each has a separate pack and all simultaneously play the same game, the winner being the first to complete his suites, or run out of cards, whichever seems more appropriate. A scoring system may be devised to make the result more interesting. A further step in this direction is represented by Racing Demon and other race games, in which all can play to one another's suites.

A more advanced type of competitive is that which works on the 'dictation' principle, such as Dictation itself or the better known Poker Squares. Here each player plays a separate game, but only one player (the dictator) has a shuffled pack. As he turns a card and plays it in his own game, he calls out what it is, and everyone else turns the same card from their own pack and plays it to theirs. The player who produces the best result by arranging his cards most skilfully is the winner.

Even better are the games that work on the 'ordering' principle of most patiences but are specifically designed for two, such as Russian Bank and Spite and Malice.

The following is a select collection of multi-player patiences ranging from the hilarious (Grabbage) to the highly skilled (Spite and Malice). Omitted are a number of old games, mechanical exercises and 'fortune-tellers' that are non-competitive, or give no opportunity for skill, or are not patiences by any stretch of the definition.

Racing Demon

and other race games

Any number of players
One pack each

Racing Demon in English, Race Canfield in American, Pounce, Scramble and other names – all denote a fast and furious family game that probably remains widely popular despite an overall decline in the status of Patience. The rules are simple: each player has a complete pack, which must be distinguishable by its reverse colour or design from everyone else's, and plays a game of Demon (Canfield). The winner is the first player to get rid of the thirteen cards of his reserve pile. The only difference in play is that each player may build from his own game onto any other player's suit-sequences whenever he has available a card that will fit. With this addition, follow all the rules of Demon described on page 149.

Any one-player patience can be played in exactly the same way: each plays his own game but may build on anyone's suites, and the winner is the first to play off all his cards. That said, there is no need to detail similar race games or give them special names.

Grabbage

Hasty Patience

Two or more players
One pack each

This hilarious game is guaranteed to draw complaints from the neighbours if played late at night. It should be played with old cards; for when a suite is built up to the King, in the words of Whitmore Jones, 'It is generally thrown on the floor, as this game allows no time for small ceremonies.'

Object To be the first to get rid of all one's cards by building them on suites to which all players contribute.

Play All play simultaneously, holding their packs face downwards. Turn cards rapidly one by one from stock and build them if possible or discard them face up to a personal wastepile if not. Always play a turned Ace to the centre to start a new suite. Using cards turned from hand or from the top of your wastepile, build suites upwards from Ace to King regardless of suit. If two try to play simultaneously to the same suite, the card to reach it first stays put. Suites are discarded when complete. When a player runs out of cards, he turns his wastepile face down to form a new one.

Pirate

Two players
One pack each

If you think Grabbage is silly, wait till you have played Pirate!

Object To capture a majority of ships (suites).

Preliminaries Each takes a complete pack shuffled by his opponent and cuts it. The lower cut plays to found Aces and build them upwards in suit, the other to found Kings and build them downwards in suit. These suites are called ships. Neither may play to the other's ship.

Play Both hold their packs face down and play simultaneously. Turn cards from stock one at a time and play them if possible or discard them face up to a personal wastepile if not. The top card of the wastepile may be built on a ship when it fits. A base-card (Ace or King) is played to the centre and built in suit as the appropriate cards turn up. When the two ships of a given suit meet in the middle, the first to play the connecting card captures both. (For example, if one has built spades up to the Six and the other spades down to the Eight, the first to play a spade Seven captures.) If both play it simultaneously, the two ships are sunk and belong to neither player.

When a ship has been captured or sunk the two players start a second ship in the same suit but playing in opposite directions – i.e. the former Ace-up player now plays King-down, and vice versa. (Thus both players may be building different suits in opposite directions at the same time!)

When one player runs out of cards, he stops play and watches the other carefully. Whenever his opponent turns a card required by the watcher for one of his own ships, the watcher may claim it and put it in place. When a capturing card is turned, the first to claim it captures both ships – which, as before, are sunk if both claim simultaneously.

Note The first to capture five suites wins, or four if one is sunk. It may be agreed not to sink ships but to credit those claimed simultaneously to the winner of the next.

Conjugal

Two players
One pack each

To paraphrase G. B. Shaw, two-player games are popular because they combine the maximum of temptation with the maximum of opportunity. So married couples may be assumed to start off with Honeymoon Bridge, progress from there to Conjugal Patience, and from there to Spite and Malice. (Divorce, see page 217, is, appropriately, not a two-player game.) Of these it must be admitted that Conjugal is the least interesting.

Preliminaries Each player takes a complete 52-card pack, shuffled by his opponent, and deals six cards face up before him as a reserve. The rest are held face down as a stock.

Object To be first to get rid of all one's cards by building them onto eight thirteen-card suit sequences compiled by both players.

Play Each in turn plays as many cards as he can from his reserve to the centre. An Ace is taken to start a suite, and on it is built the Two, Three and so on of the same suit up to the King. Any reserve card may be built on any suite if it fits. He then fills vacancies in the reserve with cards drawn from the top of his stock, and continues building if possible. Eventually, when his reserve consists of six unplayable cards, he concludes his turn by discarding any one of them face down to a personal wastepile and filling that vacancy from stock. (The space-filler is not available for building until his next turn.) When either player's stock is empty, he takes the wastepile as a new one. Agree beforehand whether or not it should be shuffled before use. If not, the last discard will be the first stock-card, and all cards will come out in reverse order of placing – a point to remember whenever discarding during the game. What little skill there is consists in selecting each discard and holding back possible builds if they may prove to be to the opponent's advantage.

Note In the above account, 'he' is a pronoun of common gender meaning 'he-or-she'. On the same morning that I wrote this, a correspondent in the *Guardian* newspaper pointed out that in Old English the word 'woman' was masculine in gender and therefore took the equivalent of 'he/him/his'. How sensible.

Progressive

Two players
Two packs

The skill of this unusual game, like that of Dictation, lies in the way each player arranges the cards in his tableau. But intriguing complications are caused by the fact that both are playing in turn to the same sequence.

Preliminaries Shuffle both packs together and take fifty-two cards each as a stock, which is to be kept face down.

Object To be the first to play off all one's cards to the centre.

Play Each in turn faces the top card of his stock and plays it to the centre if possible or discards it face up to any one of four wastepiles if not. Playing it entitles him to turn the next card; discarding it automatically ends his turn.

Centre building The first to turn an Ace must play it to the centre of the board. Cards are then built on it in sequence, regardless of suit, until it reaches the King. This is followed by another Ace, and the cycle continues until one player runs out of cards. At each move a player may build off as many playable cards from his wastepiles as he wishes before turning a card from stock.

Discarding A turned card not playable to the centre is discarded face up before its player. Each player maintains up to four wastepiles, which may be spread in columns so that all cards are visible. Discards are made regardless of rank or suit.

Obligations It is obligatory to start the centre run as soon as the first Ace is turned. After that it is not compulsory to play any playable card. Once a card is turned from stock, it must be immediately built or discarded – i.e. it is not permissible to look at the next turn-up before deciding whether or not to play from the wastepiles.

Turning the wastepiles When a player runs out of stock cards, he gathers up his wastepiles and consolidates them into a new stock. (Agree beforehand whether to gather them up at random and shuffle them, or whether to pile them on one another from left to right and turn the newly consolidated stock without disturbing the order of cards.) As soon as one player has only four cards left, or fewer, he merely turns them all face up, at which point it will usually be obvious which player has the win.

Dictation

Two (or more) players
One pack each

Almost any form of Patience can be played by the 'dictation' method, one of the most popular being Poker Squares. This lesser-known game is particularly compulsive.

Preliminaries One player, the dictator, shuffles his 52-card pack; the other arranges his pack face up in an orderly manner so that he can rapidly pick out any specified card.

Object Each plays a separate game of the patience called Sir Tommy, but using cards turned up in the same order. The winner is the player who completes the greater number of thirteen-card suites, which are built up from Ace to King regardless of suit. Neither person plays any card to his opponent's suites or layout.

Play At each turn the dictator turns the top card of his pack, announces what it is, and plays it to his own game. His opponent selects exactly the same card from his pack and plays it to his own game. When both are ready, the dictator turns the next card, and so on.

Whenever an Ace turns up each player puts it before him to start a suite, and may then build on it as many cards as may be available to him on his layout. Unplayable cards are discarded face up to a layout which may contain up to four piles, spread into columns so that all are visible. Any card may be placed on any pile regardless of rank or suit, and it is not obligatory to start all four piles at once: some may be held open until their player wishes to use them. No card may be transferred from one column to another, or to a column vacancy, but the exposed card of each column may be built on a suite at any time.

When all the cards have been called, each player will endeavour to complete his suites by playing off exposed cards.

Score The following system is recommended. Each player scores the combined face values of the uppermost cards on his suites, counting for this purpose Jack 15, Queen 20 and King 25. Thus a game completed up to the four Kings scores the maximum of 100, whereas four suites headed by (say) K–J–9–3 would score 52 – which is quite a good average result, in my experience.

Poker Squares
Any number of players
One pack each

A separate entry is included here for Poker Squares because it is a very good game in its own right. The rules of play are exactly the same as those of so-called Poker Patience as described on page 232. The difference is that each person plays his own game in accordance with the 'dictation' method – namely, one player has a shuffled pack, turns cards from it one by one, announces what each card is, and plays it to his own square. Every other player draws the same card from his own pack and plays it to his own square. When twenty-five cards have been called and played in this way, the winner is the player whose Poker Square attains the highest value.

Russian Bank
Dispute, Duplex, Robuse, Stop, Wrangle
Two players
One pack each

Russian Bank goes back a long way and has been popular with many nationalities, as indicated both by its miscellany of names and by its liability to minor but numerous variant rules from place to place. It is also recorded under the names Crapette, Crepette and Cripette; but Whitmore Jones gives the latter as a different species of the same genus and I think it useful to preserve the distinction.

Layout Each player takes a full 52-card pack shuffled by his opponent and deals a pile of thirteen cards face down to form a reserve, of which the top card is then turned face up. He then deals four cards face up in a row to start a tableau, and holds the remaining cards face down in his hand as a stock.

Object To be the first to get rid of all one's reserve and stock cards by entering them into the game, either on the tableaux or on eight thirteen-card suit sequences to be built up between the two players.

Play That player starts whose top reserve card is higher in rank. (If they are equal, shuffle the reserves and turn a new card.) At each turn a player makes as long a sequence of moves as he can in accordance with the rules below. When he can get no further, or is stopped by his opponent for contravening a rule of play, the other starts his turn.

Available cards Cards available to the player in turn are: the top card of his reserve, the exposed card on any of the eight tableau positions, and the top card of his stock. But he may not turn the stock-card until he has played any other available cards required by the rules and filled any vacancies that may exist in a tableau.

Building suites If an Ace is available, he must play it to the centre of the table to start a suite. These are to be built up in suit and sequence to the Kings. If he can add an available card to any suite he must do so, and, given the choice, he must build from his reserve rather than from the tableau. Having played from his reserve, he must turn the next card face up at some time before the end of his turn.

Packing the tableau If the player in turn cannot play to the centre, he must pack his top reserve card on the tableau if possible, and may (but need not) carry out any other packing that may be possible between the eight exposed cards of the tableau. The tableau must be packed in descending sequence and alternating colour, only one card being moved at a time. If he leaves a tableau position vacant, he must fill it at once either from elsewhere in the tableau or from his reserve (or, when this is gone, from his stock).

Turning from stock When he can make no more moves from the existing position, the player must turn the top card of his stock and may use it for packing, building, or loading onto his opponent (see below). If he uses it, he must then do any other building that may be done, and play his reserve card if possible, before turning the next. As soon as he turns an unplayable card he must discard it face up to a single wastepile. This act ends his turn (even if he notices, too late, another move that was open). The two players keep their wastepiles separate.

Loading If no building is possible, the player may disadvantage his opponent by loading an available card onto his wastepile or reserve, provided that it is of the same suit and next in sequence, either up or down. (Ace and King are not consecutive.) This does not end his turn.

Turning the wastepile When a player plays his last stock card he must form a new stock by turning his wastepile upside down, but may not do so until it is next his turn to play.

Stopping If a player contravenes any of the above rules (expressed in terms of 'must' or 'may not'), his opponent may call 'Stop', point out the contravention, and start his own turn. The usual penalty for a false challenge is the transfer of the challenged player's top reserve card to the top of his opponent's reserve.

Scoring The first to play all the cards of his reserve, stock and wastepile scores 30 for game, plus 1 for each card in his opponent's wastepile and 2 for each in his reserve.

VARIANTS Many variant rules may be encountered. The only one worth noting is that older accounts of the game require packing to be carried out in suit instead of alternating colour. This increases the opportunities for packing, but counterbalances it by reducing the opportunities for building long runs on the suites. Sometimes the reserve consists of only twelve cards. There is a one-pack version, in which each starts with twenty-six cards. Suites are built regardless of suit.

CRIPETTE Essentially the same, but start by shuffling both packs together and taking half each. Each player's reserve is then laid out as twenty cards in four rows of five (the reserve itself being known as 'Cripette', apparently a proper name, but of unknown identity). All cards of the Cripette are simultaneously available for play.

Spite and Malice

Two players
Two packs with Jokers

Spite and Malice attracted a well-deserved following in the 1970s through the publication of a study of the game by Bridge expert Easley Blackwood, who saw it played by two fellow-passengers on a cruise. Although it is clearly related to Russian Bank, the author did not know of any possible antecedents. A combing of the collected Patience works of Mary Whitmore Jones, however, turns up three games of remarkable similarity dating from the nineteenth century, and they are given below as variants. Spite and Malice (aptly named, as you will see) is one of my favourite two-hand card games, and I introduce it here with considerable enthusiasm.

Preliminaries The game requires two full packs, one containing 52 cards and the other 56 by the addition of four Jokers. It is convenient to use packs with different colour backs, and, ideally, the four Jokers should all be of the same back colour. However, it does not matter too much if there are two of each colour, nor, since many packs now contain three Jokers as standard, if you play with three instead of four.

Deal Shuffle the 52-card pack and split it in two. Each player takes his twenty-six cards and lays them face down on the table beside him as a reserve. Shuffle the 56-card pack, deal five cards each to form the two playing hands, and place the rest face down within reach of both players to form a common stockpile.

Object To be the first to get rid of all one's reserve cards. They can only be played off by being built on Ace-to-King suites which are to be built up on the table between the two players. Leave enough room to take eight suites. The suites are to be built in sequence from Ace to King, regardless of suit.

Play Each player turns up the top card of his reserve. We shall call this the upcard. As each upcard is played off the one below it is turned to become the new upcard. Whoever has the higher-ranking upcard moves first. (If equal, shuffle the reserves and turn a new upcard.) At each turn a player makes as long a sequence of moves as he can in accordance with the rules below. Sometimes a player in turn finds that he cannot or will not move: in this case his opponent plays again. It is a cardinal rule of play throughout the game that no move is obligatory unless otherwise stated, and neither player is forced to play to his own disadvantage.

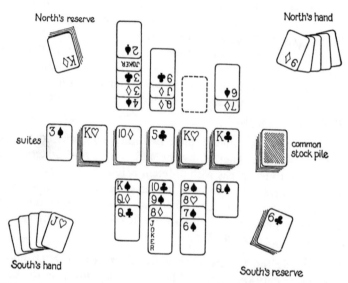

SPITE AND MALICE South can play off his reserve Six, followed by Joker (Seven), Eight, Nine, Ten from column two, Jack from hand, and either of his Queens. Unless his next reserve card is a King, however, this enables North to play off his reserve King. South will therefore take it no further than the Jack, hoping that North does not hold a Joker or the eighth Queen (seven being accounted for).

Available cards Cards available to the player in turn are: his upcard, the five cards in his hand, and the four exposed cards of his tableau, which has yet to be started. Whenever his upcard is an Ace he must play it to the centre to start a suite, and when it is a Two he must build it on an Ace if there is one waiting. Higher ranks, however, are not forced in this way.

Building suites Apart from playing any obligatory upcards, the player may use any available cards to start or add to a suite in the centre. If there is an Ace in the centre and he has an exposed Two, he is obliged to cover the Ace – though he may do so from the hand if he wishes. He may not take any cards from his opponent's reserve or tableau, nor add any to them.

The tableau Having played as far as he can or will, the player may (but need not) make one discard face up to the table to start or add to his tableau. If he does, he may do nothing else but draw from the stock as described below. The tableau may contain up to four piles of cards, spread towards him in columns so that all are visible. Any card may be used to start a column, but after that each succeeding card must be either of the same rank or one lower. (For example, on a Ten may be placed another Ten or any Nine.) Only the exposed card of each column is available for building. Cards may not be transferred from one column to another, and the space made by playing off all the cards from a column may be filled only with a discard.

Drawing from stock If the player succeeds in playing all five cards from his hand, he draws five more from the top of the stock and continues play. If not, he signifies the end of his turn by drawing as many cards as he needs to restore his hand to five.

Jokers A Joker may be used to represent any desired card. When played to a suite it must represent the next required rank and may not be retaken. When played to a tableau column it is not necessary to say which rank it represents. (This makes it possible, for example, for 10-Joker-Joker on a tableau to be followed by Ten, Nine, Eight or Seven ad lib.) An exposed Joker may be taken for building on any suite, no matter what rank it may have represented on the tableau. It is not compulsory to consider a Joker as an Ace or Two in circumstances where it is obligatory to play either rank.

Replenishing the stock When the stockpile contains fewer than twelve cards, the player who has just drawn must replenish it by taking all the suites that have been built up to the Kings and shuffling them in (very thoroughly) to form a new stock. If the stock runs out before any suites have reached this stage, he gathers up *all* the suites as far as they have gone and shuffles them together to form a new stock.

Blocked game The game is blocked if neither player is able to make a move. In this case it must be restarted as follows: gather up all the cards in the suites, the tableaux, the hands and the stock, shuffle them all together, deal five cards each, and play again. As before, the player with the higher upcard begins. If these are equal, the player whose proper turn it was begins. The game is also blocked if neither player is willing to make a move. In this case, however, the player who first refused to play is obliged to set it going again, if he can, by playing an Ace or a Two. If he cannot do so, his opponent must play an Ace or a Two, and if he cannot do so either then all the cards except those of the reserves are gathered up and shuffled as described above. For this purpose a Joker need not be counted as an Ace or Two, and neither need play an Ace or Two if he is prepared to play something else.

Scoring The game ends as soon as one player plays the last card of his reserve. He scores one point for each card remaining in his opponent's reserve. I prefer a scaled-up system as follows: count one point for the first card in his reserve, add two for the second, three for the third, and so on. (Four left, for example, would score ten to the winner.)

CARBOUCHE is the inexplicable name given to each player's reserve in a substantially similar forerunner of Spite and Malice. It is played like Spite and Malice but with the following differences. No Jokers are used, and, for their reserves, one player takes all the red cards of one pack and the other all the black. Both reserves are to be shuffled before being set down. The lead is made by the player with the lower-ranking upcard. Each player's tableau may be packed in any way he likes, without regard to rank or suit. Each time a suite is finished, shuffle it into the stock immediately. If the stock runs out and the game blocks, the player in turn may draw any card from his tableau to set the game going again, or, if he cannot, his opponent may do so. It is obligatory to play from the reserve instead of from the tableau where the choice exists.

OBSTRUCTION can be played by any number of players, each of whom starts with a complete 52-card pack. Deal eight cards face down to form a reserve called 'the obstruction', and place the rest beside it to form a stock. Turn the top card of the obstruction face up. The winner is the first player to play off all the cards of his obstruction by building them on suites made at the centre of the table by all the players together. Each in turn must use his upcard to start or continue a suite if possible, and continue as far as he can. He then builds as many exposed cards as he can from his tableau. When unable to play from either source, he turns the top card of his stock, and if this enables him to continue he may do so. Eventually he will turn an unplayable card from the stock, which he must then discard to his tableau. The tableau may consist of up to four piles or columns, as at Spite and Malice, but a discard may be made to any of the columns regardless of rank or suit as at Carbouche. If anyone contravenes a rule or makes any other obvious error, the others say 'We obstruct' and transfer one card each from their reserves to that of the defaulter, whose turn then ends. (The game may block before anyone has won. In this case the winner may be held to be the player with fewest cards left in his obstruction, and a tie be broken either by position or by the rank of the tied players' upcards.)

DOWAGER'S PATIENCE This is a two-player game similar to Obstruction, but with a different objective: this time the player who crowns a suite with the King captures the suite, and the winner is the player who captures the greater number. Each takes a complete pack shuffled by his opponent, deals the first eight cards face down as a reserve, and turns the top one face up. Each in turn must start by playing his upcard if possible, turning up the next immediately and playing it too if he can. Suites are built up between the two players from Ace to King regardless of suit. He then turns four cards at a sweep from his stock, packs them in any way he pleases on a personal tableau containing up to four piles or columns, then builds exposed cards onto the suites as far as he can. He must play his upcard in preference to a tableau card whenever possible. If both capture the same number of suites, the winner is the player with fewer cards left in his reserve. Or it may be agreed that the winner is the first to capture a predetermined number of suites in as many deals as it takes.

FINIS CORONAT OPUS
(I have reached the end of my patience)

Select Bibliography

Only those sources are listed which have provided material for this book.

BERGHOLT, ERNEST: *A New Book of Patience Games*, Routledge, 1941.

BLANCCOEUR, COMTESSE DE: *Le Livre Illustré des Patiences*, Brussels, c. 1860–70.

CADOGAN, LADY ADELAIDE: *Illustrated Games of Patience*, 1870.

CAVENDISH (= HENRY JONES): *Patience*, De la Rue, 1890.

DALTON, BASIL: *The Complete Patience Book*, John Baker, 1948.

HARBIN, ROBERT: *Waddington's Family Card Games*, Pan, 1972.

HERVEY, GEORGE: *Teach Yourself Card Games for One*, Hodder & Stoughton, 1965.

HOFFMAN, PROFESSOR (= ANGELO LEWIS): *Illustrated Book of Patience Games*, Routledge, 1920 – an English version of Blanccoeur.

KING, TOM: *Thirty-One Patience Games*, Foulsham, c. 1920.

MOREHEAD, ALBERT, and MOTT-SMITH, GEOFFREY: *The Complete Book of Patience*, Faber & Faber, 1950.

MOYSE, ALPHONSE: *150 Ways to Play Solitaire*, U.S. Playing Card Co., 1950.

PHILLIPS, HUBERT: *The Pan Book of Card Games*, Pan, 1960.

TARBART (pseud.): *Patience Games*, De la Rue, 1905.

WHITMORE JONES, MARY: *Games of Patience*, Series 1–5, Upcott Gill, 1899 – *New Games of Patience*, Upcott Gill, 1911.

Index

of games, variants and alternative titles

The index is in strict alphabetical order. For example St Helena and St Louis are listed between St— and Sto—. Initial 'P' stands for 'Patience' where it is part of the title.

Entries in ordinary type are main headings in the text.
Entries in SMALL CAPITALS refer to variants which in the text are also headed in SMALL CAPITALS.
Entries in *italics* are alternative titles: in each case the main title is also given.

About the Author

David Parlett was born in London and grew up in Wales. He was a language teacher and involved in technical journalism and public relations before turning to full-time freelance writing with a specialization in games. He has invented several published board games and is the author of six books on cards and card games, as well as two on linguistics. He is a consulting editor to *Games & Puzzles* magazine and a consultant to a British playing-card company. He is married, has two children, and lives in South London.